Andrew Duncan Senior

Physician of the
Enlightenment

Edited by
JOHN CHALMERS

National
Museums
Scotland

Published in 2010 by
NMS Enterprises Limited – Publishing
a division of NMS Enterprises Limited
National Museums Scotland
Chambers Street
Edinburgh EH1 1JF

ISBN: 978 1 905267 30 9

Publication layout and design by
NMS Enterprises Limited – Publishing.
Cover artwork by Mark Blackadder.
Cover images:
    (front) Henry Raeburn's portrait of Andrew
    Duncan is by courtesy of the Royal College
    of Physicians of Edinburgh); (back) the
    drawing of proposed new Asylum is by
    courtesy of the Royal College of Physicians
    of Edinburgh; the image of Arthur's Seat is
    from *Old and New Edinburgh* by James
    Grant (London: Cassell & Co. Ltd, 1881-83).

Printed and bound in the United Kingdom by
Thomson Litho Ltd, East Kilbride, Glasgow.

ACKNOWLEDGEMENT

*The Douglas Guthrie Trust, administered by the
Scottish Society for the History of Medicine, and
The Strathmartine Trust, have made generous
awards towards the cost of publication.*

For a full listing of NMS Enterprises Limited –
Publishing titles and related merchandising:

www.nms.ac.uk/books

Contents

Acknowledgements

Grateful thanks are due to the many individuals who have given invaluable help and advice in the preparation of this book. First, my gratitude goes to those whose articles about Andrew Duncan and his time were the inspiration for the compilation of this biography. These include Mike Barfoot, Connie Byrom, Iain Chalmers, James Gray, Matthew Kaufman, Morrice McRae and Ulrich Tröller. The names of several of these individuals appear as authors of chapters, but their contributions have been much wider for they have all had a say in the concept as a whole.

Andrew Duncan left most of his papers to the Royal College of Physicians of Edinburgh. Iain Milne, Librarian of the College has made a huge contribution by locating appropriate textual and illustrative material from his unique knowledge of this most valuable resource. The willing help of Assistant Librarian, Estela Dukan, has been much appreciated.

Grateful thanks are due also to the librarians of Edinburgh University Library Centre for Research Collections, Royal College of Surgeons of Edinburgh, Royal Botanic Gardens, Royal Society of Edinburgh, National Library of Scotland, Edinburgh Central Library, British Library, Wellcome Library and St Andrews University which have been major sources of information. The Aesculapian and Harveian Societies kindly allowed access to their minute books which are held in the library of the Royal College of Physicians of Edinburgh.

Adrian Sinfield read the entire text and made many useful suggestions particularly with regard to the organisation of the book. John Forrester deserves particular thanks for his help with Latin translation and for his ability to trace the source of obscure Latin passages. Sir Fred O'Brien kindly commented on matters relating to the law. Warren McDougall drew our attention to the existence of the Charles Elliot papers within the John Murray Archive. Leslie Hodgson confirmed the location of the grave of Andrew Duncan Jr. George Anderson, President of the Royal Caledonian Horticultural Society, John Byrom and Carol Smith and Anna Buxton were most helpful with their advice about this Society. Dr Robert Kennedy gave useful advice regarding the Royal Edinburgh Hospital. Lt Col. Richard Callander, Secretary of the Royal Company of Archers, kindly corrected errors relating to that subject, and Alan D. C. Smith gave advice about the dispute involving James Hamilton Jr. Stana Nenadic identified the coade stone relief of the Good Samaritan from the Royal Public Dispensary.

Mathew Kaufman, author of chapter III, is grateful to Dr Donald Thomson of the General Practice Teaching Unit, University of Edinburgh, for allowing him access to documents, collected by him over the years, relating to the activities of the Royal Public Dispensary.

James Gray, author of chapter VIII, thanks Dr Mike Barfoot, staff of the Centre for Research Collections, Edinburgh University Library, Professor M. H. Kaufman and Mrs Elizabeth Singh of the Library of the Royal Medical Society and Mr Iain Milne, Librarian, and staff of the Royal College of Physicians of Edinburgh, for their help and permission to consult material in their care, and Dr Sandy Buchan, Dr Elizabeth McCall Smith, Dr Hilary Watkinson and Dr Sandy Buchan, past and present secretaries of the Medico-Chirurgical Society of Edinburgh.

Gwyneth Chalmers gave encouragement and help throughout the book's long gestation. Alison Milne kindly proof-read the text.

The Douglas Guthrie Trust, administered by the Scottish Society for the History of Medicine, and the Strathmartine Trust, have made generous awards towards the cost of publication.

To Lesley Taylor and Lynne Reilly at NMS Enterprises Limited – Publishing, we owe a great debt of gratitude. Without their help the book would not have seen the light of day.

John Chalmers
Edinburgh 2010

Foreword

I am delighted to welcome this excellent book about Andrew Duncan, an outstanding and visionary physician of the age of the Enlightenment in Edinburgh. The son of a Fife shipmaster, Duncan rose to become Physician to the King and was twice President of the Royal College of Physicians of Edinburgh. He was intensely competitive, applying – albeit unsuccessfully – for appointment as Professor of Medicine in St Andrews within months of obtaining his medical degree. He became a loved and admired teacher in Edinburgh, but had powerful enemies who felt he was too focused on health and insufficiently scientific. His determination and tenacity are exemplified by his eventual success in being appointed to the Edinburgh University Chair of the Institutes of Medicine 14 years after having been rebuffed for the same post.

His humanity and innovation are shown by his championing of public health – or as he termed it 'medical police' – as an important part of the responsibilities of doctors and at least as important as the care of the individual patient. Against considerable opposition he eventually succeeded in creating a chair of 'medical police and jurisprudence' in the University of Edinburgh, a model taken up elsewhere in the United Kingdom thereafter. His distinction was rewarded by honours from around the globe.

Duncan was a very sociable man with impressive organisational vigour. He was a prodigious founder of clubs and bodies including medical dining clubs, a gymnastics club, the Royal Edinburgh Hospital and the Royal Caledonian Horticultural Society. He clearly loved channelling his energy into running things: he was President of the Medical Student Society of the Royal Medical Society on no fewer than six occasions and Secretary of the Harveian Society of Edinburgh for 46 years – so presumably he was good at it! These particular societies gave him free reign to play the prankster and buffoon, a role enjoyed by many but which may have contributed to the views of some of his detractors.

Andrew Duncan was one of the most notable Edinburgh physicians. John Chalmers and his co-authors have added facts to the myths and character to the facts in this fascinating book about my distinguished predecessor.

Professor Sir Neil Douglas
President, Royal College of Physicians of Edinburgh

The Chronology of
Andrew Duncan Senior

BORN   17 October 1744, at Pinkerton, near Crail, Fife.

1759-62 Student at St Andrews University, graduating MA.

1764-68 Studied medicine at University of Edinburgh.

1765   Joined the (Royal) Medical Society.

1767   President of the (Royal) Medical Society. Served as president a further five times between 1769 and 1774.

1768-69 Surgeon on East India Company's ship *Asia*.

1769   Graduated MD at St Andrews University.

1770   Licentiate of Royal College of Physicians of Edinburgh.
       Unsuccessful application for Chandos Chair of Medicine at St Andrews University.
       First publication: *Elements of Therapeutics*.

1771   Married Elizabeth Knox (1751-1839). They have 12 children.
       Elected Fellow of Royal College of Physicians of Edinburgh.
       Elected to Royal Company of Archers.
       Created Knight of the Beggar's Benison.

1773   Launched and edited *Medical and Philosophical Commentaries*.
       Founded the Aesculapian Society. Secretary for 54 years.

1774-76 Locum Professor of Institutes of Medicine.

1774   Elected member of the American Philosophical Society.
       Initiated as a Freemason, Canongate Kilwinning Lodge.

1776   Failed in his application for Chair of Institutes of Medicine.
       Commenced his extramural course of lectures in medicine which continued until 1790.
       Public Dispensary for Sick Poor established.

1778   Founded the Harveian Society. Secretary for 46 years.
       Obtained Royal Charter for the Royal Medical Society.

1783   Founder member of the Royal Society of Edinburgh.

1789   Awarded gold medal of the Royal Medical Society.
       Published *Edinburgh New Dispensatory*.

1790   Appointed to the Chair of Institutes of Medicine.
       Elected President of the Royal College of Physicians for the first time.
       Proposed establishment of a lunatic asylum in Edinburgh.

1795	Began course in medical jurisprudence.
1804	Dispute with James Gregory.
1807	Responsible for creation of Regius Chair in Medical Jurisprudence. Andrew Duncan Jr first professor.
	Lunatic Asylum given Royal Charter.
1808	Given Freedom of the City.
1809	With Patrick Neill, founded the (Royal) Caledonian Horticultural Society. Duncan permanent vice president.
1813	Edinburgh Lunatic Asylum opened.
1818	Public Dispensary given Royal Charter.
1819	Andrew Jr joined father as joint Professor of Institutes of Medicine, resigning his Chair of Medical Jurisprudence.
1821	Appointed First Physician to His Majesty in Scotland.
	Appointed Professor of Materia Medica.
	Founder member and first President of the Medico Chirurgical Society.
1824	Elected President of the Royal College of Physicians of Edinburgh for the second time.
1825	Dispute with James Hamilton.
1827	Climbed Arthur's Seat on morning of 1 May for the last time, having done so for more than 50 years.
DIED	5 July 1828, aged 83.

Introduction

Now lend your lugs, ye benders fine,
Wha ken the benefit of wine,
And you who laughing, scud brown ale,
Leave jinks a wee, and hear a tale.

From Andrew Ramsay's *Monk and the Miller's Wife*,
quoted by Andrew Duncan

… one of the curious old Edinburgh characters. He [Andrew Duncan] was a kind-hearted and excellent man; but one of a class which seems to live and be happy, and get liked by, its mere absurdities. He was the promoter and the president of more innocent and foolish clubs and societies than perhaps any man in the world, and the author of pamphlets, jokes, poems, and epitaphs sufficient to stock the nation – all amiable, all dull, and most of them very foolish. But they made the author happy; and he was so benevolent and so simple, that even those who were suffering under his interminable projects checked their impatience and submitted. Scientific ambition, charitable restlessness and social cheerfulness made Duncan thrust himself into everything throughout a long life. Yet, though his patronage was generally dangerous, and his talk always wearisome, nobody could ever cease to esteem him. He was even the president of a bathing club, and once at least every year did this grave medical professor conduct as many of the members as he could collect to Leith, where the rule of the club was that their respect for their chief was to be shown by always letting him plunge first into the water. He continued till he was past eighty, a practice of mounting to the summit of Arthur's Seat on the first of May, and celebrating the feat by what he called a poem. He was very fond of gardening, and rather a good botanist. This made him president of the Horticultural Society, which he oppressed annually by a dull discourse. But in the last … of them he relieved the members by his best epitaph. … After mentioning his great age, he intimated that the time must soon arrive, when, 'In the words of our inimitable Shakespeare, you will all be saying, "Duncan's in his grave".'

Thus Henry Cockburn described Andrew Duncan.[1] Cockburn's description highlights the amiable buffoonery which was certainly one of Duncan's characteristics, but does less than justice to the achievements of a remarkable medical figure, whose influence continues to this day. Other contemporary commentators view him more favourably. One of his students wrote, 'His zeal in the prosecution of medical science was never surpassed, and his numerous attempts to be of service to his fellow creatures ... deserved the most unbounded praise'.[2] Another student, who in general tended to be critical of the medical school and its professors, highlighted Duncan's amiable nature and concern for others:

> I cannot forbear from mentioning, that I always heard the poor both in the Infirmary, and in the city of Edinburgh, speak in terms of the greatest gratitude and affection of Dr Duncan, as one, whose humanity and benevolence to them were ever active and unlimited, shrinking from no toil and no expence [sic], so that those, who were in affliction and in distress, might be relieved and comforted. ... his behaviour and conduct were uniformly such, as entirely to win the esteem and affection of his students, who never, to this day, mention his name with out reverence and honour.[3]

Andrew Duncan lived during the period which has become known as the Scottish Enlightenment, when it was said that one could 'stand at what is called the *Cross of Edinburgh*, and can, in a few minutes, take fifty men of genius and learning by the hand'.[4] When he attended the University of Edinburgh it had superseded Leyden as the pre-eminent medical school in Europe and attracted students from throughout the western world. He was taught by an outstanding faculty which included William Cullen, John Gregory, Alexander Monro *secundus*, and Joseph Black, who were making tentative efforts to advance medicine from the traditional teachings of Galen and Boerhaave. Students were being encouraged to learn from observation and experience rather than dogma.

Duncan flourished in this heady environment. He may not have had many original ideas, but he had a flair for identifying among the many new concepts, those which might be of greatest benefit to medicine and to Edinburgh. Having selected these, he promoted them with relentless endeavour and usually with a successful outcome despite sometimes the inertia and even the opposition of his colleagues.

Among his many achievements was the founding of the successful journal *Medical and Philosophical Commentaries*. Duncan's *Commentaries* went from strength to strength and continued, with changing titles, for nearly 200 years. He may have got the ideas of a Dispensary for the Sick Poor from

Lettsom's London Dispensary and the Edinburgh Lunatic Asylum from similar developments in Montrose and elsewhere, but his great contribution was to see the need for these facilities in Edinburgh and to bring them into being in the face of considerable difficulties. Perhaps Duncan's greatest contribution was the establishment of the Chair of Medical Jurisprudence and Public Health in Edinburgh in the face of opposition from the University Senate. These academic disciplines had existed in the continent for some time, but the Edinburgh chair was the first in Britain and became the model for other universities to follow. The City of Edinburgh recognised Duncan's contributions by awarding him the Freedom of the City.

At a time when the medical profession was riven with professional jealousies between physicians and surgeons, Duncan founded the Aesculapian and Harveian Societies, designed to promote unity in a convivial atmosphere. These and the Royal Caledonian Horticultural Society, which he also founded, survive to this day.

In this book the authors have attempted to bring to life the many facets of Andrew Duncan, a man much loved for his geniality and benevolence of character. The contributors are authorities on the period during which Duncan lived and several have published papers on topics related to Duncan, but in journals that are not easily accessible to the general public, for whom this book is intended. This volume is the first to give a full account of Andrew Duncan whose many achievements surely merit his being included among the luminaries of the Enlightenment.

The first chapter gives a biographical overview of the man; subsequent chapters expand on different aspects of his life and contributions in more detail.

Throughout the text 'Andrew Duncan Sr', 'Andrew Duncan' or 'Duncan' refers to the subject of the book. His son, Andrew Duncan, is identified by the addition of 'Junior'/'Jr', or referred to simply as 'Andrew'. 'Royal College of Physicians' refers to the College of Edinburgh unless otherwise stated.

The conversion of values in Duncan's day to present-day values has been calculated from the Composite Price Index 1753 to 2003 published by the Office of National Statistics in *Economic Trends*, no. 604, pp. 38-46 in 2004. In 1750 £1 was equivalent to £140 today, but inflation had reduced the value to £68 at the time of Duncan's death in 1828.

Notes

1 Cockburn (1909), pp. 273-74. Henry Cockburn (1779-1854) was a leading Scottish judge and a shrewd commentator on Scottish events and individuals during his lifetime.

2 Bower (1817-30), vol. III, p. 27.

3 Bristed (1803). John Bristed was a medical student in Edinburgh in 1801-1802.

4 Smellie (1800), pp. 161-62.

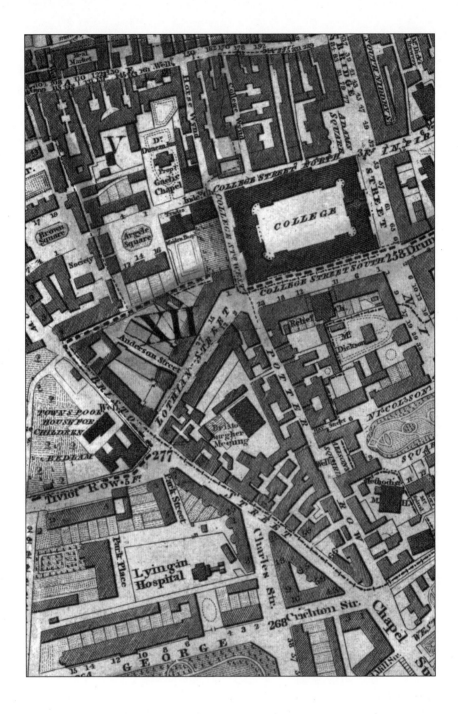

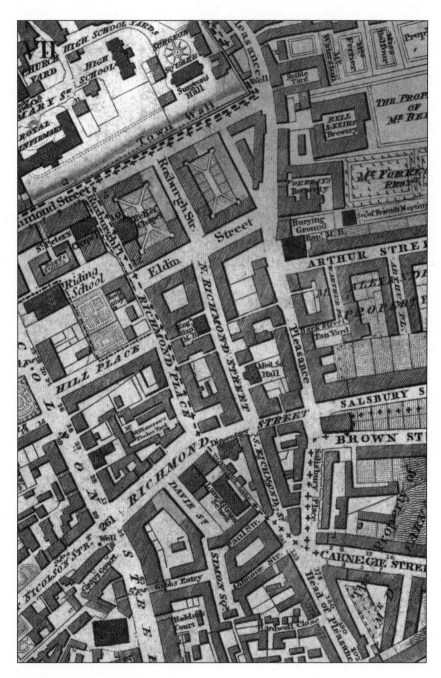

EDINBURGH

Kirkwood's map of Edinburgh (1821) shows the location of Adam Square and Bristo Street, the Public Dispensary on Richmond Street, the Royal Infirmary and Surgeons' Square.

VIVAT · VERITAS

Duncan of Ardounie

DUNCAN OF ARDOUNIE

The armorial bearings of the Duncans of Ardounie,
first registered in 1698 to Alexander Duncan,
Commissioner of Supply for Forfarshire.

(NISBET: *HERALDIC PLATES*)

CHAPTER I

Andrew Duncan Senior (1744-1828)
A Biographical Overview

JOHN CHALMERS

No amount of perseverance will make a poet of a man in whom the divine gift is not born. Samuel Smiles 1867[1]

... at Edinburgh at this time ... there happen to be collected a set of as truly great men, professors of the several branches of knowledge, as have ever appeared in any age or country. Benjamin Franklin 1776[2]

Family history and early life

Andrew Duncan was born on 17 October 1744 in Pinkerton, a small farm near the fishing village of Crail in the East Neuk of Fife, about eight miles from St Andrews. His father, also Andrew (1713-91), was a shipmaster based in St Andrews, where he became a Baillie. He may, however, at the time of Andrew's birth have lived in Crail, where Andrew received his early schooling.

Information in the family bible[3] traces the family back to a younger son of the owner of the estate of Ardounie in the County of Forfar. This younger son, also Andrew, was educated at University of St Andrews from 1570 to 1575, and became a professor (regent) there before becoming a minister at Crail. His son William was a shipmaster based in Anstruther, who married Margaret Drummond of the family of Hawthorndean in Midlothian. Sadly William was lost at sea, leaving two daughters and one son, the father of the subject of this book.

The vessels from the East Neuk of Fife traded extensively with the continental North Sea ports, Spain and Scandinavia, and rarely to more distant destinations in America and the West Indies. Duncan's father is on record as the master of two ships, the *Concord of St Andrews* and the *Concord of Crail* which traded with Trontheim [*sic*], Oporto, Bergen and Hamburg.[4]

Andrew Duncan's mother, Katherine Vilant, was descended from Nicholas Vilant, a French protestant refugee, who came to Scotland in the early 17th century and worked as chamberlain to John, Earl of Strathmore.

He is said to have lived to the age of 106.[5] The Vilant family played a prominent part in University of St Andrews during the 18th century, providing professors of humanity, mathematics, philosophy and civil history, a librarian, and even a tailor to United College. Katherine was the daughter of William Vilant (1660-1757), Professor of both Humanity and Civil History and Principal of St Mary's College at University of St Andrews, who owned the Pinkerton farm. William Vilant's eldest son inherited the farm, but had to sell it to pay his debts. Duncan regarded this as fortuitous, for otherwise he might have inherited it and would have become a 'petty Fife Laird in place of an industrious physician'.[6]

A touching letter exists from Andrew's mother, Katherine, to her husband (26 February 1755, St Andrews):

> *My Dearest Sweetest Life*
> *I received yours and was very glad to hear my Dear, that you was in good health and as you desired. … I am very sorry for my Dear Life that you should be tossed at sea in the winter season and especially in this tempestuous and stormy weather, but hopes and prays that the Almighty will ever direct and protect you in every circumstance of life and I hope you'd be safely arrived by the time this comes to your hand and be sure to write me my Dearest Jewel as soon as you can. … My father, the bairns and all our other friends are very well and have their kind love to you.*[7]

Duncan retained the local Fife accent throughout his life. One of his English students commented that his lectures were 'delivered in broad Scotch, with such a wearisome drawl, that it requires no very nice musical ear to be actually tortured and agonized at the doctor's tones'.[8]

Duncan had a fondness for writing doggerel, and in his old age planned to write a poetic autobiography in seven cantos[9]:

1   *Infancy – the School boy.*
2   *Youth – the Collegian.*
3   *Virility – the East Indian Surgeon.*
4   *Early Matrimony – the Private Lecturer.*
5   *Industrious Exertion – the Father of a Family.*
6   *Advanced Manhood – the Active Professor.*
7   *Old Age – the Venerable Doctor.*

Only the first is extant, which from the biographer's point of view is unfortunate for personal details about his life are scant. From a poetic standpoint, however, one wishes that he had chosen a more prosaic style:

> *At Pinkerton I first drew breath,*
> *And breathe I must until my death.*
> *With Sandy Don I went to school,*
> *Like other boys to play the fool.*

Duncan ends his first canto

> *Thus, then, I pass'd my boyish years,*
> *The favourite friend of many peers;*
> *And, while I added to their joy,*
> *Was styl'd by all,* The Smiling Boy.

and completes it with a footnote which gives a great deal of insight into his character and outlook on life:

> *I can say that I was remarkable for being a good-natured boy, and I have
> ... retained the character of being a good-natured man during the whole
> course of my life.*

False modesty was not one of Duncan's failings! No record can be found of the proposed further six cantos of his autobiography. It is doubtful if they were ever completed.

Duncan describes his schooling, first in Crail where Sandy Don, the schoolmaster, introduced him to Latin and a love of poetry which were to remain dominant interests throughout his life. His schooling was continued at St Andrews Grammar School where his teacher, Richard Dick, a noted Latin scholar, further instilled Latin with the 'powerful aid of taws [*sic*]'.[10]

Among his schoolfellows at that time were the brothers Thomas and Henry Erskine, sons of Henry David, 10th Earl of Buchan. The younger brother, Thomas, became Lord Chancellor of Great Britain:

> *... but of all my school-fellows, my earliest, my most intimate, and most
> affectionate friend, was ... the late Honourable Henry Erskine. My friend-
> ship with him commenced when we began together to learn the rudiments
> of the Latin language at Dick's school; and it continued without the slightest
> shadow of interruption till the day of death. Perhaps there are but few
> instances of friendship which have been of longer duration, more steady,
> or more sincere: and I shall always consider it as one of the unavoidable
> calamities attendant on a long life, that I have survived my best friends.*[11]

The name of Henry Erskine will recur throughout this narrative. He became a leading advocate in Edinburgh, Dean of the Faculty of Advocates, and

Lord Advocate for Scotland on two occasions during brief Whig administrations, when he was able to use his influence to assist Duncan in several of his endeavours.

Duncan enrolled at St Salvator's College in University of St Andrews in February 1760 at the age of 16 and obtained a Master of Arts degree in 1762. The University in those days was a small and intimate institution; only 25 students matriculated in Duncan's year. His professsors included the mathematician David Gregory, one of the distinguished family of Gregorys, which produced no less than 16 professors of mathematics and medicine in five generations.[12] Duncan certainly enjoyed his time at the University, as noted in 'Thanks returned by an octogenarian physician, to his friends in the county of Fife, particularly in the ancient city of St Andrews in 1823':

> ... *I had the honour and happiness of being a student: and I can also with truth add, that I had the honour and happiness of being a favourite pupil. The only return I can now make for their* [the professors] *warm patronage and fatherly friendship is my earnest prayer,* Requiescat in pace.

At St Andrews, Duncan was to be introduced to golf which remained a major recreational activity throughout his life.

Medical studies

Duncan left no record of his medical training. In *The Story of the University of Edinburgh* (p. 406), Alexander Grant states that Duncan spent the years 1762-68 as a medical student at the University. Although this has been widely quoted, six years seems excessively long at a time when the average student took three to four years to complete his studies. The records of the University of Edinburgh show that Andrew Duncan first matriculated in 1764 and renewed his matriculation annually until 1768. At a meeting of the Royal Infirmary Committee in 1818, Duncan stated that 'my first connection with the Royal Infirmary was in the year 1764 when I commenced my medical studies at Edinburgh',[13] and he later stated that he spent the first 20 years of his life in St Andrews which would take him up to 1764.[14] There seems no doubt therefore that Duncan spent not more than four years as an undergraduate at Edinburgh, commencing in 1764.

The gap years

How then did Duncan occupy himself from 1762-64? Perhaps he was engaged in helping his father in his shipping business, or working on his grandfather's farm at Pinkerton while he made up his mind about his future career. Nor do we know what motivated Duncan to study medicine. There was no tradition of this discipline in his family and no one to guide him in his course of studies. There was no fixed curriculum of medical education at that time and it was left largely to the individual student to map out his course. Trainee physicians attended university, and trainee surgeons the Incorporation of Surgeons (the Royal College of Surgeons after 1778), but it was not uncommon for surgical apprentices to attend university classes and for medical students to gain surgical experience. Duncan may have been undecided as to whether to become a physician or a surgeon.

It is quite possible that he may have crossed the Forth to visit Edinburgh during this period to see what was on offer. He may also have attended some of the medical lectures, for many students made private arrangements with the professors without matriculation. Another possibility is that he explored a surgical apprenticeship. The Incorporation of Surgeons offered a training in surgery and medicine to young men who bound themselves to individual surgeons, either as an apprentice indentured for five years, or as a 'servant' for a period of three years. These formal arrangements were recorded in the Incorporation minutes. There is no record of Andrew Duncan making such an arrangement, but less formal attachments appear to have occurred, for in 1770 the Incorporation passed a resolution forbidding masters to take into their shops any students not properly bound.

While these suggestions are totally speculative, it might explain why Duncan remained on friendly terms with his surgical colleagues at a time when surgeons and physicians were at loggerheads over a number of issues (see chapter XII). The Aesculapian and Harveian Societies, which he founded, were designed to create harmony and friendship between the two branches of the profession. It may also be relevant that this is the pattern of medical education which Duncan Senior devised for his son, Andrew Duncan Junior. Duncan Sr insisted that Duncan Jr should commence his studies, at the age of 14, with a period of surgical apprenticeship to Alexander and George Wood, the sons of his friend Sandy Wood.[15]

The university student

In 1764, when Duncan first matriculated at the University of Edinburgh, he was taught by an outstanding faculty. An American contemporary, Benjamin Rush, who became Duncan's friend, wrote that the Medical School was 'now in the zenith of its glory. The whole world I believe does not afford a greater set of men than are at present united in the College of Edinburgh.'[16] This included William Cullen (1710-90), Professor of Institutes of Medicine (Physiology), one of the first to teach in English rather than Latin; John

Gregory (1724-73), Professor of Practice of Medicine; Alexander Monro *secundus* (1733-1817), Professor of Anatomy and Surgery, the second of three generations of Alexander Monros who held the Chair of Anatomy for 126 years[17]; John Hope (1725-86), Professor of Botany and Materia Medica, who was responsible for the introduction of the Linnaean system of classification of plants into Scotland; and Joseph Black (1728-99), the distinguished Professor of Chemistry, famed for his discovery of carbonic acid gas and the principle of latent heat. Professor Thomas Young taught midwifery, which was not a required part of the curriculum; and it is fairly certain that Duncan did not attend his lectures, for he regarded midwifery as a suitable occupation for a '*Sage Femme* – a Houdy-wife', but not for doctors (see chapter XIII).

The Edinburgh Medical School at that time was regarded as the leading medical school in the world and attracted students from England, Europe and America. The Scottish students came mainly from middle-class families, as knowledge of classical languages was required as well as an ability to pay the fees. There were, however, some outstanding examples of students from impoverished backgrounds qualifying for entrance by dint of hard work and success in obtaining a bursary.

A few students boarded with the professors, but the majority lived in lodgings in the vicinity of the University. A typical room cost about £10 to £20 for the winter session of six months, or £40 for the entire year. For this the student obtained his meals, a fire and candles. He also had additional expenses including clothing, quills, paper, books and class fees, so that his entire cost for a year would be in the order of £100 (*c*.£11,500 in modern values). Many survived on much less, but a few, particularly those from afar, enjoyed a much more affluent existence which enabled them to visit taverns, concerts and the theatre. None of the students could afford to be married; and of course there were no female students for company, apart from a few who were allowed to attend the midwifery classes. An Oxford writer regarded this extra-collegiate life with disapproval, as the vulnerable young student was exposed to every temptation and could sink into debauchery, which a few no doubt did.

Although Duncan has left no record of his time as a medical student, it is possible to imagine what his life was like from the writings of contemporaries. Thomas Ismay,[18] who commenced his studies in 1771, wrote to his father that he had found lodgings opposite the college with the widow of a professor, for which he paid £10 per quarter. For this he received tea twice a day and a hot dinner and supper.

The dinner generally consists of a large Tirene of Soup, *which I like extremely well, a Dish of Boiled Meat and another of Roast. Their Mutton*

6

and Beef is very good. Veal I have not seen any yet; Puddings only one. Generally to Supper, Fish, Eggs, Beefstakes or what you please.[19]

He was also supplied with candles and a fire. Financial constraints meant all work and no play, which he felt was not conducive to his health. (He died at the end of his first winter session and was buried in Greyfriars Churchyard.) Ismay described a typical day thus:

I rise about 7, read till 9, then go to Dr Cullen's Class, come back at 10, then breakfast and transcribe the Notes which I have taken at his Lecture. From 12-1 walk in Infirmary, from 1 to 3 attend Dr Monro. Then come and dine, and as you may suppose I am very hungry. From 4 to 5 attend Dr Young, from 5 to 6 transcribe the notes I have taken of Dr Young or Dr Monro's lectures; from 6 to 7 attend Dr Innis's Private Demonstrations [Innis was Monro's dissector], *from 7 to 9 transcribe the Lectures I have borrowed and at 9 get Supper; from 10-12 write Lectures; besides every Tuesday and Thursday from 5 to 6 o'clock I attend the Clinical Lectures.*[20]

Ismay found Professor Monro very good natured. 'He has about 300 Pupils which pay him three guineas each, so you may judge of his Yearly Income. Besides he is called to all Extraordinary Cases in Town. Generally when a Person is given up by the Physicians, Dr Monro is called in.' Professor Cullen also had a very full class and was 'accounted very clever, but deals too much upon Theory'.[21]

Professor John Gregory, who alternated with Cullen in giving courses in the Practice of Physic and Institutes of Medicine, was better liked 'as he only regards Theory so far as is Requisite for Practice'. Professor Young was

very clever, and has a great many Preparations; he is upon Midwifery. Dr Hume, upon the Materia Medica, has the fewest Pupils; ... Dr Hope is a fine Man; He lectures upon Botany; and is also one of the Physicians that attends the Royal Infirmary. In short, they are all Fine Men; and it is supposed to be one of the First Universities for Physic now in Europe, I suppose there may be 500-600 Students of Physic [medicine], *which consist of Scotch, English, French, Dutch, Irish, and from almost every Kingdom in Europe; besides a great many from America.*[22]

Ismay had to ask his father to send 'a hundred or two quills as they were three pence per hundred in Edinburgh and he used a great many as he had to write five or six sheets of paper every day'.[23]

Duncan's programme was probably similar to that of Ismay, although perhaps less intense, for he had four years from 1764 to 1768 in which to attend the various classes. The medical course was quite flexible. Students could attend the courses on offer as and when they chose. Professor Hope's class-lists for 1764 indicate that Duncan enrolled for botany at a fee of two guineas, and for materia medica, which Hope also taught, at a fee of two guineas and two shillings. During this period he attended the wards of the Royal Infirmary for three years.

During his undergraduate days, Duncan was an enthusiastic member of the students' (Royal) Medical Society, of which he became president. Throughout his life he maintained a close interest in the society which then, as now, played a valuable role in the educational experience of many medical students.

Some students spent a year or more in a foreign school such as Leyden or Paris. However, there is no evidence that Duncan studied abroad and he probably did not have the means for doing so. He was, however, acutely aware of the advantages of such experience. He encouraged and financed his son, Andrew Duncan Jr, to travel extensively to further his medical education in European centres including Göttingen, Vienna, Pisa and Naples (see chapter VI).

Postgraduate experience

From 1768 to 1769 Duncan served as surgeon on the East India Company's ship *Asia*. He is known to have entertained his friends with accounts of his adventures, but alas has left no record of these. The *Asia*, according to the East India Company's records, was a small vessel of 657 tons launched in 1763. Duncan's voyage from 6 April 1768 to 4 July 1769 was the *Asia*'s second to China, where it visited Whampoa and Bocca Tigris on the Pearl River and returned via the Cape of Good Hope and St Helena. Duncan refers to the fevers he experienced on the Canton River and in Java, which he treated with cinchona bark, then a popular remedy for fevers in general and intermittent fever, presumably malaria, in particular.[24] Duncan commented on the quality of the grapes which he tasted in Constantia in South Africa. Throughout his life he carried a piece of gold, acquired during his voyage, as a memento.[25] The Captain, Robert Preston, offered Duncan £500 to be ship's surgeon on the next voyage, which Duncan declined, even though £500 amounted to about five years income of a professional man at that time.[26]

Duncan's Doctor of Medicine degree

In Duncan's day it was not necessary for a medical student to have a degree in order to practice medicine and few troubled to undergo the ordeal and expense of obtaining a degree, although if they had any academic pretensions a MD degree was desirable. On the completion of his medical studies at the University of Edinburgh, Duncan did not sit the examination for a MD degree. The reputation of the Edinburgh Medical School at this period depended not only on the quality of its professors, but on the high standing and rigorous requirements of its MD degree. Candidates were required to have studied medicine for three years or more (many did more), at least one of which must have been spent at the University of Edinburgh. The required subjects were anatomy, surgery, chemistry, botany, materia medica, pharmacy, medical theory and practice. Attendance at clinical lectures at the Royal Infirmary was also obligatory.

The lectures in Duncan's time were mostly given in English, but the examination was conducted in Latin – a deterrent for many, although Duncan would not have found this a problem. The first part took the form of an oral examination by one of the professors, at his home. If the candidate passed this, a further oral examination in Latin was conducted by two or more professors in the University library. Next, the student had to write a commentary on an aphorism of Hippocrates simply to prove that he had some knowledge of Greek. Then he had to give a written answer to a medical question and submit two case histories. Finally, he had to submit and defend a thesis in Latin. Many of the students had to take cramming courses from 'grinders' to acquire the jargon required for degree examinations, and some engaged the help of classical scholars to translate their theses into Latin, the going rate being ten guineas.[27] It was alleged that theses could even be bought! The theses were mostly very mundane, a notable exception being Joseph Black's 'De Humore Acido a Cibris Orto et Magnesia Alba' (1754) an account of his preliminary studies which led to the discovery of carbon dioxide. Only a minority of students actually took the exam; the examination fee of £10 (equivalent to £1000 today) was beyond the means of many. When Duncan was a student, only 20 individuals sat the degree exam. In 1827, when the Medical School was at its peak with over 2000 students, only 160 took the MD degree.

While Duncan undoubtedly fulfilled the necessary conditions to sit the Edinburgh MD, he chose an easier course. On his return from his East Indian voyage, he obtained his MD degree at University of St Andrews which, although it had no medical school at that time, was empowered to grant this degree, sometimes without examination, to applicants who had studied elsewhere and had suitable letters of recommendation and were able to afford the fee.[28] In Duncan's case the customary fee of £10 was waived because he was 'the Grandchild of a Master (professor) and a young man of great merit'.[29] His thesis was 'De Alvi Purgantium Natura et Usu',[30] 'On the nature and use of (agents) that purge the bowel'. Duncan, 50 years later, was to poke fun at the Scottish universities, St Andrews and Aberdeen, which made their money by selling degrees, and became a staunch champion for the integrity of the Edinburgh MD (see chapter XIII). Duncan's respect for the Edinburgh MD became so great that he had the theses of his students bound in volumes, with leather backings embossed with the crest of his family heraldic device – a greyhound and the motto *Vivat Veritas*. In these volumes the contents are listed in his handwriting and some are inscribed to Duncan by the author. Edinburgh University Library (EUL) possesses 150 of these volumes, each containing about ten theses, and the numbering of the volumes suggests that another 100 existed at one time.

Application for the Chair of Medicine at University of St Andrews

The year 1770 was an eventful one for Duncan. He became a licentiate of the Royal College of Physicians of Edinburgh and published his first book, *Elements of Therapeutics*. In that year he applied for the Chandos Chair of Medicine in St Andrews. There were four candidates. Duncan was supported by warm testimonials from John Gregory and William Cullen, who wrote, 'I will pawn my credit upon it, that he will make an ingenious Professor and an able practitioner of physic'.[31] Despite these recommendations, the chair was awarded to James Flint, a physician from Dumbarton.

Duncan did well to fail in his application, for the chair was a sinecure.[32] Having no medical faculty, the professor's lectures were simply an optional subject in the arts curriculum and Duncan's talents would have been wasted had he succeeded.

Marriage

On Sunday 19 August 1770 the banns of Andrew Duncan and Elizabeth Knox were proclaimed at the Lady Yester Kirk in Edinburgh and the wedding took place on 4 February 1771. At that time the announcement of banns was a legal requirement prior to a marriage and usually the wedding took place soon thereafter; the unusual six-month delay between the proclamation of banns and marriage is unexplained. Elizabeth Knox (1751-1829) was the daughter of John Knox, a surgeon in the service of the East India Company and a descendant of the brother of John Knox, the reformer of the Church of Scotland. Although Duncan rarely refers to his wife in his writings, the fact that they had twelve children suggests a happy relationship (see appendix II).

At a meeting of the Royal Company of Archers in 1822, in response to a toast in his honour, Duncan replied that 1771 had been a memorable year, for three good things had happened to him. He had married Elizabeth Knox, he had been nominated for membership of the Royal Company of

Archers, and he was created a Knight of that most ancient Order of Merit, the Beggar's Benison (a society dedicated to sex, see chapter X). It is of interest that he should bracket together his marriage with membership of a distinguished society and a sex club as being his most memorable sources of fulfilment. In that year he also became a Fellow of the Royal College of Physicians of Edinburgh, of which he was later to be elected president for two terms. The Duncan family home at that time was in Bristo Street, near to the Chapel of Ease, where his family vault remains to this day.[33]

Becoming established

Now fully qualified and married, Duncan settled down to establish himself as a physician in what was a very competitive market. The only physicians entitled to treat patients in the Royal Infirmary were two salaried physicians-in-ordinary and a panel of visiting physicians nominated by the Royal College of Physicians. The professors of medicine attended in rotation the patients in two wards set aside for teaching purposes. Apart from the Lying-in Hospital founded by Alexander Hamilton, Professor of Midwifery, no other hospital beds were available to the remaining physicians, whose practice was restricted largely to home visits, consultations and advice given by correspondence. Wealthy private patients, able to pay a fee, were scarce, and private practice was dominated by the surgeon apothecaries, who were entitled to dispense drugs. This was a privilege denied to the Fellows of the Royal College of Physicians – one of the many sources of irritation between the two branches of medicine (see chapter XII). To make a success of private practice, a physician had to have good connections or establish a reputation over a period of years. Duncan, lacking any influential friends or relations, was aware that success and financial security demanded some extra entrepreneurial effort.

Publishing enterprises

Duncan had been invited to contribute the section on 'Medicine' for the first edition of the *Encyclopaedia Britannica,* which no doubt explains why he matriculated at the University of Edinburgh for two years after he obtained his St Andrews MD in 1769. Access to the University library was then restricted to matriculated students and members of the teaching faculty, and his commission for the *Encyclopaedia,* would have required extensive library access. The *Encyclopaedia,* which was first published in 1771, became a great success and is one of the most notable and enduring legacies of the Scottish Enlightenment. Subsequent editions followed with regularity and with ever increasing size. Duncan made a major revision of his entry in the fourth edition (1809). In the first edition, his section had amounted to 112 pages and relied heavily on William Cullen's teaching. In the fourth, his entry was 299 pages and included an account of medical history, dating back to ancient Greek, Roman and Arabic sources. There was a section on what we would now call physiology, and a greatly expanded section on medicine and on his pet topics of medical jurisprudence and medical police. His identity as the author was not revealed until the introduction to the fifth edition (1817), although he does give a clue in page 302 of the fourth edition when he refers to the death of his favourite son from *Cynanthe Trachealis* or the croup (see page 98).

It is doubtful whether his contributions to the *Encyclopaedia Britannica* brought him much wealth, and being anonymous probably brought him little renown, although no doubt his local colleagues were aware of his involvement. Another enterprise was to bring him much more fame and fortune. Realising that it was difficult for the average doctor to keep abreast of the medical literature, he founded in 1773 the ground-breaking and financially successful *Medical and Philosophical Commentaries* (see chapter II). At this early stage of his career he must have made his mark and gained the respect of his colleagues, for the Aesculapian Society which he started in the same year attracted some of his most distinguished contemporaries and flourishes to this day. These were remarkable achievements for a young doctor aged only 29, and they undoubtedly brought his name to the attention of the medical profession within the city and beyond. Perhaps Duncan's fondness for joining and creating clubs and societies was prompted by his need to make social contacts for professional advancement, although his outgoing and friendly disposition would naturally have led him towards this end.

Locum professor

When John Gregory, Professor of the Institutes of Medicine, died in 1773, Edinburgh Town Council considered five possible candidates for the vacant chair, including Andrew Duncan.[34] On the advice of the medical faculty, Dr Alexander Monro Drummond was appointed to the vacancy. Dr Drummond, who at that time lived in Italy as physician to the King of Naples, did not appear to want the chair, nor did he want to live in Edinburgh. In the interim the Council appointed first Francis Home and then Andrew Duncan as locum professors, a role which Duncan fulfilled from 1774 to 1776.[35] When it became apparent that Drummond was not returning, the chair once more came up for consideration. Andrew Duncan and James Gregory, the son of John Gregory, were the principal candidates. Nepotism won the day and the Lord Provost chose James Gregory, a recent graduate aged only 23. It has been suggested by Alexander Bower that the five-year delay in replacing Drummond had been simply a delaying tactic to allow James Gregory time to qualify to succeed his father,[36] but if this was so, Duncan was quite unaware of the stratagem.[37]

Duncan was bitterly disappointed to have failed and aired his grievances at some length in *Medical Commentaries,* where he outlined his plans for the future. He pointed out that it was improper that the appointment should have been made without discussion within the medical profession. Indeed no discussion had taken place even within the Town Council, for the Lord Provost offered no other name than Gregory's for consideration, although Duncan had declared his candidature for the chair.[38] In the event, James Gregory proved to be a very satisfactory choice and filled the chair with distinction until 1790 when Duncan eventually succeeded him. Nevertheless the circumstance of his appointment was to rankle with Duncan for the rest of his life and no doubt contributed to his dispute with Gregory, relating to the Royal College of Physicians. Duncan wrote:

> I have … the satisfaction of being able to retire from this arduous task [as locum professor] *with ease in my own mind, and I hope not without some additional credit in your estimation. … I was not without hopes that by my exertions here, I should still have been able to hold the office of teacher in the University, and I had no hesitation in offering myself a candidate for the chair lately vacant. In that competition I had indeed no powerful connection, no political interest to aid my cause, but I thought that my chance for success stood on no infirm basis when it was rested on what I had done to deserve it. … I can no longer act in an equally conspicuous capacity, yet I hope I may hereafter be employed as a teacher in one not less useful. It is my intention to dedicate my labours to the service of students of medicine.*[39]

Extramural teaching

Despite losing his university connection, Duncan was determined to continue teaching which he enjoyed and which provided an important source of income. In 1777 he advertised his 'Independent course of lectures on the Theory and Practice of Medicine outwith the walls of the University'. The course was designed to cover 'the whole fundamental principles of the healing art … within the short space of six months'. This he accomplished by 'avoiding minutiae and matters of mere curiosity'.[40] A year later he added a course of materia medica in the summer months. His extramural courses were very popular and attracted ever increasing numbers of students until his eventual appointment to the Chair of Institutes of Medicine in 1790. To accompany his lectures he published outlines of his courses in two volumes entitled *Heads of Lectures on the Theory and Practice of Medicine* and *Heads of Lectures on Materia Medica*. In the introduction to the former, Duncan offers the following advice, which is perhaps still relevant today:

> *It is not from having spent in thoughtless dissipation a certain number of years at schools of medicine; it is not from having repeatedly paid fees to the most eminent teachers, nor from the charm of academical honours, that disease can be cured. This is to be accomplished only by new medical knowledge; which cannot be acquired without diligent, nay unwearied, exertion.*[41]

In order to conduct his large classes, Duncan required suitable accommodation. In the incredibly short period of one year he had built a substantial 'medical academy' at 10 Surgeon's Square between the old Surgeon's Hall and that of the Medical Society. This contained a commodious teaching room and several other apartments which were designed to be used by students for experimental inquiries on medical and philosophical subjects. It is a measure of Duncan's success that he had the resources to build this teaching facility at the age of 33.

Duncan was banned from using his medical academy in Surgeon's Square for the purpose of seeing outpatients there. Certain members of the Royal College of Surgeons (which was the feuar) insisted that an appropriate clause be inserted into his feu to confirm that his house would not be used in any way that might become a nuisance to the neighbourhood. Until it was built, however, the College allowed Duncan the use of its hall for two hours in the day, twice a week, for three months, in order to lecture there on cases of patients with chronic diseases.[42] When Duncan became Professor of Institutes of Medicine, he no longer required his medical academy and sold the building to other extramural teachers. In 1800 John Barclay acquired the property and used it as his anatomy school, together with his partner and eventual successor, Robert Knox. It was to this building that Burke and Hare delivered bodies for dissection.[43] The extramural course in anatomy conducted by Barclay and Knox attracted many more students than the university course conducted by Alexander Monro *tertius*, whose teaching lacked the inspiration of his forebears.

Duncan was the first physician to establish a significant extramural course of medicine, but a tradition of such teaching in Edinburgh had commenced in the 16th century with the founding of the Incorporation of Surgeons, and surgery continued to be taught outwith the University in Duncan's day. The Monros, *secundus* and *tertius*, the Professors of Anatomy, were also nominally Professors of Surgery, but did not operate or teach the subject. So successful were some of these extramural courses that they became an increasingly important feature of medical education in Edinburgh. Some of Edinburgh's most distinguished doctors started their careers as extra-mural teachers, including John and Charles Bell, Robert Liston, John Lizars, Sir William Ferguson, Sir John Fraser, Henry Littlejohn, Sir James Young Simpson, James Syme and Sir David Wilkie. The popularity of these courses led eventually to the establishment of the independent extramural School of Medicine conducted by the Royal Colleges of Physicians and Surgeons in Edinburgh from 1895 to 1948.[44]

Dispensary for the Sick Poor

To supplement his lectures, Duncan needed access to patients. In 1776 he established the Dispensary for the Sick Poor (see chapter III) with the dual purpose of providing a much needed facility for the underprivileged, as well as providing cases for teaching purposes. Examples of the type of patients presenting to the Dispensary are given in *Medical Cases selected from the records of the Public Dispensary at Edinburgh*, published by Duncan in three editions (1778-84). In the preface he gives the background to his extramural lectures, which he states were started at the request of several students of medicine,

> ... on the cases of patients subjected to chronical diseases. With this view, I then proposed to give medicines gratis to a few patients only who might be the subject of lectures. But the number of indigent individuals, who made daily application to be admitted to the benefits of this institution, soon led to the establishment of a Public Dispensary in Edinburgh.

Students attending Duncan's lectures paid two guineas per session for each of the courses on theory and practice of medicine, one guinea for materia medica and for the lectures on the Dispensary cases, with half a guinea towards the supply of medicines for the Dispensary. Duncan recruited Dr Charles Webster to assist with teaching and running the Dispensary.

Students, including Charles Darwin (uncle of Charles Darwin of evolutionary fame), also assisted in the running of the Dispensary and were responsible for taking the case histories, although they had to pay five guineas for the privilege. Duncan emphasised the importance of accurate history-taking and record-keeping and learning from these. During its first year 19 patients per month were seen, increasing to an average of 320 per month over the 52 years of Duncan's involvement. By the time of his death, 200,000 patients had been treated in his clinic. The Dispensary was granted a Royal charter in 1818.

There are no details about the size of his private practice during this time. Later he kept a record of his private patients from 1801 to 1806. The practice declined progressively from 209 in 1801 to 124 in 1806.[45] The numbers seem small – four a week or less, but competition was intense, and Duncan had many other conflicting interests at that time. Perhaps, before he obtained his chair, he may have had a larger practice.

Becoming a professor

In 1790 Cullen retired from the lucrative Chair of Medical Practice and was succeeded by James Gregory, who vacated his Chair of Institutes of Medicine. The reason for Gregory's move was that the course of Medical Practice attracted many more fee-paying students.[46] Andrew Duncan was appointed to the Chair of Institutes of Medicine that Gregory had vacated and for which he had applied unsuccessfully in 1776. In this year he was also elected President of the Royal College of Physicians for the first of his two presidential terms.

At last Duncan achieved his ambition of becoming a member of the medical faculty. He was at that time the only holder of a medical chair who was not the son of the previous occupant. Nepotism was the accepted norm, and between 1786 and 1807 eight of the ten appointments to medical chairs at the University of Edinburgh went to sons of medical professors.[47] In his new role Duncan immediately lent his authority to raising funds for the rebuilding of the new University College by approaching the medical alumni of the University, particularly those from overseas.[48]

In 1792 Duncan moved from his home in Bristo Street to a grander dwelling in Adam Square, more in keeping with his new status as a professor and college president. Adam Square, although so called, consisted only of three substantial adjoined houses built by John Adam in 1764. The central house was the grandest, having paired bow-fronted windows, and had been occupied until his death by Robert Dundas (1713-87), Lord President of the Court of Session and half-brother of Henry Dundas (1743-1811) who became the first Viscount Melville. In 1821 this house became the Watt Institution and Edinburgh School of Arts – a precursor of Heriot-Watt University. Duncan occupied the most southerly of the three houses, across North College Street from the New College of the University which was then being rebuilt. In 1820 the Great Hall of the New College was completed and Duncan was invited to be the first promoter for the MD degree in the new building. He gave his address in Latin to the 117 successful candidates. The Principal, the Rev. Dr Baird, concluded the ceremony with a particularly energetic prayer. Adam Square was demolished during the building of Chambers Street in 1871.[49]

Each professor was allowed a free hand in deciding the contents of his course. The boundaries of the different chairs were not clearly defined and there was much overlap, which may explain why some courses were more popular than others. According to the *Guide for gentlemen studying medicine at the University of Edinburgh*, Duncan divided his course into three parts: (1) nature, properties and diseases of the various parts of the human body, (2) therapeutics, and (3) medical jurisprudence. The *Guide* stated:

> *Dr Duncan is entitled to the warmest encomiums for having introduced into his course a regular view of medical jurisprudence. In questions concerning the effect of poison, manslaughter, violation of chastity, child murder, etc. the lives or fortunes of the parties may depend on the decision of the practitioner. … The third part of Dr Duncan's course should therefore, be considered as more valuable than the others.*

Duncan occupied his chair until his 82nd year, but in his latter years was supported first by the appointment of his son Andrew Duncan Jr and later by Dr William Pulteney Alison as conjunct professors. At the age of 70 he relinquished the teaching of therapeutics to Dr Alison, who was to succeed him, but continued to teach the Philosophy of Medicine until his last year, delivering five lectures a week. At the same time he gave up examining students for the MD degree. It had become a major commitment, examiners being involved for three hours a day for ten weeks prior to the graduation of successful students, which interfered with their other professorial duties.

Duncan took his teaching very seriously. He wrote in 1818 that he had

> *… although aged 74 delivered 120 lectures without interruption … though attentive in discharging his duty as a medical Practitioner and fond of active amusements in the open air, yet he has made it an invariable rule during the whole course of his life, never to postpone his business as a lecturer.*[50]

He made a great mistake, however, by continuing to lecture when well past his prime. Robert Christison, who attended Duncan's lectures in 1816, described him as

> *… an aged, most amiable, benevolent, but by this time rather feebleminded man. He … contrived to make it appear as if the physiology, pathology and therapeutics of Gaubius*[51] *and the previous century were the physiology, pathology and therapeutics of the present day, and the existing doctrines those of the historical past. Little therefore was to be learned from him. But he was so kindly and warm-hearted a man in manner, had done so much practical good in his day, and was so attentive to his students, whom he invited in succession once every week to a dull enough tea-and-talk party, that he was universally respected and respectfully listened to.*[52]

Christison also attended Duncan's ward rounds:

> *It so happened that several times in succession, I found the old Doctor in the act of proceeding to the same bed, that of one Christian Jack, plainly a familiar holdfast, long past yielding any new clinical instruction ... and gave out* [for the benefit of students who were expected to take notes] *'Christian Jack. – As yesterday. –* Continuentur medicamenta' [continue the treatment].[53]

Duncan's tea parties were held usually on Sunday evenings. Invitations were sent to 20 or 30 of his students at a time. Charles Darwin, author of *The Origin of Species* and nephew of the Charles Darwin referred to on page 15, attended Duncan's lectures and his tea parties which he found dull occasions. In a letter to his sister Susan he wrote, 'Next Friday we are going to the old Dr Duncan, & I hope it will be a pleasanter party than the last; ... What an extraordinary old man he is, now being past 80, & continuing to lecture. Dr Hawley hints that he is rapidly failing.' Charles and his brother Erasmus had presented Duncan with a letter of introduction from their father on their arrival in Edinburgh in October 1825.

Duncan was happily unaware of his failing powers. In a letter to his grand-daughter Eliza in India (1 November 1825), he wrote:

> *I began in the 82nd year of my age my winters labours, or rather my winters pleasures for the 57th Winter Session. I had a numerous and respectable audience, and according to the account of some of my old pupils who were present, I never lectured more distinctly or with greater animation in the course of my life.*[54]

In a letter to Charles Wightman (5 April 1826), he wrote:

> *I have great reason to thank God for the blessings bestowed on my old age. ... While I enjoy, to a sufficient degree,* mens sana in corpore sano *for such public duties* [lecturing] *... Mrs Duncan and my three unmarried daughters, my present messmates, and the nurses of my second childishness although not of mere oblivion, join in requesting to be kindly remembered to you etc.*[55]

Duncan was very proud of his longevity, and in almost every letter and lecture after the age of 70 he rather tiresomely referred to it. Christison calculated the average age at death of the 78 members of the *Senatus Academicus* who had died after 1820 and found it to be 66.4 years, whereas their actuarial life expectancy from the time of their appointment was about a year less. Duncan at 83 was by no means the oldest. Sir David Brewster,

Principal of the University, lived to 86, and Alexander Monro *secundus* and *tertius* reached 84 and 85 respectively. Principals of the Scottish universities did better, outliving their life expectancy by 8.9 years. Christison concluded: 'severe mental exercise is favourable to longevity to a remarkable degree'.[56]

Medical jurisprudence and public health

Medical jurisprudence was a subject close to Duncan's heart and a popular feature of his lectures. In 1795 he commenced a campaign to have a Chair of Medical Jurisprudence established. In a 'Memorial to the Patrons of the University' (Edinburgh Town Council) he made his case, detailing the topics to be considered under this heading. These were in two main parts, the first being what would now be regarded as Forensic Medicine. The second, which he referred to as Medical Police, he defined as 'the application of the principles deduced from the different branches of medical knowledge, for the promotion, preservation and restoration of general health' – or what we would now call public health.

The Town Council rejected Duncan's proposal. His left-wing political leanings counted against him in his dealings with the Tory Council, just as it delayed his attempt to found a lunatic asylum. In 1806, following the death of William Pitt, the short-lived 'Ministry of all the talents' was formed with Whig representation. This window of opportunity, with the help of Duncan's friend, Henry Erskine, the Lord Advocate, enabled a Regius Chair of Jurisprudence and Medical Police to be created. The Town Council was powerless to resist a crown appointment and Duncan was able to have his son, Andrew Duncan Jr, appointed as first professor.

The introduction of the teaching of public health into the medical curriculum was a first in this country and may be regarded as one of Duncan's greatest achievements. A full account of this chair is given in chapter VI.

Duncan and the Royal Infirmary

Teaching of medical students had been a feature of the Royal Infirmary since soon after it opened in 1741. Students paid 7½ guineas a year for the privilege of attending the wards. (Surgical apprentices paid only 5 guineas.) After 1783, when attendance at the Infirmary for at least a year was made an obligatory part of the medical curriculum, the student fees represented up to 25% of the hospital income.[57] For their money, students were allowed to follow the attending physician and attend lectures. They were obliged to remove their hats in the operating theatre in deference to the surgeon and to avoid obstructing the view of others. The medical staffing at consultant level consisted of two salaried physicians-in-ordinary. Two wards, each with

14 beds, were set aside for the use of the medical professors who worked in pairs, each alternating for three months during the academic term. The professor in charge had the choice of the patients admitted each day in order to select the most suitable for teaching purposes.[58] Other physicians were denied the opportunity of having patients admitted and could only attend, if requested, in an advisory capacity.

Duncan spent three years attached to the hospital during his student days. During his locum professorship in 1774-76 he enjoyed the teaching experience so much that he continued with extramural teaching thereafter, making use of the outpatients at his Public Dispensary for teaching purposes. When he finally achieved his professorial chair, he once more had access to the inpatients in the teaching wards alternating with James Gregory. Duncan stated that he was so conscientious that he attended the hospital three times a day. The anonymous student records of his ward rounds mentioned on page 58 indicate the quality of his teaching and detailed knowledge of his patients. After 1818 he gave up clinical teaching in favour of his son, Andrew Duncan Jr.

The Royal Infirmary in Duncan's day was highly regarded. John Howard, the English philanthropist and prison reformer, wrote in 1784:

> I could not but admire the Royal Infirmary of Edinburgh. Few hospitals in England exceed it in airiness and cleanliness. Great attention is paid to the patients, and their complaints are very accurately minuted. The success of this institution is evident from the few that die in comparison with the number admitted.[59]

By 1817, however, things must have deteriorated. In that year John Wigham (1781-1862), a wealthy cotton manufacturer and generous benefactor, at a meeting of contributors to the Royal Infirmary, criticised the lack of management, particularly with regard to diet and cleanliness. Wigham, while acknowledging that the medical care was above reproach, reported that he was much surprised to witness the pitiful quantity of porridge and bread given to each patient, with a limited amount of milk and beer (the latter of very poor quality). Relatives had to bring in food contrary to the rules of the hospital. There was no cutlery or plates for the patients. The linen was filthy, with some patients having lain seven to eight weeks without a change of sheets. Hands, face and feet were seldom washed – there was only one towel available in each ward – and some of the beds were swarming with lice. Patients had caught the 'itch' while in the hospital. He was also critical of the nursing care. There was only one nurse in each ward and they were untrained and poorly paid, receiving only £5 per year.[60]

Duncan reacted with a letter to Wigham:

Now in the 74th year of my age I have had an opportunity of witnessing the practice of medicine in three different quarters of the Globe[61] and it is my sincere belief that there does not exist a charitable institution on the face of the Earth in which the sick poor have a better chance of recovery than in the Royal Infirmary of Edinburgh. If I be examined before you I trust I shall be able to convince you that you are much mistaken and have been mis-informed respecting that Hospital.[62]

A meeting of the Contributors to the Royal Infirmary was held in January 1818 to consider Wigham's complaints. A number of individuals connected with the hospital were called to give evidence. Duncan presented a declaration respecting the Infirmary which he opened by stating:

My first connection with the Royal Infirmary was in the year 1764 when I commenced my medical studies at Edinburgh and during the [54] years ... I have had many opportunities ... respecting that charitable establishment, ... as a student ..., as a clinical professor ... having occasionally the charge of the clinical wards for more than [30] years and ... as an official manager of the Royal Infirmary for ... two years while I was President of the Royal College of Physicians.[63]

During his evidence Duncan, in reply to questioning, stated that he thought the diet was highly proper for a hospital. He thought that the quality of the porridge was very good, as well as the milk. He had never heard a patient complain of having had too little. He had frequently seen the beef and it likewise was good. The beef was dressed in the ward so that the patient received it hot and the way he liked it. He had never seen the beef thrown upon the beds of the patients. He frequently ordered clean linen for his patients. He did not think it prudent for the nurse to wash each patient on admission, but the clerk could order this when appropriate. He also found the nurses to be very attentive and humane.

In general the other witnesses gave similar evidence, although some were more critical. It was noted that because of the age of the hospital – one of the first to be built in this country outside London – its design was rather dated when compared with newer hospitals. It was also observed that in 1817, the year in which the alleged deficiencies had been noted, there had been a severe influenza epidemic which had put increasing pressure on the resources of the hospital. The funding was also recognised to be less than ideal.

As a consequence of the enquiry, a number of recommendations were made regarding improvement of laundry facilities, catering and fund-raising. Wigham remained a generous contributor to the hospital.

President of the Royal College of Physicians of Edinburgh

Duncan was elected President of the Royal College of Physicians for the first time on 2 December 1790. At his first meeting he proposed that committees be appointed to examine the possibility of establishing a lunatic asylum, the introduction of general inoculation against smallpox, the creation of vapour baths, and the improvement of facilities for cold bathing. The Asylum Committee recommended the creation of a powerful body of trustees to raise the necessary funds and supervise the planning. It was to be many years before this ambition was realised (see chapter IV). The Inoculation Committee was more effective; by advertising in the press and obtaining the support of the clergy, the uptake of inoculation was increased at least temporarily.

The therapeutic benefits of various types of bathing was a favourite hobby-horse of Duncan's. William Buchan, in his widely read *Domestic Medicine*,[64] had recommended the benefits of cold bathing: 'By it the body is braced and strengthened, the circulation and secretions promoted and, were it conducted with prudence, many diseases might thereby be prevented.'

The properties of bathing presented problems. The *Edinburgh Courant* of 30 May 1761 reported under the heading 'Leith Bathing in Sea Water':

> *This sort of bathing is much recommended and approve of, but the want of a machine, or wooden house on wheels, ... to undress in, and to carry those who intend to bathing to a proper depth of water, hath induced many in this part of the country to neglect the opportunity of trying to acquire the benefits to health it commonly gives.*

The Cold Bath Committee recommended that a large basin be created on the shore at Leith, which would be filled with sea water at every tide. It should be divided into two parts, one for women and children and the other for men and boys. The Vapour Bath Committee recommended that the managers of the Royal Infirmary should add a vapour bath to their existing hot and cold baths. History does not relate whether either of these recommendations was acted upon.

Another College initiative during Duncan's first term as president was an attempt to establish the means of obtaining reliable mortality statistics, a subject which the College was to continue to promote until this objective was achieved in the Birth and Death Registration Act of 1836. Duncan, on his own initiative, compiled a report of deaths and epidemics within the City of Edinburgh and environs in 1810, which he submitted to the College as an example of the value of such information.[65] There were three epidemics that year: *Cynanche Parotidea* (mumps), *Pertussis* (whooping cough) and *Scarlatina Angiosa* (scarlet fever). All were mild; the distribution demonstrated spread by contagion. Duncan's experience convinced him that having any of these diseases conferred life-long immunity from further attacks. The deaths were recorded separately for children and adults (the age limit of childhood was not stated). The numbers in each category were about equal overall, but there was considerable variation from one churchyard to another, which may reflect social circumstances. Adults outnumbered children in Greyfriars, Canongate and West Church, while the reverse occurred in Calton, Chapel of Ease and Leith.

McCrae attributes the relative lack of success of Duncan's presidential initiatives to the prevailing political situation. The disturbances within France preoccupied the political leaders and made them suspicious of and resistant to new initiatives.[66]

His second term as president, from 1824-25, was unremarkable and it was not extended for a second year as was customary. At that time he was 80 and much involved in his dispute with James Hamilton (see chapter XIII). Duncan did involve himself with one initiative concerning the inadequacies and deterioration of the condition of the Royal Infirmary. His old friend and golfing companion, Sir William Fettes (1750-1836), a very wealthy merchant and philanthropist, had offered to contribute towards the establishment of new hospital. Duncan wrote to him, in his capacity as President of the College, urging him against this proposal as it would compete with the charitable donations to the Royal Infirmary which was always short of funds and badly needing refurbishment and enlargement. He recommended that it would be a better plan to establish a Lock Hospital and a Hospital for Incurables. A 'Lock Hospital' would be used for the incarceration of dissolute females affected by venereal disease until their cure was complete, 'thus removing the source of venereal contagion and affording protection to imprudent youths'.[67] Why infected imprudent youths should not be similarly confined was not explained.

Duncan's letter to Sir William Fettes provoked an angry printed letter of response from Dr Richard Poole who had been one of the prime movers in promoting the idea of a new hospital.[68] He ridiculed Duncan's statements that 'for nearly a century past [the Royal Infirmary] has contributed very essentially both to the honour and interest of the city of Edinburgh' and that it was 'justly considered that first Hospital in Europe for Clinical Lectures' which were 'one of the most important branches of one of the most eminent schools of Medicine in Europe'. He insultingly suggested that it would be better if Duncan's beloved old Royal Infirmary should become the Lock Hospital and Hospital for Incurables, and be replaced by a new hospital.

There is no record of Duncan's response, if any, to this letter. In the event none of the various proposals was carried out and Sir William left his vast fortune to the founding of Fettes College. Another 54 years were to elapse before the new Royal Infirmary was opened on a site in Lauriston Place in 1879. Poole was to become a major critic of Duncan again in connection with the Edinburgh Lunatic Asylum.

The Edinburgh Lunatic Asylum

One of Duncan's achievements which gave him greatest satisfaction, and which was mentioned in his citation for the Freedom of the City, was the foundation of the Lunatic Asylum. As mentioned above, his first action on becoming President of the Royal College of Physicians was to establish a committee to advance this idea. The timing, however, was not auspicious. The politicians and the public were too much preoccupied with the unrest in France at that time to involve themselves in domestic matters and the Asylum appeal got off to a very slow start.

Once his mind was set on a course, however, Duncan pursued it relentlessly. His opportunity came once more with the change of government in 1806 and the assistance of Henry Erskine, then the Lord Advocate, who was instrumental in obtaining government finance and a Royal charter from King George III. The foundation stone was laid in Morningside in 1809 and the Edinburgh Lunatic Asylum was opened in 1813. From small beginnings it has grown into the present-day Royal Edinburgh Hospital.

Duncan's literary interests

The University library was accessible only to matriculated students and members of staff. Before Duncan's professorial appointment he would have been obliged to buy his books. A ledger exists in the archive of the publisher John Murray, recently acquired by the National Library of Scotland, which details Duncan's transactions with the Edinburgh bookseller and publisher Charles Elliot from 1782 to 1786. Among the books bought by Duncan were Fergusson's *Poems*, four volumes of Pennant's *British Zoology*, Chambaud's *Fables Choisies* and a number of contemporary medical texts. An account of Duncan's relationships with his publishers, John Murray in London and Charles Elliot in Edinburgh, is given in chapter II.

As a professor, Duncan was entitled to borrow books from the University library. A register exists of professorial borrowings during the years 1790-1805.[69] Duncan's entries occupy several pages and display a catholic range of interests, although the register is difficult to read because of heavy scoring out when a volume was returned. Among those identifiable are many medical books, including Benjamin Rush's *Inquiries*, and texts on anatomy and medical jurisprudence. Duncan's wider interests are indicated by the borrowing of Samuel Johnson's *Journey to the Hebrides*, Erasmus Darwin's *Zoonomia*, Somner's *Antiquities of Canterbury*, the works of Pliny and Aristotle, and many books on natural history including several volumes of Buffon's *Histoire Naturelle*, Catesby's *Natural History of Carolina, Florida, and the Bahama Islands*, and others on ornithology, conchology, medical botany and mineralogy.

Most curious among the borrowings are books of sonatas and quartets by Pleyel.[70] Nowhere does Duncan mention that he had any musical skills or interests – perhaps these were borrowed on behalf of members of his family, or for his friend Henry Erskine who was known to be a competent violinist and owner of a Cremona violin. Catesby's *Natural History*[71] was probably borrowed for his daughter Elizabeth. Andrew Duncan Jr, writing to his father from London on 23 February 1795, said, 'Bess complains that she has got nothing to draw. You might get Catesby's *Natural History of Carolina* from the College Library [for her].'

Freedom of the City

On 7 September 1808 the City of Edinburgh admitted Andrew Duncan and James Gregory as Burgesses and Guild Brethren – the equivalent of the Freedom of the City. This honour was awarded to those who had made substantial contributions not only to the capital but to the nation and the world. Duncan's award specifies that it was given in recognition of 'his unwearied attentions to the Public Dispensary and of his great exertion for the establishment of a Lunatic Asylum in this Metropolis'.[72] Distinguished visitors such as Benjamin Franklin were similarly honoured. During the 19th century other medical recipients included Edward Jenner 1804, Thomas Hope 1817, Sir James McGrigor (Director General of the Army Medical Department 1826), Sir Astley Cooper 1837, Sir James Young Simpson 1869 and Lord Lister 1898. In recent times the award has rarely been made, the last medical recipient being the much respected neuro-surgeon Professor Norman Dott in 1962.

Duncan was the recipient of many honours, including his appointment as first Physician to the King in Scotland in 1821, for which he received an honorarium of £100 per annum. Duncan's international reputation was further recognised by his election to membership of the Medical Society of Denmark, the Royal Medical Society of Paris, the American Philosophical Society, the Medical Society of London and the Cesarian University of Moscow.

Recreations

Duncan was a keen advocate of the healthful benefits of regular exercise and, despite his busy professional life, he found time to practise what he preached. His membership of the Royal Company of Archers and the Honourable Company of Golfers indicates his enthusiasm for these sports.

One of Duncan's great hobbies was gardening, which led to the founding of the Royal Caledonian Horticultural Society in 1809. In one of his lengthy discourses to the society, he attributed his love of gardening to his grandfather, William Vilant:

> ... a Professor at St Andrews who enjoyed good health, and who amused himself in the cultivation of his garden, even till his ninety-sixth year of his age, I consider myself as indebted for a hereditary pleasure in the garden. ... and when you consider, Gentlemen, that I am still able in the seventy-ninth year of my age, now to address you from this chair, with vigour both of mind and body, very little impaired, you may, I think, view me as a living example of the healthfulness of Horticulture.[73]

In another discourse he said, 'Horticulture, as a relaxation from laborious profession, has, during the whole course of a long life, been my favourite amusement ...'.[74] Duncan tried, unsuccessfully, to persuade the University to found a Chair of Horticulture.

Duncan's garden was on St Leonard's Hill, about a quarter of a mile from his home, 'between the basalt columns at the foot of Arthur's Seat and Duddingston Lake' with 'Hinc Sanitas' ('from here health') inscribed at the entrance[75]: 'In that small garden I may be found almost every good Summer morning, before breakfast, obtaining from it both amusement and health.' He kept occasional records of the produce from his garden:

> In the year 1808, from my garden the extent of which is one million and an half of square inches, I had five Currants, two Gooseberries and a half the tenth part of an Apple, and the 235th part of a Pear for every square inch, exclusive of Broccoli, Cabbage, Turnip, and other useful vegetables. And in addition to all these, there was an unmeasurable crop of weeds and not a few caterpillars.[76]

He recorded the annual produce of his two Jargonelle pear trees, which ranged from 53 dozen in 1803 to a miserable three dozen in 1812. His apple trees were brought from Ireland and included a Murray Pepsin and a Crofton Pepsin. The garden also contained a hot-house, but the grapes it produced were nothing like the quality of grapes his son Andrew Jr obtained in Vienna.[77] In 1826 Duncan's garden was appropriated for the Edinburgh-Dalkeith Railway which commenced construction that year and opened in 1831. It was a horse-drawn railway connecting the collieries around Dalkeith with the city. He sent the last produce from the garden – ten fine apples – to the Caledonian Horticultural Society (see page 163).

Duncan's wife Elizabeth, a background figure, hardly mentioned in her husband's writings, must have shared his horticultural interests. She emerges in her own right as the winner of the two awards for her currant wine at a meeting of the Caledonian Horticultural Society in 1821 (see page 162).

Retirement

In 1823 Duncan announced in the press that he was retiring from visiting patients and would confine his medical practice to giving advice by correspondence. Shortly after, he qualified this announcement by stating that he would continue to visit friends, clergy, colleagues or students gratuitously, as in the past: 'I shall think myself amply compensated by the satisfaction which must always result from exerting my best endeavours for the removal or alleviation of the disease of my friends.'[78]

In his old age Duncan took up yet another cause. His four sons and five grandsons had been educated at the High School in Edinburgh, which by then had become overcrowded in its site in High School Wynd. Duncan did not think the classes should exceed 100 pupils! There was talk of rebuilding it elsewhere, and in a letter to Edinburgh Town Council he advocated the establishment of a second school to be located in the New Town:

> Old as I am, for in a few weeks I shall enter the eightieth year of my age, I do not despair of living to see these two schools mutually striving, by fair and open rivalship, to excel each other, and to teach the rudiments of Latin and Greek at Edinburgh, with every advantage to the rising generation.[79]

At that time the Town Council was considering a proposal by Henry Cockburn and others for the building of a new school. Whether Duncan's letter carried any weight is unknown, but the Council gave its approval and the Edinburgh Academy was built in the New Town in 1824. The High School was rebuilt on Calton Hill in 1829.

Duncan had a curious reverence for Arthur's Seat. In his discourse to the Caledonian Society of 1820, he effused, 'It is from the hand of the Great Architect of the Universe; and, to the thinking mind affords demonstrative evidence of the infinite power, wisdom, and goodness of the Creator'.[80]

He first recorded his habit of climbing Arthur's Seat, his 'Parnassus of Modern Athens', each May-day morning on 1 May 1807: 'My winter's labours in the University are always concluded in the last week of April: And ever since I have been a Professor, on the 1st May. ... I have treated myself with a walk to the top of Arthur's Seat before breakfast.'

He was sometimes accompanied by his grandchildren and greeted at the top by his students, or children from the Orphanage Hospital of which he was a governor. On reaching the summit he would declaim a poem which he had written for the occasion. On 1 May 1826 he read a poem addressed to his friend the Duke of Gordon, then the oldest living peer and President of the Royal Caledonian Horticultural Society.[81]

> Once more, good Duke, my duty to fulfil,
> I've reached the summit of this lofty hill,
> To thank my God for all his blessings given,
> And by my prayers, to aid my way to heaven.
> Long may your Grace enjoy the same delight,
> Till to a better world we take our flight.

To which the Duke replied:

> I'm eighty-two as well as you, And sound in lith and limb;
> But deil a bit, I am not fit, Up Arthur's Seat to climb.
> In such a fete I'll not compete – I yield in ambulation;
> But mount us baith on Highland shelts, Try first who gains the station.
> If such a race should e'er take place, none like it in the nation;
> Nor Sands of Leith, nor Ascot Heath, could show more population.

Clearly a couple of spirited old men. Duncan climbed the hill for the last time in 1827. Again he sent a poem to the Duke of Gordon, who replied on 5 May 1727 that he could not respond in verse: '... my wretched muse, has for some time past, been very lethargic.'[82] He wished Duncan health and vigour to climb Arthur's Seat for many succeeding years and 'add to your poetry'. The Duke died six weeks later and Duncan a year later, but not before he had composed yet another poem in anticipation of one more climb. In this he refers to a fall on 5 June 1827, while walking across the road from Adam's Square to the Senate Hall.

> But now my legs have failed, my head went round,
> And I tumbled senseless to the ground.
> Let then this Warning Bell teach me to know,
> That the next stroke may be the fatal blow.[83]

Although Duncan enjoyed robust health into old age, he mentions that he had suffered from recurrent fevers associated with headaches since child-hood. In the early days they had responded to cinchona bark, but in later life this had less effect. In 1774 he acquired a typhoid-like fever due to conta-gion from sitting at the bedside of a medical student. As he reached old age he seems to have become aware of his declining mental acuity: 'With a man ... past his 70th year ... life must be considered as very precarious, especially after mental exertion,' he wrote, quoting from Ecclesiastes, '... of making many books there is no end and much study is a weariness of the flesh.'[84] Perhaps this is best revealed in his annual discourses with which, according to Henry Cockburn, he oppressed the Caledonian Horticultural Society. These discourses, which were delivered annually from 1810-25 and dis-cussed more fully in chapter IX, reveal a progressive intellectual decline, becoming increasingly repetitive in the pursuit of unrealistic ambitions.

With some justification, Duncan regarded the establishment of the Royal Public Dispensary and the Edinburgh Lunatic Asylum as his greatest achievements. In his discourse to the Royal Caledonian Horticultural Society in 1823, he said:

> There is at least some chance that a prediction of my truly amiable and most excellent friend, the late Hon Henry Erskine, may at my death be fulfilled. When I was assiduously and successfully employed in promoting the estab-lishment of the Public Dispensary and Lunatic Asylum of Edinburgh, two establishments now confirmed by Royal charters ... he applied to me, with a very slight alteration, the lines of a justly celebrated British Poet applied to a distinguished British Patriot.
>
> > And you, good Doctor, with your latest breath,
> > Shall feel your ruling passion strong in death;
> > Just in that moment, as in all the past,
> > 'Improve my country, Heaven, shall be your last.'

This quotation is typical of many adulatory comments that Duncan made about himself and his achievements, and had printed for wider circulation. He revelled in the friendship and admiration of his peers, and in his associ-ation with people of rank. In the preface to a letter to a friend, on the death of the Duke of Gordon,[85] he makes the following revealing observation:

> So much have his Grace's letters to me, flattered my vanity, that I find it impossible for me to resist the temptation of transmitting some of them to posterity, by means of the printing press. By being put in print they may be long preserved in all the principal public libraries of Edinburgh and may con-vey to posterity the amiable manners of one of the first Dukes of Scotland.

The family man

Little has been discovered about Duncan's family. He had twelve children (listed in appendix II), of which three boys and four girls are known to have survived into adult life. Of the boys, Andrew Duncan Jr, who followed in his fathers footsteps, is best documented and is referred to repeatedly in this book. Alexander and John both became officers in the Bengal Infantry, Alexander reaching the rank of general. Only one of the girls married; the others continued to live in the family home, which also served as home to the children of the Bengal-based Alexander. Duncan wrote in 1826[86]:

> I am surrounded at home by a promising race of grandchildren. I have already sent out three to their father in Bengal, and all of them have obtained excellent outgoings in the service of the East India Company; the eldest in the medical line,[87] the second in Infantry, and the third in Artillery. I have still five other East India grandchildren under my roof, and five European grandchildren residing with parents in Edinburgh. In addition to these I have one great grandchild, whose great-grandmother, still enjoying good health, is one of my family. Possessed of all these inestimable jewels, I do not know a man in Britain that is richer than I am.

The East Indian grandchildren were those of General Alexander Duncan who had twelve, all of whom were sent home to Edinburgh for their education. In a letter to his father dated 19 March 1813, he wrote:

> Your accounts of my dear children delight me when I look to their happy situation and compare it with the situation of the children of some of my acquaintances in this country, at expensive public schools without friends or relations to look after them. I consider myself more than fortunate. I cannot express what I feel. I can never in anyway repay my parents and my sisters for the kindness and the care you have all of you taken of my darling children.[88]

The separation must have caused great sadness.[89] When seeing off Eliza, Francis and Henry on the *Fort William* to London on 23 November 1814, Alexander wrote, '... poor little souls their little hearts are yet breaking for their Mamma and in a few hours I too must steal away from them ...',[90] yet the house in Adam Square must have been a busy but happy second home. Duncan, in a letter to Alexander in India on 6 February 1826, wrote, 'We had accordingly last Thursday a dancing and supper party of about 50 young folk'; and his daughter Elizabeth added, 'I never saw a set of better dancers or happier creatures'.[91] The occasion was the departure of his grandson, also Alexander, newly-qualified in medicine, to join the East India Company.

Religion

At a time when religious belief was accepted without question and religious practice was the norm, Duncan adopted a conventional attitude to Christianity. In his writings and poetry he makes frequent religious references.

He was a member of the Buccleuch Church (then the Chapel of Ease of St Cuthbert's) in the graveyard of which his family vault remains. His concern for the welfare of mankind is certainly consistent with Christian teaching. In his discourse to the Horticultural Society in which he refers to his grandfather, William Vilant, Duncan states:

> From him, also, I derive a warm affection to the Church of Scotland. And I may, without hazard of contradiction, say, that few men in Scotland have a stronger attachment to the Established Church. Although I have made it an invariable rule to abstain from all party politics in Church matters, yet I have I believe, been oftener as Member of the General Assembly of our National church than any man living.

To be a member of the General Assembly of the Church of Scotland implies that he was an elder of his church and selected as a representative. He must have impressed the congregation with the sincerity of his devotion.

Duncan's death and his legacy

Duncan died on 5 July 1828, aged 83. His splendid civic funeral, described in chapter XV, indicates the respect with which he was held by the community.

Duncan left the bulk of his library to the Royal College of Physicians where it remains today. It included 70 volumes of manuscript lectures by the founders of the Edinburgh Medical School, Drs Monro *primus*, Rutherford, Alston, St Clair and Plummer, which Duncan had purchased from John Murray for seven guineas, and 100 volumes of *Practical Observations in Medicine* which consisted of his case records used in teaching, handwritten mostly by Duncan. His other assets, which included £7034-13/7 in cash and shares (about £500,000 in present-day value), his house in Adam Square, and other property in Edinburgh and St Andrews, were left to his widow and children.[92]

Duncan's most important legacies, however, which survive to this day, are the Royal Edinburgh Hospital, which evolved from his Edinburgh Lunatic Asylum, the General Practice Teaching Unit (the successor of his

Royal Public Dispensary), and the Aesculapian, Harveian, and Royal Caledonian Horticultural Societies. Perhaps his introduction of public health as
an academic subject in the medical curriculum may be regarded as of greater
significance than any of the above.

DUNCAN'S GARDEN

The location of
Duncan's garden *Hinc
Sanitas*, from Robert
Kirkwood's Map of
Edinburgh (1817).

(REPRODUCED BY PERMISSION
OF THE TRUSTEES OF THE
NATIONAL LIBRARY OF
SCOTLAND)

Notes

1   Samuel Smiles in his biography of Thomas
    Telford (1867). Telford, the great engineer,
    was contemporary with Andrew Duncan
    and like Duncan fancied himself as a poet.
    Both men were inspired by Robert Burns.
2   Sachse (1956), p. 56.
3   One of the treasured possessions of the
    Library of the Royal College of Physicians of
    Edinburgh (RCPE) is the Duncan family
    bible. It is an excellent example of the
    'Bassandyne Bible', of which only five

copies exist. It was the first English translation of the bible to be printed in Scotland
by Thomas Bassandyne and Alexander
Arbuthnot in 1576-77. In the fly pages are
notes on family genealogy mostly written
by Andrew Duncan. Enclosed in the bible is
a letter from Harvey Cushing, the leading
American neurosurgeon of his day, dated
22 June 1826, declining to buy the bible
which had been offered to him for £26-5/-
by an Edinburgh book dealer; and another

letter from George Duncan, Earl of Camperdown, to whom Cushing had forwarded the information about the book. The Earl also declined to buy it as he could not find any family link between his branch of the Duncan clan and that of Andrew Duncan.

4   Dobson (2008a and b). Smuggling was widespread around Scotland's shores and there is one report of Duncan and his ship *Concord of Crail* being arrested in Leith on suspicion of smuggling during a journey from Rotterdam to Bergen with a cargo of tobacco and soap. There was no report of further action being taken, so presumably he was cleared, *Caledonian Mercury*, 3 February 1752.

5   The Edinburgh University Library (EUL) acquired an archive of material related to the Duncan family in 2008. At the time of writing it has not been catalogued and items from this source will be identified simply as Duncan Archive. An epitaph relating to Nicholas Vilant, Duncan's long lived forebear, is contained in the Duncan Archive:

> Kind France gave to me birth and tender life. / Fair Scotland blessed me with a tender wife. / Sixty six years a bachelor was I, / Forty years more I lived in wedlock's lie. / And in my marriage to increase my love / Of children eight a father I did prove. ...

6   Duncan (1818b), p. 13.
7   Duncan Archive.
8   Bristed (1803), p. 580. Another student, Sylas Neville, wrote that 'Dr Duncan speaks with much fluency, but his Scottish dialect and other circumstances make his manner very disagreeable to me' (Cozens-Hardy, 1950).
9   Duncan (1818b), pp. 10-25.
10 *Ibid*, p. 20.
11 *Ibid*, pp. 22-24.
12 In later life he was to be involved in a bitter controversy with another Professor Gregory (see chapter XII).
13 Entry in notebook (RCPE Library, Ab.3.70).
14 Duncan (1823) in 'Thanks returned by an octogenarian physician to his friends in the County of Fife, particularly the ancient City of St Andrews'.
15 Duncan Jr, however, did not value the experience highly. He wrote 'that apprentices must spend a great deal more time on mere manual operations than is required for mastering them; that leisure hours for study are cut up and frittered away by frequent calls for occasional service'.

16 Butterfield (1951), p. 41.
17 Monro *secundus* was even more distinguished than his father who was one of the founders of the Medical School in 1726. He was a brilliant lecturer and made a number of original anatomical contributions. The foramen of Monro in the skull is still known by his name. During his 50 years in the chair it is estimated that he taught 40,000 students. Although Monro *secundus* taught surgery as well as anatomy, he never carried out an operation on a living patient, and was a Fellow and one-time president of the Royal College of Physicians. This caused much resentment in the Royal College of Surgeons which tried to persuade the University to establish a Chair of Surgery independent from anatomy. This was opposed by Monro and when a Regius Chair of Surgery was established in 1803 it was so hedged with restrictions to avoid impinging on Monro's territory that complete independence of the Chair of Surgery was not achieved until the appointment of James Syme in 1833.
18 Ismay (1936/7), pp. 57-61.
19 *Ibid.*
20 *Ibid.*
21 *Ibid.*
22 *Ibid.*
23 *Ibid.*
24 His son, Andrew Duncan Jr, was to isolate an active principle from cinchona bark which he called cinchonin (see Duncan Jr [1803], pp. 225-28). Now named quinine, it is a therapeutic agent for malaria to this day.
25 Another object which he kept throughout life was his father's penknife: 'It was the first knife with which I made a good pen. It devolved to me at his death, and I intend to keep it carefully till mine.'
26 The voyage which he missed was a westerly circumnavigation lasting 18 months calling at Madeira, Rio, Madras, Calcutta, Kedgeree, St Helena and Ascension. The *Asia* foundered in India during its next voyage. Captain Preston went on to become managing owner of nine vessels and inher-

ited his father's baronetcy, becoming Sir Robert Preston of Valleyfield, Edinburgh.

27 Bristed (1803), p. 584.

28 Jean Paul Marat, one of the leaders of the French Revolution, practiced as a physician in London and was awarded the degree *in absentia* in 1775.

29 University of St Andrews, minutes of 20 September 1769, pp. 78-79. One of the signatories to his MD certificate was his uncle Nicolas Vilant, Professor of Mathematics.

30 Published in Latin by Balfour, Auld and Smellie, Edinburgh (1769) (RCPE Library).

31 Doig, *et al.* (1993), p. 204.

32 The Chandos Chair of Medicine and anatomy was established by James Brydges, 1st Duke of Chandos, in 1721 with an endowment of £1000. It still exists, but since 1875 has been a Chair of Physiology.

33 Bristo Street extended from Bristo Port to Chapel Street and was the main road to the south from Edinburgh. It disappeared as a result of building developments of the University of Edinburgh in the 1970s.

34 Edinburgh Town Council minute of 21 April 1773.

35 The Edinburgh Town Council minute of 26th October 1774 stipulated that this appointment 'shall not give any claim of preference in the case of a vacancy'.

36 Bower (1830), vol. III, pp. 198-200.

37 Edinburgh Town Council as governors of the University had the responsibility of appointing professors from its foundation in 1621 until the Universities Act of 1858. Cockburn (1874), vol. I, pp. 106-108, was very critical of this procedure: 'I am clear that the nomination of professors by a board of ordinary tradesmen, called a town-council, ... has been and always must be, very dangerous ... the mere necessity of cultivating them must always be a degradation.'

38 *Medical Commentaries* (1776) 4, pp. 99-100; see also Watson (1937/8), pp. 160-63.

39 *Medical Commentaries* (1776) 4, p. 103.

40 *Ibid*, pp. 105-106.

41 Duncan (1801a); Duncan (1801b); Duncan (1801c).

42 Creswell (1926), p. 61.

43 The resurrectionists, William Hare and William Burke, provided bodies for Knox's anatomy school. At first they obtained subjects who had died of natural causes, but later they found it less laborious to obtain their bodies by smothering (burking) their victims after plying them with drink. In all they murdered at least 16 victims before they were caught. Their trial in 1828 caused great public interest. Hare turned King's Evidence and Burke was convicted and publicly hanged before massed crowds. Although Knox was found innocent of any involvement, his reputation suffered and this episode marks the decline of his fortunes.

44 Guthrie (1965) gives an excellent history.

45 Entry in notebook cited in note 13.

46 Rosner (1991) recorded that 61% of students attended Medical Practice compared with 37% attending Institutes of Medicine.

47 Bristed (1803), pp. 574-75, when criticising the appointment of Alexander Monro *tertius*, wrote: 'It is the great cause which has made its [the University's] fame decline, and its utility decrease. There is but one medical chair at this day [1800] in Edinburgh, which is not filled up, like an estate, that descends from father to son; the folly and the injustice of such a measure must be apparent to everyone. Because the father is a cobbler of notoriety, does it necessarily follow that the son must also mend a shoe well. ...'

48 *Medical Commentaries* (1790), 2nd series, 15; pp. 410-20.

49 A full history of Adam Square is given in Mowat (2002), pp. 93-101.

50 Duncan (1818b), p. 63.

51 Hieronymus Gaubius, *c.*1705-80, a physician practicing in Leyden, published *Institutiones Pathologiae Medicinalis* in 1758 with subsequent editions. Duncan thought highly of this work and recommended it to his students.

52 Christison (1885), vol. I, pp. 75-76.

53 *Ibid*, p. 84.

54 Duncan Archive, British Library (Mss Eur F568).

55. Duncan Archive, British Library.

56 Christison (1885), vol. I, pp. 422-26.

57 Risse (1986), p. 38.

58 For a description of the teaching wards, see Duncan Jr (1818).

59 Risse (1986), p. 25.

60 'Report of the Committee of Contributors to the Royal Infirmary of Edinburgh appointed to enquire into the Estate of the Hospital, 5 January 1818' (RCPE Library).

61 This comment must refer to his travels on the *Asia* when he visited China and South Africa.

62 Duncan papers (RCPE Library, Ab.3.70).

63 *Ibid.*

64 Buchan (1772).

65 'Report presented to the Royal College of Physicians of Edinburgh respecting contagious epidemic diseases which have prevailed in that City and its neighbourhood during the year 1810' (RCPE Library).

66 McCrae, 2007, pp. 118-31.

67 Letter to Sir William Fettes, 1 November 1825 (Edinburgh University Library [EUL]).

68 Letter to Andrew Duncan Sr regarding the establishment of a New Infirmary (1825) (Edinburgh: A. Constable and Co.).

69 Receipt Book, II, 1790-1805, for the Principal and Professors borrowing books from the College Library (EUL).

70 Ignaz Joseph Pleyel, a pupil of Haydn, was an Austrian pianist, violinist and composer. Now virtually forgotten, his compositions in Duncan's day were popular with aspiring violinists.

71 Mark Catesby was an Englishman who travelled extensively in the Eastern United States, studying and painting the new fauna and flora he encountered. His beautifully illustrated book *The Natural History of Carolina, Florida and the Bahama Islands,* was published between 1731-47. His original watercolours are now in the Royal Collection. The RCPE Library and EUL both possess copies of this rare work.

72 Duncan's father was also honoured by being made a freeman of Dundee in 1768 and of Dunbar in 1778.

73 Duncan (1823) 'A discourse to the Caledonian Horticultural Society'.

74 Duncan (1822) 'A discourse to the Caledonian Horticultural Society'.

75 *Ibid.*

76 Duncan's Miscellanies (RCPE Library).

77 Duncan Jr wrote to his father from Vienna on 20 October 1795: 'I bought a bunch of grapes weighing a pound and a half for a halfpenny, and grapes like which your hothouse produce nothing better.'

78 'Letter to Rev. Andrew Brown, 1823'.

79 'Letter to John Waugh, 1823'.

80 Duncan Archive.

81 *Ibid.*

82 *Ibid.*

83 'Letter to a friend, 1827'.

84 'Conclusions of a clinical lecture, 1815'.

85 'Dr Duncan Sr, in the 83rd year of his age, has addressed the letter to a friend on the death of His Grace Alexander, Duke of Gordon (1828)'.

86 'Letter to Charles Whightman, 5 April 1826' (EUL).

87 This was Alexander Duncan, who as a medical student aged 19, won the swimming medal at the *Ludi Apollinares* of 1823.

88 Duncan Archive, British Library (Mss Eur F568/1).

89 It is hard nowadays to imagine the extent of the separation. Exchange of letters between Britain and India could take seven months. Furlough was uncommon. Alexander wrote on 7 August 1813: 'The time I trust is fast approaching when my income will be doubled and if my life be spared for sixteen or twenty years ... I may be able to revisit my native country and pass many happy days yet amongst you all.' His hope was fulfilled; he lived to spend many years of happy retirement in Gattonside in the Scottish Borders.

90 Duncan Archive.

91 *Ibid.*

92 Duncan's properties at the time of his death included his house in Adam Square, his previous tenement property in Bristo Street, and an acre of land in St Andrews which he inherited from his father. National Archive of Scotland: Testament and Inventory Edinburgh Commissary Court (16.1.1829 CC8/8/152) and Inventory Trust Depositions Edinburgh Sheriff Court, (SC70/1/39, pp. 791-801).

CHAPTER II

Medical and Philosophical Commentaries and its Successors

IAIN CHALMERS, ULRICH TRÖHLER
AND JOHN CHALMERS

I am the more zealous of having the publication perfect as your own reputation and the reputation of Scotland are in some measure invested.
John Murray to Andrew Duncan (letter, 7 January 1773)

Andrew Duncan began his publishing career in 1772, with observations on the use of mercury for treating venereal disease. Thereafter he produced a substantial published output – on therapeutics, materia medica, pathology, reports of cases seen at the Edinburgh Public Dispensary, and biographical commentaries on his colleagues. However, Duncan's most successful publishing venture was his *Medical and Philosophical Commentaries* (hereafter the *Commentaries*). In *Commentaries*, Duncan endeavoured to meet needs which remain inadequately met even today: namely, how doctors can be helped to cope with cascades of clinical literature.[1]

There had been some attempts in the 17th century to respond to the needs of busy people for relevant research information. *Weekly Memorials* (1682) and *Medicina Curiosa* (1684) contained abstracts of articles and books published elsewhere. The contents of the former were mostly non-medical, however, and the latter ceased publication after only two issues.[2] In 1733 a publication entitled *Medical Essays and Observations* was launched by 'a society in Edinburgh' which had been instituted in 1731 for the improvement of medical knowledge. The secretary of the society was Alexander Monro *primus*, the first Professor of Anatomy at the University of Edinburgh, and he was almost certainly the author of the preface. As explained in the preface, this initiative reflected a concern that, because the preparation and publication of a book was a major undertaking, important observations were not being reported because doctors were not prepared to take on the work of communicating them in book format.[3] In addition, there was a felt need for a publication specifically for medical matters, and one which considered the applicability of observations made in other parts of the world to the climatic and other circumstances of Scotland.

Each issue of the new periodical was to contain registers of climatic measurements in Edinburgh and accounts of the diseases which had been epidemic and 'most universal' there; observations and essays on medical subjects; figures illustrating instruments, pathological specimens, etc.; and lists of medical books, published or in press. Each volume also included accounts of 'the most remarkable Improvements and Discoveries in Physick' which had been made since the previous issue. This element comes nearest to the purposes of Andrew Duncan's *Medical and Philosophical Commentaries*, but it only used between one and ten per cent of the pages in each volume of *Medical Essays and Observations*, which was principally a vehicle for clinical and pathological case reports.

Medical Essays and Observations was published in five volumes until 1744, after which the disruption caused by the Jacobite rebellion meant that no further volumes were published. In 1754, *Essays and Observations Physical and Literary* was launched, inspired by the example of *Medical Essays and Observations*, again by 'a society in Edinburgh'. It appeared in three volumes (the last published in 1771), and published papers that had been 'read before the society'. In addition to medicine, *Essays and Observations Physical and Literary* covered topics as various as astronomy, botany, earthquakes and the benefits of shallow ploughing, but it had no section specifically designed to comment on advances or recently published books.

Although *Medical Essays and Observations* must have had some influence on Andrew Duncan's decision to launch *Medical and Philosophical Commentaries*, the principal model for his plan for the new publication seems likely to have been *Commentarii de rebus in scientia naturali et medicina gestis* – a periodical containing abstracts of scientific and medical books published in Leipzig, Germany, which appeared between 1752 and 1798.[4]

Duncan's *Commentaries* was the first English-language journal of abstracts of books relevant to busy clinicians. Between 1773 and 1780, over 1000 copies of each quarterly issue came out in three editions simultaneously in Edinburgh, London and Dublin.[5] This large circulation suggests that its readership included all types of 18th-century practitioners – university trained physicians, barber-surgeons, apothecaries and the new type of surgeons with Scottish or continental MD degrees. It became sufficiently well regarded to justify translation into languages other than English [preface, vol. 6, 1779]. In 1780 it was renamed *Medical Commentaries* (the new title reflecting its clinical contents), and it went on to be published annually until 1795.

Finding a publisher

Andrew Duncan had two principal publishers – John Murray in London and Charles Elliot in Edinburgh (their publications for him are listed in

Appendix One). The archive of the publishing firm of Murray, recently acquired by the National Library of Scotland, contains many references to the relationship between Duncan, Murray and Elliot. These give an interesting insight into a cut-throat and competitive industry, and also reveal an unflattering aspect of Duncan's character.

John Murray (1737-93), the founder of the eminent publishing house, was born in Edinburgh and attended the High School and University there. After trying his hand at a variety of jobs, including serving as an officer in the Royal Marines, Murray bought the bookselling and publishing house of William Sandby in Fleet Street, London, in 1768. Without any experience or training in publishing, he proved to be a shrewd businessman and rapidly established himself as one of the leading London publishers with a special interest in medical works. Edinburgh had several eminent publishers with whom Duncan had a friendly relationship, but when first seeking a publisher for his own works he chose John Murray. London had the advantage of greater prestige and a larger potential market.

Duncan's favoured Edinburgh publisher was Charles Elliot (1748-90) who established his business in Parliament Square in 1771 (James Boswell and Robert Burns were among his customers). Like Murray he specialised in medical publications, including works by William Cullen, James Gregory, Alexander Monro *secundus* and Alexander Hamilton.

The Murray Archive contains copies of 109 letters sent by Murray to Duncan between 1773 and 1786, mostly business letters concerned with publications. There are no letters from Duncan to Murray, although the content of Duncan's letters can sometimes be inferred from Murray's replies. The Murray Archive also contains the archive of Charles Elliot which came into the possession of the Murray family through the marriage of John Murray II, with Elliot's daughter Anne in 1806. The Elliot Archive contains no letters to or from Duncan, for the two men lived close together and must have communicated personally, but the copies of Elliot's letters to others contain many references to Duncan's publications.

The copy letters from both the Murray and Elliot Archives are haphazardly punctuated and capitalised. In the interest of clarity these have been edited lightly here, but without altering the text. The letters have been quoted at length, for they give a vivid account of the sometimes stormy relationship between Duncan, Murray and Elliot.

In 1772 Murray had published Duncan's *Observations on the operation and use of mercury in the Venereal Disease.* He began publication of *Medical and Philosophical Commentaries* the following year.

The early letters from Murray,[6] although businesslike, are written in a friendly manner and contain many personal asides:

JM to AD, Jan 7th 1773

I was duly favoured with yours by your brother[7] who is to dine with me to-day and whom you need not doubt my readiness to serve, were but my ability equal to my inclination. ...

I have communicated the Plan of our new intended Publication [the Commentaries] to several people here who are of opinion that it may succeed if it is in some measure extended ... the greatest care should be taken of the Composition and Language of the first number. I mention this particularly as the age we live in requires it and as your proposals are extremely incorrect. ... I am the more zealous of having the publication perfect as your own reputation and the reputation of Scotland are in some measure invested.

It was arranged that the *Commentaries* would be published quarterly and sold to the public at 1/6.[8] The rate to booksellers was 1s to 1s 2d. The four annual numbers were bound into volumes selling at 6s. Duncan was to receive £15 for each number (£1450 in present-day value).

JM to AD, 28th Jan 1773

If I am fortunate enough to establish the work after the first 4 numbers, you will if my agreement of £15 per no. is judged to [sic] small, have an opportunity of making your own terms. ...Who ever built a house at the estimate price?

Duncan was to have the *Commentaries* printed in Edinburgh. One thousand copies were to be printed in the first instance, some to be retained in Edinburgh by the booksellers Kincaid and Creech for local sale, and the rest shipped to Murray in London.

The launch and development of the *Commentaries*

The first volume of the *Commentaries* was dedicated to William Robertson, Principal of the University of Edinburgh, for his efforts on behalf of the 'celebrated School of Medicine'. The journal was announced as having been prepared by a 'society', of which Duncan was the secretary. However, it is clear from the correspondence that Duncan *was* the society and he deserves all the credit. There is a hint in the preface to volume 3 that he received some assistance from his friends, for he apologised for the delay, which he attributed to his teaching commitments and the absence of his friend Dr James Hamilton Sr. He apologised again for the delay in the preface to volume 4,

... because the greater part of his time has been occupied in academical labour. He has also suffered no inconsiderable distress from circumstances

of a more private nature ... the death of a beloved daughter [his first born, Katharine Elisa, aged 3].

In the preface to volume 16, 1792, he acknowledges for the first time the assistance of his son Andrew Duncan Jr, then a medical student. His father introduced his contribution with the following notice:

Notwithstanding his youth and want of experience in literary composition, I yet trust, that he has not failed in retaining the sense of the Authors whose writings he has analyzed: And, if the language which he employs should sometimes appear deficient in accuracy or perspicacity, the Indulgent Reader will I hope, permit me to offer for him, the apology which the illustrious Haller made for his son 'Condonandum aliquid juveni octodecim annorum.' ['Make some allowance for a youth of eighteen.']

Duncan's editorial introduction to the first issue of *Commentaries* has a remarkably modern ring:

Medicine has long been cultivated with assiduity and attention, but is still capable of farther improvement. Attentive observation, and the collection of useful facts, are the means by which this end may be most readily obtained. In no age ... does greater regard seem to have been paid to these particulars, than in the present. From the liberal spirit of inquiry which universally prevails, it is not surprising that scarce a day should pass without something being communicated to the public as a discovery or an improvement in medicine. It is, however, to be regretted, that the information which can by this means be acquired, is scattered through a great number of volumes, many of which are so expensive, that they can be purchased for the libraries of public societies only, or of very wealthy individuals. ...
    No one, who wishes to practise medicine, either with safety to others, or credit to himself, will incline to remain ignorant of any discovery which time or attention has brought to light. But it is well known that the greatest part of those who are engaged in the actual prosecution of this art, have neither leisure nor opportunity for very extensive reading. (Introduction, vol 1, 1773)

The introduction goes on to explain how the new journal would help doctors to learn about 'new discoveries, without the necessity of examining a great variety of books', and thus help them to improve their practice.

A scheme, better calculated for saving time in reading, and expense in purchasing books, is a concise view of the books themselves. It cannot indeed be alleged, that, from this or any other plan, the same advantages will be obtained as from a careful perusal of original works. But, by this means, those who have not leisure for extensive reading, may easily become acquainted with every thing proposed as a discovery in medicine, and with the principal arguments by which it is supported.

Duncan pays tribute to the Leipzig *Commentarii* which had begun publication 20 years earlier. He noted that it took little account of British books, however, and that it was not up-to-date, sometimes taking years to review the books it did cover. This lack of currency was exacerbated by the fact that issues of the journal were often available in Britain only a considerable time after publication. So, Duncan's introduction to the first issue of the *Commentaries* explains that his new journal 'will comprehend four sections, treating of the following subjects: An account of the best new books in medicine, and those branches of philosophy most intimately connected with it; medical cases and observations; medical news; and a list of new medical publications'.

He made clear that, of these four sections, the first – an account of the best new books in medicine – was to be the principal feature of the journal. The fourth section of the journal was a kind of 18th-century *Index Medicus*. As the editor put it:

The last section will consist of a list of new medical books ... for the satisfaction of those who may be deprived of other methods of information ..., published, both in this and other countries, during the three preceding months. We cannot, indeed, pretend that this list will in any case be a complete one; but it will be our endeavour to render it as much so as our situation will allow; and we are hopeful we shall be able to obtain intelligence of every material book.

Sorting the wheat from the chaff

The first and many of the subsequent editorial prefaces during the first decade of publication of the *Commentaries* stress the efforts made to be impartial, and they invite comments and suggestions for improvements from readers. This editorial policy was set out in the introduction to the first issue:

As it is not our intention to offer any opinion with regard to the general characters of the books, we shall, on every occasion avoid, as much as possible, either applauding or condemning any author. Our chief aim will be to give such a view of books as may enable every reader to judge for himself.

At the beginning of the second decade of publication, however, 'critical appraisal' of the books reviewed was introduced:

> [Those] *whose chief pleasure consists in the perusal of ingenious and useful publications ... will now find our analysis of books interspersed with observations on the degree of credit which we think they deserve. Where ... we have had occasion to differ from authors of the first eminence, our sentiments, though stated with freedom, are yet, we trust, expressed with that respect which is due to merit, and that diffidence which the nature of the subject demands: And this line of conduct, it is our intention steadily to pursue.* (Preface, vol. I, [2nd decade], 1786)

The following year, the editor judged this innovation to have been a success:

> *We are happy to find, that the alteration we have made in our plan, by not confining ourselves to a mere analysis of new books, but by candidly offering our opinion of their contents ... has met with the approbation of some of our most valuable correspondents. And we trust that those criticisms which are contained in the present volume, neither show a want of due deference to the assertions of others, nor inattention to facts.* (Preface, vol. II [2nd decade], 1788)

In order to understand what the editors rated important as 'a discovery or an improvement ... in medicine' (Introduction, 1773) one needs to be aware of the approach then being taken by British physicians and surgeons who wished to find their way out of 'the labyrinth of therapeutics' and improve 'the evidence of medicine'.[9] This quest included quantitative assessment both of procedures that had been in largely unchallenged use for centuries, and of therapeutic innovations. This involved comparing groups of patients who had received different forms of active treatment, as well as comparisons with observations of the natural history of conditions in untreated patients. Examples included comparison of immediate with delayed amputation after limb injuries, and the use of cinchona bark (quinine) for 'ship fever' and childbed fever.

These comparisons were made prospectively as well as retrospectively. Army and navy institutions and the new voluntary hospitals and dispensaries afforded opportunities for research: there were large numbers of comparable cases, the hierarchical order of the institutions meant that patients were expected to obey instructions, and staff had to report results of treatment in numerical terms to administrative authorities. 'The test of arithmetical calculation ought not to be evaded,' wrote John Millar, a protagonist of this movement of 'arithmetic observation' in 1777.[10]

This 'proto-statistical' enterprise was intended to encourage the adoption of new standards of evidence for inferring therapeutic success, and deplored the common practice of relying on single-case reports, or excluding from case series those cases judged to have been treatment failures. These issues were discussed in 18th-century Britain and had relevance during an era when there were quite a few innovations in both medicine and surgery.[11]

It would require very detailed historical research to establish the criteria used by Duncan to choose books for review in the *Commentaries*, but there is no doubt that he supported those efforts to improve the methodologies used to assess the effects of clinical practice.[12] Although the journal did not review the third edition of James Lind's book[13] (which contained the celebrated account of his prospective trial of six remedies for scurvy) or Millar's books on *Practice in the Medical Department of the Westminster General Dispensary and On the Management of Diseases in the Army and Navy*,[14] John Clark's *Observations on the Diseases which Prevail in Long Voyages to Hot Countries*[15] was included twice, the second time with some very flattering remarks. Thomas Percival's and John Coakley Lettsom's investigations of mortality in and around Manchester[16] and at the Aldersgate Dispensary in London,[17] respectively, were reviewed equally well, as were Matthew Dobson's observations on 'fixed air' in therapeutics[18] and William Black's on smallpox.[19]

Thomas Fowler's and William Withering's works were the subject of repeated methodological comments. On reading Fowler's first book on tobacco,[20] the reviewer thought that his manner of introducing this new medicine 'may justly be considered as a discovery of very great utility'. He agreed with the author that still more facts were necessary, but concluded that whatever further workers would find out, 'Fowler was still entitled to much praise as a faithful and industrious observer' (*Commentaries*, 1786). Withering's now classic *Account of the Foxglove*[21] – that is, the introduction of digitalis for treating certain forms of dropsy [oedema] and heart disease on the basis of a large case series – earned similar appreciation (*Commentaries*, 1786). Both authors were again quoted in relation to Fowler's second and third *Medical Reports*[22] on the effects of arsenic (Fowler 1786) and of blood-letting in acute rheumatism, respectively. Fowler received a rare and favourable comment: 'We cannot too highly applaud the industrious zeal with which he has endeavoured to render hospital practice subservient to medical improvement' (*Commentaries*, 1795). In a review over 50 pages long, Gilbert Blane's *Observations on the Diseases incident to Seamen*[23] also received approving comment concerning the necessity for mass observation, and extensive methodological passages on 'arithmetic observation' were reprinted completely (*Commentaries*, 1788).

Although most of the editorial Prefaces in the *Commentaries* thanked those who had submitted clinical observations and solicited more such submissions for the second section of the journal, the principal focus of the journal remained the critical appraisal of books published in its first section:

> *Some ingenious friends, on whose approbation we put a high value … were of opinion, that too large a proportion of our last volume was occupied with the analysis of new books. In the present volume, this fault is not corrected. … We flatter ourselves, that … candidly offering our opinion, respecting the facts and doctrines which new books contain, those even who are possessed of the original works, may still peruse our account of new books with pleasure and advantage; while to those who do not possess these works, this section of our publication must convey much useful information, which they could not otherwise obtain, without both considerable labour and expense. These considerations will, we trust, be a sufficient apology for still continuing our work on the former plan.* (Preface, vol. III [2nd decade] 1788)

What might have been the origins of this attack of Duncan's editorial policy? Possibly some contributors of individual case reports may have been motivated to press for a change so that they would see their names in print. Yet Duncan stuck to his principle of concentrating on reviews rather than case reports.

Duncan's relations with his publishers

The *Commentaries* had been an immediate success and some of the early numbers required reprinting. Duncan must have asked Murray for an increased payment, but this was refused (although as a sop, Duncan was offered 12 free copies of each number for his own use).

JM to AD, 29 August 1774

> *… hope that you will take particular care of yourself in order to confirm your health and to insure against relapse. …I would willingly offer you more money for the* Med. Com *did the state of matters admit it. … The truth is my offer at first (considering the Work was to be established and that all the risk was to be mine) was too much. … I agreed to pay a price upon the supposition of their success and it will be hard to deprive me of the reward now that the work promises one. … It is pleasant to hear Dr. Rush and others tell you that many copies of the Com. would sell at Philadelphia, Charlestown and New York.*

Murray detailed the costs of each issue of the *Commentaries*:

14 reams of paper	£10-10/0
Printing of 7 sheets	£7-7/0
Advertising	£10-10/0
Copy money (to Duncan)	£15-0/0
	£43-7/0

Murray's profit ranged from about £10 to £15, depending upon how many were sold to the trade and how many directly to the public.

Advertising was an item which Murray regarded as very important. He insisted, to Duncan's annoyance, that the covers of the issues belonged to the publishers to use for advertising purposes, which led to the first of many prickly letters.

JM to AD, 17 May 1777

I always conceived that the cover of any periodical publication was the Bookseller's. ... If you ... insist that no advertisement whatever shall be printed upon the cover ... I cannot agree to it the impropriety of such a request, which not only fetters me inconveniently ... but which also denotes your want of faith in me. ... I would much rather keep the Commentaries *than not, yet I am not disposed to fight for them ... and I can relinquish them with a quiet conscience whenever you shall be disposed to carry them from me.*

Duncan's views did not however prevent him from using the *Commentaries* freely to advertise his own publications and teaching arrangements.

Goods were sent between London and Edinburgh generally by sea, which could take five to ten days. Stagecoach or wagon was quicker but more expensive, and the goods tended to get chafed by the jolting of the coach. Duncan paid £1-2/6 for the carriage of 300 copies of *Commentaries* by wagon. For reasons of economy, parcels for several recipients were often packaged together and the first named was asked to distribute them. In this way Duncan acted as an agent for Murray in Edinburgh. He was frequently asked to carry out small commissions, sending him goods from Edinburgh or seeking purchasers for items that Murray would like to sell, such as the engravings of Dr John Hunter[24] (who had thought highly of the *Commentaries*, in which many of his papers are reproduced).

Murray dealt with other items than books. He would sell anything that might bring a profit, including inks, wines, Irish linen, game birds and Tassie[25] medallions. He also sold lottery tickets, and the correspondence records that Duncan purchased several. In 1776 he bought a whole ticket, and in 1777 one half and two quarter tickets. The half ticket cost £7-11/- and the two quarters £7-14/- (smaller fractions of tickets were available). The potential prize was £20,000, but, alas, Duncan was not successful.

Murray was well informed about the medical politics in Edinburgh, and at the time when Duncan was applying for the Chair of Institutes of Medicine he wrote:

> *JM to Mr Chas. Gordon, Canton, China, 26 December 1774*
>
> *Dr Duncan this year occupied Dr Drummond's chair at Edinburgh as Professor of the Practice of Physic. If Dr Drummond casts up who has been long missing, Dr Duncan must resign the chair, but if that event does not happen the latter I think stands a chance of succeeding him.*

> *JM to AD, 25 June 1776*
>
> *You have my best wishes for your success in the Professorship. I hope however that you have not hitherto lain upon your oars, but have been active by preserving your solicitations. Without your own industry your merit will not be so much recognised. ... Pray acquaint me with what success Mrs Duncan carries on business and if our friend Creech is going to get married.*

It is intriguing to speculate on what business Mrs Duncan was engaged. Perhaps it was the common practice in professional households of giving lodgings to students. It is known that the family did take in boarders, one of whom was a Swiss national, Baron Benjamin Constant (1767-1830), who was to play a prominent role in the French Revolution.[26]

> *JM to AD, 9 August 1776*
>
> *I felt as a friend for the disappointment you met with .... [in failing to get the Chair of Institutes of Medicine]. I believe you have been a bad politician. You have proved deficient in your sacrifices to flattery. Your stubbornness on inflexible honesty is no match for it. Now however that the election is over and past it is a folly to regard it. ... Happily to digest a repulse has more merit in my eyes than moderately to enjoy good fortune. ... Smellie[27] is very irregular and the most unsatisfactory correspondent I ever met with. ... I am glad of the credit your work has acquired in Germany.*

These letters indicate the warm relationship between the two men at that time.

Duncan's extramural classes prospered after his unsuccessful bid for a chair and Murray congratulated him (5 December 1776): 'I hear your success this winter is beyond conception and congratulate you upon it, even altho the *Commentaries* may be retarded by it'.

Times must have been hard for Duncan in 1778, for he kept pressing Murray for an advance of payment. Murray responded (25 July 1778), 'I shall honour your draft of £25 when it appear[s]. Times are really bad otherwise you would find me disposed to give you every indulgence. Meantime, bad as they are, I hope you will not be prevented from putting in execution your design of visiting London and making your friends here happy'.

During 1778 Murray's irritation with Smellie's delays reached breaking point. He wrote asking Smellie to ask Duncan to get another printer if he couldn't keep to time.

JM to Smellie, 26 July 1778

Let me therefore entreat of you to finish it without delay or honestly to give it up. I cannot forgive a disappointment and I pray for both our sakes that you will not put me to the proof. My interest is <u>very</u> much concerned. Your behaviour will show whether you regard my interest.

JM to AD, 19 November 1778

I am favoured with Mr. Smellie's letter and with yours in answer to mine upon the subject of printing the Commentaries *here ... yet it was not the opinion of the instant. I had long weighed the matter and the necessity of the alteration. ... I am by no means Mr. Smellie's enemy or less his friend than ever. I should act as I do about the* Commentaries *in any other printers hands at such a distance, and I see so many real advantages and conveniences that will result to me from the printing here, that I have real pleasure and satisfaction in thanking you for the readiness you express to oblige me. ... The printing here will remove a heavy load from my breast which has long incommoded me. ...*

A letter of 24 December 1778 indicated that issue no. 21 was being printed in London.

Duncan's dispute and reconciliation with John Murray

During 1779 the cordial relationship between Murray and Duncan came to an abrupt end. Murray had had the effrontery to publish another journal, the *Foreign Medical Review*, without consulting Duncan. To some extent it covered the same ground as the *Commentaries* and Duncan was incandescent. Before he had even seen a copy he must have written an angry letter to Murray. Murray tried to send an emollient reply. He didn't think the journal would continue and he took it on simply 'to prevent it falling into worse hands'. The correspondence tells the story:

JM to AD, 27 April 1779

... I write this fully because there seems to be a little jealousy excited by it in your letter which surprises me, for surely after so long an acquaintance you cannot suspect that I would act clandestinely either against you or the Commentaries. *The idea if* <u>entertained</u> *is an imputation upon the confidence one friend should impose in another.*

Duncan must have approached Charles Elliot to find a new publisher. Elliot wrote on 17 April 1779 to his cousin James Sibbald,[28] who was spending that year in London to learn the book trade.

I have just now I believe a fair chance of purchasing the property of Dr. Duncan's Medical Commentaries *if I incline, not that Mr. Murray has given them up but that the Doctor is determined for certain Reasons to give him up. This is an undertaking, however, I would not chuse to engage in altogether myself, owing to the greatest part being sold in London which would oblige me to send quantities there on commission which I by no means like, more particularly in a publication that is to continue like it. I would most willingly take one half if I could get a creditable London Bookseller to take the other. Therefore I beg you will immediately meet with Mr. Longman and ask him if he inclines to take the one half while I keep the other. ... Assure him at the same time they need have no scruples on account of interfering with Mr. Murray, the Doctor being determined to part with him, although he knows nothing of it. Therefore you will not mention the subject to any person but the necessary ones and beg of them not to speak of it till something is done in it. Although I authorise you to make such an offer I am not absolutely certain of it myself having made no bargain but the Doctor assures me none shall have a preference.*

Will you please buy from Mr. Murray two copies of No 1st of the Foreign Review *... to be published on the 15 currt. ... You will please send off immediately ... and state them private inclosed. Don't say who the numbers are for anything whatsoever to Mr. Murray. The above are for Dr Duncan and I fancy it is on account of Murray's engaging in this publication without acquainting Dr Duncan. However it is no business of yours or mine.*

CE to James Sibbald, 3 May 1779

... If you have come to no terms with anybody about the Medical Commentaries *don't say anything more about them till you hear further. I imagine Murray and Dr Duncan will make it up. ...*

Murray inevitably heard what was going on behind his back and wrote to Elliot on 10 May 1779:

Your behaviour respecting the Medical Commentaries *which I have had a hand in establishing, I do not mean to analyse, for it will not bear it. I have only to assure you that I shall never imitate your example in any similar case. ...*

Of the first numbers of the Commentaries *I printed 1000 each. Of no 8 I printed 1500 and have continued this number since. In 1774 no 8 was printed and there remains 300 copies unsold of that number and proportional remains of all the following numbers.*

To the London trade I sell 25 nos for 27/-. ... I have given you a very honest state of the Medical Commentaries *and I now offer you my property in the first 5½ Vols already executed and all the remaining numbers without reserve that are in my ware rooms at a fair price.*

Turn over this proposal in your mind and make me an offer. In doing which it will naturally occur to you that you must value each remaining numbers at a certain price and next my property in the copy. *...*

Without the least tincture of resentment I remain very sincerely yours etc.

Elliot replied in a letter to Murray, dated 29 May 1779:

Dr Duncan upon learning your publishing the Foreign Review *was very much offended and signified in express terms to me that you should not continue to publish his* Commentaries *and the other and at the same time asked if I chose to be concerned and that my interference would make no difference as some one must publish them. The only answer I made was that the undertaking would not suit me to have it all in my own hands; that if a person in Lond. was half concerned and the publication to go out of your hands at any rate, in that case I should perhaps have no objection, but with regard to any bargain offered by the Doctor as proposal from me to him I do assure you never happened. I certainly did write to Mr Sibbald to mention the thing to one or two Booksellers in Lond. but to how many he has done it I do not know. ... I expressly desired him only to mention the subject and not to conclude anything as I had not in my power to settle anything with any person. I do assure you my dear sir that no person hates the very idea of interfering in such a case more than I do and I certainly would not have understood you had it in your power to continue. Dr Duncan no doubt has explained himself with regard to his reasons of complaint. When I instructed my friend Mr. Sibbald I did not look upon you as further concerned from what I have already mentioned and I had not doubt but offers would be made to others. Therefore Sir, do not imagine I either meant or wished to take undue advantage of you and I am certain that Doctor Duncan is incapable of it even in idea, yet I believe he felt very much upon your engagements in this said* Review.

Duncan continued to send angry letters to Murray, who replied:

JM to AD, 9 June 1779

I never engaged more innocently in any undertaking than in the Foreign Medical Review *and had I thought the thing was likely to offend you, I most certainly would have declined it. ... Were I disposed to be surprised at any thing it would be at your resenting my behaviour after the explanation and satisfaction I have given, and particularly with your declaration that the contents of my letter of the 27th Apl. had* surprised *and* offended *you and that my conduct required an apology. You say also in your note dated the 4th inst. That 'You hope upon cool deliberation I will think of another method of apologising for my conduct on this affair: that you had not fully expressed your sentiments: yet wished to say no more with regard to it, unless you are forced to it by such observations as those contained in my present letter'... I have gone over it [letter of 27th] with all the bias in your favour I am capable of and for the life of me cannot see what part you can reasonably take offence at. ...*

I am indeed surprised at your offer to continue *the* Commentaries *for me, because as they have been offered by Mr Elliot's agent to several Booksellers here, there must either be a mistake on his part or you have not retained the alternative you propose ... it is near a month since Mr Sibbald, who acts for Mr Elliot at present in London, first tendered this work to the trade here. He told the gentleman to whom he first applyed [sic] that Dr Duncan* had done entirely with Mr Murray, *that the work was now Mr Elliot's on whose part he had authority to dispose of one half. He enjoined secrecy from me. In this manner has Mr Sibbald offered the* Commentaries *to four or five booksellers at London. ...*

Your proposal for me to agree for the continuation of the next 16 numbers of the Commentaries *from No 25 to 40* for certain *at £25 each is so foreign to every calculation I have made, and every idea I entertain of the work, that it requires no time for consideration. I resign my pretensions to your labours at this price; for I cannot afford it; nor can the* work *if I have any knowledge in figures.*

Had you desired an explanation of any parts of my behaviour with which you was dissatisfied, before you had entered into engagements with another bookseller, I think it would have shewn openness and honour. And if Mr Elliot had declined concluding with you till I had been consulted, his conduct would have been praiseworthy. It is a great consolation at this parting that I cannot accuse myself of a single circumstance wherein I have been intentionally to blame respecting you, in the six or seven years of our acquaintance. And I am flattered that more respect has been paid to my name here than at Edinburgh.

JM to AD, 10 May 1779

I have received your last, and what your reasons are for saying that you remain in the dark concerning my conduct, after the ample satisfaction I have given, God alone knows for I confess my ignorance. I shall only add further on this subject that if ever you look at my letters when you are less disposed to be prejudiced against me, I am of opinion you will not be fond of the answers you have written to them.

Duncan's overreaction to a trivial circumstance was totally out of proportion and displays a character defect which was to trouble him later in his unwise contretemps with James Hamilton Jr. The *Foreign Medical Review* was not a success and Murray published only two parts.

Elliot must have been unable to find a willing partner in London, for Murray sent the following letter to another Edinburgh publisher William Creech on 16 September 1779.

Dr Duncan has taken great offence at my publishing the Foreign Medical Review *and has resolved to bring the culprit to condign punishment by withdrawing the* Medical Commentaries *from him. I thought he had settled matters with Mr Elliot but as you tell me he has made proposals to you, I send you enclosed my last letter to him upon the subject of that work as also part of a letter I wrote at same time to Mr Elliot thinking he was to be the favoured bookseller. And the offer I made to him I now make to you.*

You have my thanks for declining to treat with Dr D. till you heard from me upon that subject. But so far I am from wishing to prevent you from undertaking the Commentaries, *I shall be very happy to learn that you have come to an agreement with the author. … I really wish you success.*

In the event the London publisher Charles Dilly took over the publication of *Commentaries* in 1780 and 1781 and made it an annual publication.

There followed a two-year hiatus in Murray's correspondence with Duncan, but a reconciliation appears to have taken place following a visit by Duncan to London. On 1 November 1781 Murray sent a friendly letter to Duncan ending, 'Mrs Murray joins me in compts to you, Mrs Duncan and Family. I remain Dear Sir Yours etc'. In May 1782 Murray suffered a stroke. In a letter to James Gilliland,[29] his brother-in-law in Edinburgh, he described his attack:

On Friday last while I was standing in my own Shop at midday I was seized with a swimming in my head and sleepiness in my left limbs. After sometime I returned to my bed where after a puking of 24 hours, my fate was announced in its horrors and I was left in a palsy, the power of my left side

*being totally, or very near to it, taken from me. ... It is better if it can be done
to bear it with fortitude, and to conduct my business.*

Remarkably, despite his disability, which left him with permanent weakness, he continued his business almost without interruption.

On 25 February 1783, Murray thanked Duncan for his advice about the costs of education of a young man at the High School in Edinburgh. This was probably in connection with Murray's illegitimate son Archie, for whom Murray maintained a close parental responsibility. In the event, Archie was sent to an academy at Brighthelmstone where he proved a quick learner with a gift for languages.

On 16 September 1783, in response to a letter from Duncan, Murray offered to resume publication of *Commentaries* at the old terms, although the dispute still rankled. In another letter a month later, he wrote:

I shall be glad to hear from you upon the subject of the Comments. *at any
time; although with respect to my behaviour relating to them you are as
wrong as any man can be. ...*

He did resume its publication in that year, jointly with Dilly, continuing the format of an annual volume which had been established by Dilly.[30]

Further evidence of the restoration of good relations was Murray's acknowledgment of a gift.

JM to AD, 3 November 1783

*I carried yesterday to Mrs Murray ... Mrs Duncan's present; and she begs I
would offer to Mrs Duncan and You her very grateful thanks for it. ... I beg
to be considered a party in her thanks. ...*

The deaths of Charles Elliot in 1790 and John Murray in 1793 brought Duncan's association with these publishers to a conclusion, although both companies continued in the hands of relatives.

Succession

By the mid-1780s, sales of the journal had declined by 50 per cent to some 500 copies per issue.[31] Perhaps the decline in sales of the journal could be attributed to, from 1781, reducing *Commentaries* from quarterly to annual publication. Beginning in the early 1780s, successive prefaces suggested that Duncan was finding it difficult to devote the time necessary to fulfil his original ambition to provide, every quarter, an up-to-date source of reliable information for practitioners. The philanthropical Duncan had become engaged in other activities. In particular, he had founded and was practising in his public dispensary for the poor in 1776, and was actively publishing case series based on his experience there.

However, the importance of the publication continued to be appreciated. For example, a writer in the *English Review* stated, 'Were it not for this periodical [...] how many observations of great importance, might never have made their progress beyond the narrow boundaries of a single practitioner in medicine'.[32] In 1791, Duncan recruited the assistance of his son, Andrew Jr, and in 1796, under their joint editorship, *Medical Commentaries* became the *Annals of Medicine*, which followed the same editorial policy. In 1805 the new periodical, which appeared more frequently again than annually, was renamed the *Edinburgh Medical and Surgical Journal* with Duncan Jr as the principal editor. With the exception of dropping the words 'and Surgical' in 1855, the latter lasted for a further 100 years.[33]

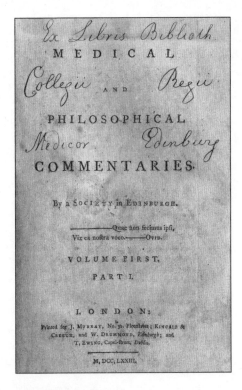

THE *COMMENTARIES*

Copy of the title page of the first issue of
Medical and Philosophical Commentaries.

(COURTESY OF THE LIBRARY OF THE ROYAL COLLEGE OF
PHYSICIANS OF EDINBURGH)

Notes

1   Chalmers and Tröhler (2000), pp. 238-43. Some portions of the text of this chapter have been previously published in this paper.

2   Colman (1999), pp. 324-26. Read also Le Fanu (1984).

3   The first volume of *Medical Essays and Observations* is dedicated to Sir Hans Sloane (president) and the Council and Fellows of the Royal Society of London. Its publication *Philosophical Transactions of the Royal Society* illustrated how short communications could be compiled and published.

4   Tröhler (2000).

5   Zachs (1998), pp. 179-80.

6   John Murray Archive (NLS).

7   Duncan had two brothers, William (1773-?) who died at sea, and Alexander (1746-89), an engineer with the East India Company who died in India. Presumably the brother referred to was Alexander.

8   Zachs (1998).

9   Tröhler (1988), pp. 31-40.

10   Millar (1777), pp. 4-7.

11   Maehle (1999); Tröhler (1987), pp. 958-61; Tröhler (1999), vol. 3, pp 235-51.

12   Tröhler (2000).

13   Lind (1772).

14   Millar (1778-79).

15   Clark (1773).

16   Percival (1767).

17   Lettsom (1774).

18   Dobson (1779).

19   Black (1781).

20   Fowler (1785).

21   Withering (1785).

22   Fowler (1786); Fowler (1795).

23   Blane (1785).

24   John Hunter (1728-93), a Scotsman who, without university education, trained as a surgeon in London and became an outstanding anatomist, scientist and teacher. He became a Fellow of the Royal Society and surgeon to St George's Hospital. He is regarded as a father of scientific surgery in Britain. His museum collection formed the nucleus of the Hunterian Museum at the Royal College of Surgeons in London.

25   James Tassie (1735-99), a Scotsman, invented a vitreous paste which could be modelled to produce stone hard miniature portraits and seals. These became very popular and Catherine the Great is said to have bought 15,000. Tassie was a good friend of John Murray, whose portrait he produced, as he did of many other notables of the time. Murray published his lavishly illustrated catalogue.

26   Bower (1830), vol. III, p. 291.

27   William Smellie (1740-95), printer of the *Commentaries*. Murray's irritation with Smellie was a recurrent theme in his letters. The printing was frequently delayed and Smellie's book-keeping was chaotic. Settling accounts frequently took many months. Perhaps Smellie's difficulties could be justified. He was not only Scotland's leading printer, but one of the outstanding figures of the Enlightenment. Educated at the University of Edinburgh, he was responsible for the first edition of the *Encyclopaedia Britannica* in 1771. He was also a journalist, and the author of the influential *Philosophy of Natural History*, a work of such standing that he applied, unsuccessfully, for the Chair of Natural History in 1775. He was a founder member of the Newtonian Club, Society of Antiquaries and the Crochallan Fencibles, a drinking club patronised by Robert Burns who wrote of Smellie:
     His uncombed grisly locks, wild-staring, thatched – / A head for thought profound, and clear unmatched; / And , though his caustic wit was biting rude, / His heart was warm, benevolent and good.

28   James Sibbald (1747-1803), a cousin of Charles Elliot, started life as a farmer. At the age of 32 he decided to enter the book trade and spent 1779 in London to learn about publishing. At the end of that year he returned to Edinburgh, first to work in his cousin's shop. He soon branched out to set up his own bookshop and lending library. He prospered and started the *Edinburgh Magazine* and a newspaper, the *Edinburgh Herald*. He bought a paper mill at Auchendinny near Edinburgh.

29   James Gilliland married Murray's sister Elizabeth. He had a prosperous jeweller's shop in Parliament Square, where Henry Raeburn was first employed (see ch. XIV). He acted as Murray's agent in Edinburgh.

30 The publishers of the subsequent volumes were: no. 10 Murray and Elliot; nos 11-14 Elliot alone; nos 15-20 G. C. J. & J. Robinson in London with Peter Hill and G. Mudie in Edinburgh; no. 20 (1795) was the last of the series. Thereafter Duncan continued the publication under the title of *Annals of Medicine*. The format was identical to *Medical Commentaries*, except Andrew Duncan Jr's name appeared as co-editor.

31 Zachs (1998).

32 Zachs (1998), p 190.

33 Johnstone, *et al.* (1954), pp. 389-90.

The publications that Charles Elliot and John Murray produced for Andrew Duncan are listed in the writings of Andrew Duncan Sr listed in Appendix I. Both men were involved with *Medical and Philosophical Commentaries*.

1773-1795 *Medical and Philosophical Commentaries*, by a society in Edinburgh. Vol First (London: John Murray; Edinburgh: Kincaid and Creech and W. Drummond; Dublin: T. Ewing Dublin). With an index. 20 vols.

Issued in four parts with separate title pages. Price 1/6 each part, or 6/- a volume. Murray lost the publication to Charles Dilly between 1780 and 1782, at which time the work began to be issued annually. From volume 7, the title changed to *Medical Commentaries*.

Charles Elliot is named as co-publisher with Murray for vol. 5 (1778), vol. 6 (1779), vol. 9 (1785), and vol. 10 (1786).

Charles Elliot is named as publisher for *Medical Commentaries*, decade second, vol. 1 (1787), vol. 2 (1788), vol.3 (1789), and vol. 4 (1790)

Elliot paid Duncan £50-8/- for *Medical Cases, Selected from the Records of the Public Dispensary at Edinburgh* and £20 for *Heads of Lectures on the Theory and Practice of Medicine*. He paid £60 for each annual volume of *Medical Commentaries* when the publication moved to Edinburgh from London. These sums, although an important part of Duncan's income, appear modest when compared with £250 for James Gregory's *Conspectus Medicinae Theoreticae*. *William Cullen's standing in the medical profession is demonstrated by the £1200 which he was able to command for First Lines of the Practice of Physic* and £1500 for *Materia Medica*.

Charles Elliot also published a portrait of Dr Duncan, painted by Weir and engraved by Trotter in 1784.

CHAPTER III

Edinburgh's Royal
Public Dispensary

M. H. KAUFMAN

*A scheme in its nature so humane and so important to society well deserves
imitation in every large city.*   Andrew Duncan 1774[1]

The establishment of the (Royal) Public Dispensary

In the latter part of the 18th century there was virtually no medical aid
available for those who were unable to pay. From time to time in the past,
charitable donations had enabled the College of Physicians to provide a
limited service. When the Royal Infirmary was first opened, it offered a free
out-patient service, but after a number of years this was abandoned because
the cost was too great.

As detailed in chapter I, Andrew Duncan, having failed in his application
for the Chair of Institutes of Medicine, commenced his extramural course in
1776. In that year he announced his intention of creating a Public Dispensary which would fulfil the dual function of providing a much needed
facility for the free treatment of the poor while meeting his teaching requirements.[2] The Royal College of Surgeons, as feuar of his teaching school, had
banned its use for the purpose of seeing patients lest it became a nuisance, so
Duncan was required to find alternative accommodation. Initially the Dispensary was conducted in rented rooms in College Wynd, where the first
patients were seen in the latter part of 1776, and later in accommodation
within the College of Physicians in George Street. Soon it became apparent
that larger premises were required, and by 1780 sufficient funds were available to buy land and build the Dispensary on a site in Richmond Street which
opened in 1785. The *Caledonian Mercury* (15 July 1780) records that beneath the
foundation stone were deposited a medal engraved with the Goddess of Health
inscribed '*Salus Publica*' (public health) and a sealed glass vessel containing
an account of the charity and lines from Alexander Pope's *Essay on Man*:

In Faith and Hope the world will disagree,
But all mankind's concern is Charity:

All must be false that thwart this one great end,
And all of God that bless mankind or mend.

The Public Dispensary is generally believed to have been the first institution of its kind in Scotland, although a comparable institution had been established in Aldersgate, London in 1770 by Duncan's friend and contemporary, John Coakley Lettsom.[3] Duncan reported the successful Aldersgate Dispensary in *Commentaries* in 1774. There can be little doubt that this was the inspiration for his Edinburgh Dispensary two years later.

To fund his Dispensary, Duncan invited contributions from the public and the churches. Students attending his course of lectures were required to pay half a guinea towards the costs of medicines supplied by the Dispensary. The fact that the medical staff served on a voluntary basis, and were assisted by free student labour, greatly helped in keeping the running costs to a minimum. Duncan obtained a Royal charter for his Dispensary in 1818, and it became the *Royal* Public Dispensary (and Vaccine Institution).

The two earliest available documents that refer directly to the activities of Andrew Duncan's Public Dispensary of Edinburgh are its first and second Annual Reports.[4] The first of these, dated 1 November 1777, was drafted by Duncan. On the last few pages a brief list of the Regulations relating to the running of the Dispensary was published. These Regulations identified which patients should be considered as acceptable to be seen at the Dispensary. They drew attention to who, among the members of the medical community, should be subscribers to the charity, and indicated who should be appointed to the committee for superintending the funds and the other business of the charity. An annual general meeting of the contributors was to be held on the last Monday of January of each year. After the Regulations were listed, it named the two physicians to the Dispensary – Dr Andrew Duncan, its founder, and Dr Charles Webster. These individuals were required to be '… in attendance at the Dispensary every Tuesday and Friday, from one to two o'clock at rooms in the College Wynd, which are at present rented for the use of the Dispensary. Advice and medicines are there given gratis, to such people in indigent circumstances, as are deemed proper patients. Those patients, who come recommended by subscribers, are admitted to the benefits of this charity, in preference to all others.'

Every person subscribing one guinea to the funds of the Dispensary is entitled to hold the rank of Governor for the space of two years after the payment is made, and for every larger sum in proportion. A subscription of five guineas constitutes a governor for life. All future appointments of physicians, or other officers to this charity, will be made by the suffrages [i.e. votes in support] of a majority of the governors. By their suffrages also, all

*such regulations as they may hereafter think necessary, shall be enacted, as
a committee appointed annually for superintending the charity.*

A later document lists the names of those who contributed at least one
guinea, or in most cases more than this amount, for the years 1778-86.[5] The
total amount received during 1778 from the 39 contributors was 121 guineas;
in 1779, 48 guineas from the 20 contributors; and in 1780, 170 guineas from
the 60 contributors.[6]

The second Annual Report contains an amended version of the General
Regulations of the Dispensary. In these two Annual Reports, the names of
all of the patients seen in the Dispensary during the first and second years
were provided, together with dates of commencement and termination of
their treatment, and, when available, information relating to the effectiveness or otherwise of their treatment. 'Effectiveness' indicated, for example,
whether the patient was considered *cured*. If the treatment given was effective, but only to a limited degree, the patient's symptoms could reasonably
be considered as *relieved*. When treatment was ineffective, the patient was
considered to be *no better*, although the full meaning of this term was
explained in greater detail in the second Annual Report (see below).

During the first year the number of patients seen in the Dispensary
between 7 November 1776 and 29 October 1777 was 222, although no
indication of the patient's clinical condition was recorded. A definitive outcome was reported in 180 cases. Individuals were either categorised as *cured*
(79), *relieved* (57), *no better* (39), or *dead* (5). The remaining 42 cases were
still under treatment at the time the first Report was being prepared.

The number of patients seen during the second year was almost double
that seen during its first year. Again no indication of their clinical condition
was given, although information on a few of these patients is available from
the analysis of a notebook[7] maintained by a student who attended during the
summer of 1778-79. The 511 patients seen fell into the following categories:
cured (221), *relieved* (110), *no better* (137), or *dead* (3); while there were 40
patients who continued to be on treatment.

According to the second Annual Report, it was thought advisable to
explain why a proportion of those seen were dismissed from the Dispensary
as *no better*. It was noted that these individuals fell into two categories. The
first group were those considered incurable, or who voluntarily withdrew
from attending the Dispensary. The second group included first those, who
for reasons that are now unclear, it was recommended should reside, for
some time, at a distance from Edinburgh. The others were those who needed
to be admitted into the Royal Infirmary, 'as changes which had taken place
in their diseases rendered confinement necessary for their recovery'.

Dr Webster also taught chemistry and pharmacy in Duncan's extramural school. He was then incumbent of St Paul's Church, Jeffrey Street, but, before his ordination to the priesthood he had qualified in medicine. Webster was succeeded by Andrew Duncan Jr. Pharmacy continued to be taught at the Dispensary which became recognised as a School of Pharmacy. In 1885 John Hill was appointed Principal of the School of Pharmacy based at the Public Dispensary. Eventually, in 1935, this School amalgamated with the School of Pharmacy at Heriot-Watt College.

Some of the patients seen in the Dispensary by Duncan during 1776 and 1777

Duncan thought it appropriate that for the benefit of his colleagues, pupils and the public, he should provide examples of the clinical conditions he saw at the Dispensary. He was encouraged to publish a series of 26 representative cases. In the preface to his *Medical Cases*,[8] he noted that these cases had all been selected by three medical students who had acted, at various times, as his assistants. While they had drafted the detailed case histories, he had complemented this information with additional remarks and observations that had previously been delivered by him in the course of his extramural lectures. He emphasised that he was initially concerned with the management of patients with chronic diseases, but had later decided that it would be particularly instructive if he published examples of those cases that were commonly encountered by general practitioners in the course of their practice.

The names of his first three assistants were Mr William Browne from Yorkshire, Mr Samuel Byam Athill from Antigua, and Mr Charles Darwin from Lichfield. In each case that was selected, Duncan recommended that his assistants should

> ... begin with giving an account of the condition of the patient, independently of his disease, briefly mentioning the age, sex, temperament, condition of life, and other circumstances, which would throw light on the nature of the patient's constitution; in the next place, to give a full description of all of the symptoms with which the patient was affected at the time of drawing up the history; then to give an account of the progress of the disease; afterwards, to enumerate those remote causes which may be supposed to have had any share, as inducing the affection; and, lastly, to mention the remedies employed before admission, and the effects resulting from these. This order, though necessarily varied by the circumstances of different cases, has been pretty generally adhered to.[9]

Duncan then followed this information with his own subsequent reports which

> ... record the practice which was employed with a view to the cure. The method which I have in general followed has been, first, to mention the obvious effects which resulted from the medicines that were used; then to give an account of the changes which had happened, with regard to symptoms before existing; next, to be taken notice of new occurrences, and of the state of the principal functions; and, lastly, to conclude with prescribing such medicines as the condition of the affection at the time seemed to indicate.

He then discussed in each case the effect of the plan that he followed. Brief details of the first few cases are provided here, as they represent examples of the range of clinical conditions that he encountered in the Dispensary. They also indicate that he was well aware of the treatments of some of these conditions as indicated both in the *Edinburgh Pharmacopoeia*, and in the earlier literature.

CASE 1: *Observations on a case of epilepsy, cured by the use of Cuprum Ammoniacum.*

The patient was an eleven-year-old boy who was first seen on 7 November 1776. He had been affected by typical grand mal epileptic fits that occurred about once per week. During these fits, which had occurred over the previous four years, he became unconscious. He had strong convulsive movements of his arms and legs, and foamed at the mouth. These fits often lasted for about half an hour. He also noted that when these attacks first occurred, they were less frequent and less severe. The boy's mother was similarly affected by fits, and over this period he had slept in the same bed with her. Duncan indicated that he had selected a formula from the *Edinburgh Pharmacopoeia*, and that the active ingredient was a particularly mild preparation of copper. He noted that copper had long been used for medical purposes, and drew attention to an inaugural MD dissertation entitled *De Cupro* published by the University of Edinburgh about 20 years earlier by a Doctor Russell.[10]

Duncan explained that while most preparations of copper were extremely poisonous, its neutral salts, particularly its ammoniacal salts, were far less virulent. Hippocrates had recommended copper salts, and more recently their use had been recommended by the German medical authorities, as well as previously by Robert Boyle (1627-91), under the title of *Ente Veneris*. Duncan later indicated that he had used this remedy in several previous cases of epilepsy with good effect in some, but by no means in all cases. Its effect in this particular case was remarkable, and more beneficial than in any of his previous cases. The patient left his mother's house, and was free from fits until the middle of June of the following year, shortly after he returned to her house. He reported that he had had no other fits, although his mother continued to have fits on a regular basis.

CASE 2: *Observations on an enlargement of the abdomen, of a doubtful nature, which terminated successfully.*

This was a girl of seven years of age, who was first seen on 8 November 1776. In this individual, the swelling of the abdomen had first been evident about five years previously. Four years later, she had a fever, and passed four round worms. About one to two months before her first visit to the Dispensary, she discharged another worm. She was treated with a range of emetics, some of which induced purging, while at a later date she was treated with a mixture containing *tincture amara*. This resulted in a considerable discharge of wind, in the way of flatus, and the swelling diminished a little, although it did not entirely disappear. Her health continued to improve, and she was discharged during the middle of March.

CASE 3: *Observations on a cutaneous affection, treated by the external application of* corrosive sublimate, *terminating successfully.*

This patient was a boy aged eight years who was first seen on 8 November 1776, whose face displayed a red scaly eruption, with a similar localised condition involving the abdomen. The patient noted that the eruption on his face often discharged matter. This condition had been present for about nine months before he was first seen by Duncan and '*no cause is assigned for it, except that of sleeping in the bed with a person, about two years before, who was afflicted with similar eruptions*'.

The patient was treated with a solution of *corrosive sublimate* externally, and of *antimony* internally, and he noted that the eruption on his face gradually declined, although soon afterwards a dry scaly eruption appeared on his scalp. When the hair was shaved off, the scalp was also treated with a similar external application, but in the form of an ointment. He was eventually discharged at the beginning of March, after his skin condition had completely recovered.

CASE 4: *Observations on a rheumatic affection cured by the use of the elixir Guajacinum Volatile.*

This patient was a married woman aged 42, who was first seen on 11 November 1776, and complained of pains in the hip, knee and ankle joints. The pain was so severe that she was unable to walk, nor could she stand upright. The pain was particularly acute '*when she begins to grow warm in bed*'. The pains first affected her about six months before she was first seen, and the affected sites were hot and red, but these features soon disappeared after '*blood letting by means of leeches*'.

This case was treated using the volatile elixir of *guaiacum* [*sic*] of the *Edinburgh Pharmacopoeia*, being very similar to the *spiritus salis ammoniaci vinosus* employed and recommended by the members of the London College. According to Duncan, '*The volatile elixir has, of late, been rendered very fashionable in* [the treatment of] *rheumatic affections, by the publication of Doctor Dawson, entitled, cases in the acute rheumatism and the gout*'.[11] The patient continued with this treatment, and was seen at intervals during December, January and February, with an excellent outcome. She was discharged, cured, shortly afterwards.

CASE 5: *Observations on a case of chronical catarrh.*
The patient was a shoemaker aged 48, and was first seen on 11 November 1776. He complained of a frequent and troublesome cough '*attended with copious and viscid expectoration, especially in the morning*', from which he had suffered for about twelve years. Duncan was of the opinion that this patient suffered from a form of catarrh that he referred to, because of its features, as a type of influenza. Such a condition, he believed, might be either acute or chronic in form, and might in due course give rise to either tuberculosis (termed *phthisis pulmonalis*) or to chronic catarrh (a disease commonly seen in older individuals), which was usually fatal. Because of the patient's age, Duncan hoped that the outcome might not be of the latter type. Duncan concluded that:

> *although by these measures the severity of his disease was alleviated, yet it continued to distress him the whole winter; and, about the end of May, when his attendance at the Dispensary was discontinued, the presumption is, that the relief which he obtained proceeded more from the change of the season, than from the influence of the medicines which were employed. ...*

CASE 6: *The history of a petechial eruption without febrile symptoms, terminating successfully.*
This patient was a girl aged 11 years, who displayed small red spots '*not raised above the surface of the skin, and neither sore nor painful. She has also on her forehead and arms, but particularly on her lower extremities, livid blotches, having much the appearance of vibices* [narrow linear marks or streaks; linear subcutaneous effusions of blood]. *These are of different sizes; some of them* [being] *as large as the surface of half a crown, others of a shilling. She sometimes complains of slight headache, and her gums have bled once or twice during these last three days. These bleedings have come*

on without obvious accident; but the discharge has never been considerable.' While Duncan admitted that he was unable to form a diagnosis, the condition fortunately terminated favourably, and the patient was then discharged from the Dispensary.

The other cases reported in his *Medical Cases* were extremely variable in nature. One was '*a cancerous affection of the breast treated by electricity*' in a woman of 62. She was not keen on the therapy prescribed for her, and decided not to continue with the treatment, and discharged herself from the Dispensary. Other cases described included a man of 47 with haemorrhoids, a 20-year-old woman with menorrhagia, and a 24-year-old woman with amenorrhoea who was treated with electricity. A six-year-old girl with *Tinea Capitis* was treated with the external application of *corrosive sublimate of mercury* and *verdegrise*. A wide range of other cases was also seen, including individuals of whom some displayed the features of gonorrhoea, while others had syphilis. Another was a child of three with hydrocephalus.

In another case (CASE 25), Duncan was particularly complimentary about his assistant Mr Darwin, and noted as follows:

> *Mr Darwin, who officiated as medical assistant at the Dispensary at the time when this patient's case was treated, and who, besides extensive knowledge in every branch of medicine, is also eminently distinguished for his acquaintance with natural history, had the first opportunity of examining this worm after it was discharged. He found it to be one of that kind which Mr Linnaeus has distinguished by the name of* <u>Taenia Lata</u>. *But he could discover no circumstances, farther than is mentioned in the history of the case and subsequent reports, from which even a probable conjecture could be formed, whether all the fragments belonged to the same worm, or to different ones.*[12]

New Town Dispensary

Other dispensaries were established in Edinburgh during the 19th century, and almost all provided free treatment to the poorest members of the population. The earliest of these institutions was the Edinburgh New Town Dispensary which was established in 1815, on remarkably similar lines to the Public Dispensary that was founded almost 40 years earlier. Duncan regarded this rival Dispensary with disfavour, particularly because it would compete for charitable funds.

At the first Annual General Meeting of the governors of the New Town Dispensary held on 4 March 1817, the managers reported the great success of their institution in fulfilling the objectives for which it was established, and the fact that they found that they were overwhelmed by patients.[13] Like those who attended the Public Dispensary, these consisted of members of the Sick and Diseased Poor who attended to obtain relief from their ills. The managers noted that because of the enormous number of individuals who had applied to them for assistance, the first house they acquired as their Dispensary was far too small, and a larger house had to be rented to accommodate their needs. This was at 13 North James' Street, Edinburgh. They also found that their expenses more than exhausted their first year's subscriptions. They therefore applied to the local churches to make an appeal on their behalf. The sum obtained from this source £266-5/- was more than adequate to free them of their financial difficulties and they hoped to continue to be able to obtain funds from this source. Their Report also noted that during the first 18 months of their existence they saw 8062 persons and 3754 of these had been seen during the previous six months.

Duncan was incensed when St Andrew's Church in George Street started collecting funds for the New Town Dispensary instead of the Public Dispensary as hitherto. A letter from Duncan to the Rev. Dr D. Ritchie, dated 7 April 1817, was published:

> I was sadly mortified to hear … from, Dean of Guild Johnston, that you did not intend to join the other Churches of Edinburgh, in making a Collection for the Public Dispensary at the door of St Andrew's Church. During the course of forty years the Public Dispensary has afforded undeniable proof that it is an Institution highly beneficial to the Poor.
>
> Its constant aim has been to have assistance to the Indigent Sick in every corner of the Town; and it has hitherto been supported by … every Parish. If you shall refuse it your countenance on the present occasion, you will not only deprive your charitable parishioners of a favourable opportunity of giving it a little aid, but you will do it a much more material injury, by supporting a doctrine which has of late been but too successfully propagated, that the inhabitants of the New Town having now a Dispensary for themselves ought to shake off all connection with the Public Dispensary, although some of those who propagate this doctrine well know, that the Indigent Sick are regularly supplied. … in the Hall of the College of Physicians immediately opposite your church door with advice and medicine at the expense of the Public Dispensary. …[14]

Dr Ritchie replied that the Session had agreed to collect for the New Dispensary only, while acknowledging that 'it may be advisable to have two houses … for accommodating the sick poor. But such is the distribution of poor and rich in Edinburgh, … the one must needs have too much business, and too little money, and the other the converse.'[15]

The governors of the New Town Dispensary believed that the reason that so many individuals had applied to them for assistance was because they, unlike the Public Dispensary, 'were open every day for advice', and possibly more importantly, if necessary 'patients could be seen and treated in their own houses'. Cockburn noted that Duncan was extremely hostile to this innovation, as he believed that patients should swallow their physic on the Dispensary's premises.[16] According to Gray, John Thomson, one of the first members of the New Town Dispensary's medical staff, introduced this innovation. Thomson's brief biography states that he was, despite considerable opposition, almost single-handedly instrumental in the establishment of this Dispensary.[17]

The governors of the New Town Dispensary also emphasised their close association with the Royal Infirmary, so that, should the need arise, patients could readily be transferred to that institution (a facility which was equally available to the Public Dispensary). Similarly, by visiting patients in their own home, they were able to persuade individuals with smallpox to get their children vaccinated, and by this means they believed that they had stopped the progress of this condition into the neighbourhood. They also attended lying-in women at their own houses, and of 369 seen, 299 were delivered and attended during their recovery.

The results of discussions between the two Dispensaries were reported in a pamphlet published at that time.[18] The managers of the New Town Dispensary noted that it was having difficulties coping with the unexpectedly large number of patients. They indicated that two possibilities were open to them. Either they could enlarge their own establishment, or enter into an arrangement with the other institution (*i.e.* the Edinburgh Public Dispensary), with the aim of dividing the town between the two Dispensaries. A meeting was therefore held to establish whether it might be possible for the two institutions to come to some agreement. According to this report, the representatives of the New Town Dispensary were in favour of dividing the town between the two Institutions, but they were not in favour of the two Institutions uniting, which might restrict the new features which they had introduced, such features being ...

1. the regular attendance upon Patients in their own houses when necessary;
2. that their Dispensary should be open every day of the week (excepting Sundays);
3. the continuance of the accoucheur (i.e. midwifery) department.

The representatives of the New Town Dispensary believed that the doctors of the Edinburgh Public Dispensary, after noting the success of the

New Town Dispensary, had decided that it would be advantageous if they also started visiting patients at their own houses. As a consequence, the number of patients who attended the Edinburgh Public Dispensary during the previous year had increased by more than 1000 when compared to former years. For these, and other reasons, the representatives of the two establishments decided that it would be in neither's interest for them to merge into a single establishment.

After these unsuccessful discussions, the two Institutions continued to function as two completely separate entities. However, shortly after the appearance of the New Town Dispensary, the activities of the Edinburgh Public Dispensary were dramatically amended, so that apart (initially) from not attending midwifery cases, both their activities and their regulations, as well as the forms of their Annual Reports, were remarkably similar. Duncan's deeply rooted antipathy to midwifery (see chapter XIII) no doubt contributed to the delayed adoption of this service by the Public Dispensary. It was only later in the 19th century that the Royal Public Dispensary began to see midwifery cases.

Although now written in slightly coded phraseology, Henry Cockburn referred to the differences that initially existed between the activities of the Edinburgh Public Dispensary (the EPD) and the New Town Dispensary (NTD) in his *Memorials of His Time*. Cockburn stated as follows:

> *The extension of the city gave rise in 1815 to the New Town Dispensary. Any such institution seems at least harmless; yet this one was assailed with a degree of bitterness which is curious now. It was a civic war. Two of its principles were, that medicines and medical advice, including obstetrical aid, were to be administered to patients* <u>*at their own homes*</u>*, and that the office-bearers were to be elected* <u>*by the subscribers*</u>*; which last, though not absolutely new, was then rare in Edinburgh. All the existing establishments* [i.e. the EPD] *had the usual interest to suppress a rival* [the NTD]. *But they disavowed this, which however was their true motive, and raised the cry against these two peculiarities. A mob selecting a doctor! The Lying-in Hospital was eloquent on the danger and the vice of delivering poor women at their own houses. The Old Town Dispensary* [i.e. the EPD], *which did not then go to such patients as could not come to it, demonstrated the beauty of the sick poor being obliged to swallow their doses at a public office. Subscribers choose managers! Impracticable, and dangerously popular! However, common sense prevailed over even this political bugbear, and the hated institution rose and flourished, and has had all its defects imitated by its opponents.*[19]

The progress of the Edinburgh Public Dispensary

Each year during its existence, Edinburgh's Royal (from 1818) Public Dispensary produced an Annual Report. That issued in 1831, prepared very shortly after Dr Duncan's death, was its 54th Annual Report.[20] It stated that this Institution 'was instituted ... for the purpose of affording medical advice and medicines gratuitously to such as have to struggle with disease and poverty. And before its venerable Founder died, he had the satisfaction to see that upwards of 200,000 individuals had partaken of its benefits'.

Information from the 1st, 2nd and 54th Annual Reports of the Edinburgh Public Dispensary appears to indicate that the clinicians at this Dispensary saw only about 19 patients *per month* during its first year, and closer to 43 patients *per month* during the second year of its operation. Numbers increased to an average of about 320 patients *per month* over the first 52 years of its existence, between 1776 and 1828 when Duncan died, and this despite the very considerable number of patients who attended the New Town Dispensary that had opened in 1815.

During the first few years of its existence, the names of only two physicians were noted in its Annual Reports. By the time of the 54th Annual Report the attending medical staff had increased to six physicians and six surgeons. The names and addresses of a phlebotomist (or cupper) and a resident apothecary were also noted, as well as four physicians who constituted the Vaccine Board.

Regulations stipulated that the six ordinary physicians and six ordinary surgeons all had to be Fellows of either the Royal College of Physicians or Surgeons. They were also required to divide the town into various districts, with one physician and a surgeon associated with each of these districts. The regulations also stated that none of the physicians or surgeons should be connected in any way with any other general dispensary. The regulations stipulated the means by which prescriptions should be signed and when they should be presented. More particularly, the medical practitioner had 'to satisfy himself of the situation of the Patient as to Poverty, &c. before he issues a Prescription to the Apothecary'. Exactly how this was to be achieved was not stated.

One of the most interesting statements in this Report of the Royal Public Dispensary ran as follows:

> *At present the benefits of the Institution are open to all who are afflicted with disease and poverty. Advice and medicines are given at the Dispensary by a Physician and a Surgeon, who are in daily attendance, to those patients whose diseases do not necessarily confine them to the house; and such cases as require it, are regularly visited and prescribed for at their own houses.*

During the last year, 6533 individuals have received its aid; making the total
number of persons who have benefited by it since the commencement of
the Institution, 232,303, — by which much relief has been afforded to
suffering humanity, and many valuable lives saved to their friends and the
community.

This is complemented by the 'Abstract of patients relieved during the
year'. This states as follows:

Medical and Surgical Patients prescribed for at the Hall of the Dispensary,	3564
Medical and Surgical Patients attended at their own houses,	2597
Number of Patients vaccinated,	372
Total during the Year,	6533

The authors of the Report of the Royal Public Dispensary were concerned that the funds they were receiving in the form of contributions from
various sources had for some time been less than their outgoings, so they
'would be obliged to diminish the benefits which the poor derive from the
Institution'. Accordingly, they appealed for 'additional funding' to support
their present level of activities, however small the individual contributions
might be. They also took the opportunity of stressing that the staff continued to provide their professional services gratuitously. In their 'Abstract of
Treasurer's Accounts' they drew attention to the fact that from 31 December 1829 to 31 December 1830, the balance due to the treasurer (*i.e.* their
deficit for the year) was £338-5/9 (approximately £24,400 in modern
terms).

The Annual Report of the Royal Public Dispensary of 1834 also stressed
the need for additional support from the public. They noted, for example,
that they had been supported of late by the collection carried out at the
various churches in the city, and that the funds obtained from this source
had been distributed to their own institution, and to the other dispensaries
in the city. They also noted an increased deficit in their funds for the year of
£624-16/6. It was noted that subscriptions and donations only provided
£165-5/9 while the dividend on their stock provided a further £36-15/-. Outgoings included the cost of medicines for use in the Dispensary of £324-13/-;
expenditure on the building, repairs, etc., £112-3/8; salaries for the apothecary and the porter, £90-19/1; the cost of printing and stationery, £37-/11;
and annual payments, such as Feu-duty, insurance, etc., £26-10/2.

An updated version of the regulations was also associated with the 1834
Annual Report, and noted that as previously each medical officer could

have two pupils, and that these had to have attended medical classes for at least two winter sessions, and attended a hospital for at least one year. All fees obtained from these students were to be paid to the secretary of the Dispensary. The regulations stated that only one of these pupils, when there were two, was required to pay to the funds of the Dispensary one guinea for every two months of attendance. The duties of the pupils were then detailed. They were required to attend the Dispensary punctually on the days that the medical officers were in attendance. They were also required to assist them in registering the patients, to visit the patients' homes and prescribe for these patients as directed by the medical officers, as well as performing any dressings or 'lesser operations' which may be required. Should they be called to a patient's house on an emergency basis, they were allowed to prescribe an appropriate emergency treatment, but had to report their activity to their medical officer as soon afterwards as possible. All the prescriptions they gave had to be furnished from the Dispensary.

It is likely that there were numerous examples over the years where difficulties and disputes occurred between the Royal Public and the New Town Dispensaries. One such example is highlighted in the Annual Report of the New Town Dispensary of 1843.[21] Just inside the cover of this report, it states as follows:

> *Caution to Contributors.*
>
> *As repeated instances have of late occurred, of Subscribers being induced, inadvertently, to pay their contributions to the Collector of another Institution, who has represented that he was authorised to receive money for 'THE NEW TOWN DISPENSARY,' the managers reluctantly feel bound to take steps, as far as possible, to prevent the repetition of such practices. They therefore intimate, that the Subscription Book of the NEW TOWN DISPENSARY has for many years been of an Octavo shape, bound in Green Leather, and is stamped on both boards, in gold letters, with a 'Die.' Of which the subjoined is an impression.*
>
> *Besides, there is an Official Certificate affixed, that the Bearer, Gavin Anderson, is authorised by the Managers to receive subscriptions.*
>
> Edinburgh, Jan. 9, 1843

The evolution of out-patient treatment

Towards the end of the 19th century, when many thousands of individuals were seen in both the Royal Public and the New Town Dispensaries, it was estimated that they were treated at a cost of about one shilling per patient. During the early part of the 20th century, despite their relatively inexpensive running cost, dispensaries tended to disappear. Some became incorporated into the out-patients departments of associated infirmaries. In Edinburgh, the passing of Part 1 of the National Insurance Act of 1911 hastened the end of many of the dispensaries. This was principally because it made the 'panel' doctor the centre of the new health service which provided free medical care to the insured workers. Dispensaries mostly departed from the scene with the introduction of the National Health Service in 1948, when the government introduced free medical treatment for all members of the population.

In the Centre for Research Collections of Edinburgh University Library there are a number of minute books of the Dispensary covering the late 19th century. The most recent dated item is a list of the medical students who attended this Dispensary between 7 January 1947 and 3 May 1948. During 1947, 102 students attended.

Establishment of the Chair of General Practice

The critical role played by the various dispensaries during previous centuries in teaching medical students how they should interact with patients still continues. The Public Dispensary building engraved by James and Henry Sargant Storer (see *figs* 7a and 7b), was demolished in 1937 and replaced with a modern building on the opposite side of Richmond Street, now known as the Mackenzie Medical Centre. This houses both the National Health Service's General Practice Unit, and the Academic Department of General Practice. It was named in memory of Sir James Mackenzie,[22] an eminent academic general practitioner whose family was associated with the endowment of the Chair of General Practice in the University of Edinburgh. With the establishment of the National Health Service in 1948, the Royal Public Dispensary in due course evolved into the University's General Practice Teaching Unit. Because of its popularity with the students, in that it revived interest in community care on the part of the Faculty of Medicine, this resulted in the establishment of a University Chair in General Practice in 1963, the first chair in this discipline in Europe.[23] Dr Richard Scott, Senior Lecturer in Public Health, became the first professor. In the same year the trustees of the Dispensary donated the remaining assets of the Dispensary to the University. Duncan would surely have approved of this satisfactory conclusion to one of his major achievements.

Opposite page:

A CLASS CARD

The card made out to Mr William Drennan and dated 1778 allowed him to attend 'Case Lectures' delivered by Andrew Duncan MD and Charles Webster MD at the Public Dispensary

(WITH PERMISSION, EDINBURGH UNIVERSITY LIBRARY, SPECIAL COLLECTIONS DEPARTMENT)

Notes

1   Andrew Duncan commenting on Lettsom's Aldergate Dispensary, *Medical Commentaries* (1774), 2, p. 95.

2   *Medical Commentaries* (1776), 4, pp. 355-57.

3   Lettsom (1774).

4   The full titles of these documents, with their Centre for Research Collections (CRC) of EUL Reference Numbers in parentheses, are as follows: 'A general view of the effects of the Dispensary at Edinburgh. During the first year of that Charitable Establishment', Edinburgh 1777 (Ref. No. O.S.36204/2/1); 'A general view of the effects of the Dispensary at Edinburgh. During the second year of that Charitable Establishment', Edinburgh 1779 (Ref. No. S.B.6104/5/3).

5   List of Contributors to the Public Dispensary of Edinburgh, 1785 (S.B.36204/2/2).

6   One guinea in 1778 is equivalent to £100 today.

7   This document is also available in the CRC, EUL (Ref. No. Gen. 553D, pp. 108-60). It should be noted, however, that relatively few of the names provided in the records correspond to those recorded by this student in his notebook.

8   Duncan (1778).

9   Duncan (1778), pp. 4-5.

10 The MD dissertation referred to by Duncan was written by Balfour Russell, (1759), p. 10.

11 Dawson(1776).

12 Duncan (1778), p. 335.

13 Anon (1817b).

14 Correspondence (1817) between Rev. Dr D. Ritchie and Dr Duncan Sr (Edinburgh: Neill), NLS 1962.12(4).

15 *Ibid.*

16 Cockburn (1856), pp. 283-84.

17 Thomson (1859), vol. 1, p. 50. First published in 1832. Now reissued, along with the 2nd volume, prefixed with a biographical notice of the author. See also Gray (1952), pp. 87-88. (For biographical notice of Dr John Thomson, see vol. 1, pp. 5-84, and for Dr William Thomson, see vol. 1, pp. 85-92).

18 Anon (1817a).

19 Cockburn (1856), p. 283.

20 Anon (1831).

21 Anon (1843a).

22 Smith (2004), pp. 596-97.

23 Thomson (1984), pp. 9-12.

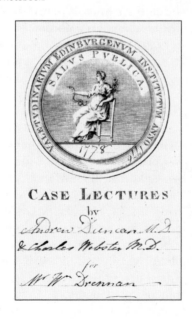

CHAPTER IV

The Edinburgh
Lunatic Asylum

JOHN CHALMERS

Rather than bear the miserable gloom
When all his comfort, all his friends are fled,
Bear me, ye Gods, where I may calmly rest
From all the follies of the night secure,
The balmy blessings of repose to taste,
Nor hear the tongue of outrage at the door.

From 'Tavern Elegy' by Robert Fergusson

The moving spirit

Andrew Duncan is probably best remembered today for his role in setting up the Edinburgh Lunatic Asylum. Certainly he regarded this, together with the founding of the Dispensary for the Sick Poor, as his greatest contributions to mankind. Yet during his lifetime the Lunatic Asylum scarcely got off the ground and he failed totally in his ambition to create a home for the mentally ill of all classes of society. He was, however, credited then and now as the prime mover of what has become a world famous institution.

In Duncan's day, provision for the treatment of the mentally ill in Edinburgh (and in the rest of the country) was woefully inadequate. When the Royal Infirmary was built in 1738, twelve vaulted rooms in the basement were set aside for the care of the insane, but these had been abandoned to other uses. The cheapest accommodation available was in the Bedlam attached to the Charity Workhouse built behind the city wall, opposite the entrance to what is now Middle Meadow Walk. It charged £8-10/- a year, later rising to £20. Other private 'mad houses' existed, but the cost was beyond the means of many, the accommodation was overcrowded, and the inmates were constantly locked in their own rooms without exercise, employment or society. In 1815 an Act to Regulate Madhouses in Scotland was passed which required annual licensing and biennial inspection by the Sheriff-Depute and medical practitioners elected by the Royal College of Physicians in Edinburgh and the Faculty of Physicians and Surgeons of

Glasgow. Houston[1] records that in 1816 there were 25 licensed madhouses in the Edinburgh Sheriffdom, of which 13 held only one or two inmates. The owners were non-medical and conditions in some were very primitive. The managers of the Montrose Asylum (the first to be established in Scotland in 1781) recognised that

> ... *the keepers of such* [mad]*houses are not possessed of the knowledge or the feeling requisite to such a charge. The idea that anything ought to be done calculated to bring about recovery hardly ever seems to enter their minds. ... the keepers seemed to ridicule the idea that medical aid can be beneficial in mental disorder. ...*[2]

One woman patient, who had been chained for many years in a room in which snow drifted through broken panes, was found with chilblains on her feet.

Charges ranged from £50 to £200 a year. Pauper lunatics who could not afford admission to a Bedlam or 'madhouse' lived in even more appalling circumstances. Mitchell (1864) records some of these.[3] Of one idiot woman, it was reported:

> *By no description can I convey an idea of the misery, filth, and degradation in which I found her. With the dog she sleeps in the ashes at the fire-side, without even the pretence of a bed. I found her half-naked, her breasts exposed, and on her shoulders nothing but a bit of sacking, shawl-ways. The house was ruinous, furnitureless, bare, wet, cold, dark, stinking, and filthy. ...*

The Edinburgh Bedlam had been opened in 1748 on the site of a smaller madhouse built in 1698 and was the first of its kind in Scotland. The accommodation was very basic, consisting of 21 bare damp cells with straw on the floor. They were unheated and lit and aired solely by openings in the doors. No treatment was offered, other than restraints to prevent inmates hurting themselves or others.

Towards the end of 1773 the young poet Robert Fergusson began to develop signs of insanity which took the form of a 'religious melancholia'. His conscience was stricken with regret for his misspent youth and he suffered from hallucinations. His condition became critical following a head injury sustained by a fall down stairs and he became unmanageable at home. He was forcibly locked up in the Bedlam where he died tragically after two months at the age of 24. As a young man, Andrew Duncan had attended Fergusson during his terminal illness, and many years later he recorded the circumstances:

*I found him in a very deplorable condition, subjected to furious insanity.
He lived in the house of his Mother, an old Widow in very narrow circumstances. Her feeble and aged state ... rendered it impossible to make any
attempt towards cure, with the slightest prospect of advantage, while he
remained at home. After several fruitless attempts to have him placed in a
more desirable situation, he was at last removed to the Bedlam of the City
of Edinburgh. There also I continued my visits to him in conjunction with
my late worthy friend Mr Alexander Wood, who had at that time charge of
the Medical Department of the Edinburgh Poorhouse and of the Bedlam
attached to it. Without a convalescence from his insanity, death soon put
an end to poor Fergusson's existence. ... His case, however, afforded me an
opportunity of witnessing the deplorable situation of Pauper Lunatics even
in the opulent, flourishing, and charitable Metropolis of Scotland. ... Since
that period ... my feeble endeavours have been steadily directed to the
erection of a well-constructed Lunatic Asylum in Edinburgh; and it is with
some satisfaction I can say, that these endeavours have been attended with
at least some benefit to the unfortunate Maniacs in Edinburgh.*[4]

The fact that 17 years had elapsed between Fergusson's death and the
commencement of Duncan's attempts to found a lunatic asylum, and 44
before he wrote the above account, must raise some doubt as to whether this
tragedy was his main inspiration. Nevertheless, this story of the founding
of the Edinburgh Lunatic Asylum has become entrenched in the history of
the institution, and Fergusson's name identifies a unit in the present-day
hospital. It is entirely consistent with Duncan's compassionate character
that he should want to establish a humane environment for this neglected
group of patients, whether or not he had witnessed Fergusson's demise. The
recurrent, well publicised, mental illness of King George III, which commenced in 1788, made the matter of insanity of topical interest. In 1789 the
College of Physicians sent the King an address of loyalty and thanksgiving
on his recovery from one of his episodes. Houston considered that this
event, which coincided with the start of Duncan's campaign, was of greater
significance than Fergusson's plight.[5]

The start of the campaign

In 1790, when he became President of the Royal College of Physicians and
thus in a position of influence, Duncan's first initiative was to propose the
founding of a lunatic asylum in Edinburgh. A committee, consisting of Drs
Home, Spens and Webster, with the president *ex officio*, was established to
look into the matter. On 2 August 1791 the committee reported their recommendations to Council. These were:

1. *That the Houses for the reception of lunatics kept by private persons in the city and neighbourhood of Edinburgh should be put under the same regulations with those in the neighbourhood of London and ... that they should ... be subject to a visitation of Commissioners appointed by the College of Physicians.* [This was achieved in 1815.]

2. *That the establishment in the neighbourhood of Edinburgh of a Lunatic Asylum similar to that of York* [Retreat] *would be of the utmost advantage to those who have the misfortune to be deprived of their reason.*

3. *That considerable funds ... might be obtained provided a respectable set of Trustees were appointed for receiving the money and supervising the building. ...*

4. *That the Lord Provost, the Lord President of the Court of Session, the Lord Chief Baron of Exchequer, the Lord Advocate of Scotland, the Dean of the Faculty of Advocates, the Principal of the University of Edinburgh, the Keeper of His Majesty's Signet, the President of the Royal College of Physicians and the Deacon of the Incorporation of Surgeons would form a Committee in whom the Public ... could not fail in placing the highest degree of confidence.*

5. *... Dr Watson's estate would be more usefully employed in a lunatic asylum than in a foundling hospital.*[6]

The College approved the recommendations, provided that the Dean of Guild and the Deacon Convener of the Trades of Edinburgh were added to the proposed list of trustees, and the president was asked to approach the Lord Provost in the name of the College and request 'that his Lordship take such steps as he shall think best for accomplishing the different objects'.

On 7 February 1792 the president reported to the Council that the proposed trustees had accepted their appointments and that the business now seemed to be in 'considerable forwardness'. In the same year a public appeal was launched by the Lord Provost, supported by many civic dignitaries and the Royal College of Physicians. Duncan proposed that the College should take a lead in subscribing to this 'useful institution' with the sum of £25.

Despite the support of the Colleges of both the Physicians and Surgeons, the public appeal, launched in 1792, made very slow progress. Contributions trickled in – only six in the first year, including the £25 from the College, and five guineas from Duncan himself. In 1794 there were eight subscribers, including James Gregory and James Hamilton Jr who were later to become involved in bitter disputes with Duncan. By 1806 – 14 years after its initiation – there had been only 21 subscribers contributing a total of about £223.

Clearly some new incentive was required. This came about in a fortuitous way.

Royal charter and government funding

In 1806 the establishment of the 'Ministry of all the talents' under George Grenville and Charles Fox gave a fresh impetus and opportunity. Duncan's friends, Henry Erskine and his younger brother Thomas, were both members of the government – Henry as Lord Advocate and Thomas as Lord Chancellor. Together with their fellow advocate and parliamentary colleague Sir John Sinclair, they managed to obtain a grant of £2000 from the Jacobite estates forfeited after the '45 rebellion (Sinclair was Chairman of the Parliamentary Committee appointed to disburse these funds which amounted to £46,454). Wards in the Asylum were later named after both Erskine and Sinclair in recognition of their efforts. On 6 May 1806, the President of the Royal College of Physicians, Dr Thomas Spens, was able to announce that he had great hopes that the plan of 1792 might now be carried into effect. The following year (11 April 1807) a Royal charter was granted for the establishment in Edinburgh of a charitable institution for the maintenance and cure of lunatics.

The charter detailed a considerably complex management structure for the proposed hospital. This was to comprise one governor, five deputy governors, and 20 extraordinary managers or trustees, consisting of the principle dignitaries of the city. In addition there were to be twelve ordinary managers and a medical board of five – the presidents of the Colleges of Physicians and Surgeons, two other physicians and one other surgeon. The underlying influence of Andrew Duncan can be seen in the various appointees, many of whom were his close friends and golfing companions. Henry Erskine and Sir William Fettes were deputy governors, and Sandy Wood and Gilbert Innes were among the ordinary managers. Duncan, himself, was appointed to the medical board.

Where the power actually lay was unclear. The medical board was responsible only for supervising the medical care of the inmates and Duncan therefore should have had little influence on the planning of the hospital itself, except during his second presidency of the College of Physicians in 1824, when he would have become one of the extraordinary managers *ex officio*. Nevertheless, it seems probable that his influence behind the scenes was considerable and a series of anonymous pamphlets regarding the Hospital was undoubtedly compiled and partly written by Duncan. These were bound in three volumes: *Address* (1807)[7], *Observations* (1809)[8] and *Short Account* (1812)[9], and were written primarily as fund-raising appeals. They detail the inadequacies of the existing facilities for the accommodation of the lunatics, the need for designated hospitals for their care, the desirability of government supervision, and the constant need for more money to achieve the purpose. The details of the admission policy to the proposed hospital were described, but with slight variation in the different reports, which was to become a source of subsequent criticism.

The *Address* of 1807, which followed the Royal charter, was the second public appeal, and it was launched by Principal George Baird of the University. It contained the following rather optimistic view of the state of psychiatric care at that time: 'It is now incontestably established by experience, that, in a large proportion of cases, skilful practice, in an appropriate institution, will either totally remove this complaint, or, to a desirable degree, will soften its violence.' It was planned that the Edinburgh Asylum should copy the model of the Quaker Retreat at York by banishing chains, stripes, and every other rough mode of treatment.

The original proposal of 1792 had stated '... as soon as sufficient funds can be obtained for that purpose, that poor patients shall be received into the Asylum, and shall be attended by Physicians and Surgeons appointed by the Trustees, without expense to them or to their relations'.

In the *Address* it was restated the proposed hospital was for 'the reception of Insane Patients from among the rich as well as the poor ...', and it was recorded that, from experience in other similar institutions, the fees paid by the rich could subsidise the poor who could be admitted at 'low terms'. The reference to free admission of the poor had been dropped.

The response to the second appeal was better than the first, although not overwhelming. It was an unfortunate time in which to conduct a public appeal. A deep financial depression had followed the ending of the war with France. In 1808/9 there were 180 subscribers, bringing the total raised to £4322 (including the £2000 from the government). Duncan wrote in the *Short Account*:

> It was confidently hoped, that the extensive publication of this work would fully awaken the attention of the Public ... to this highly important institution. It is however, a melancholy truth that the sanguine expectations of those who have interested themselves most on behalf of this charity have been by no means answered. And in place of several thousand subscribers, who it was expected, would have contributed at least 1 guinea or upwards ... the whole number of contributors in the City and County of Edinburgh ... at the beginning of the year 1812 very little exceed two hundred.

The *Short Account* gave a revised account of the proposed admission plans. Pauper patients or criminal lunatics, supported by parishes or charitable funds, were to be admitted at the rate of 7/- per week. (When this category was eventually admitted in 1842, the rate had doubled.) A middle class, with better accommodation and a more expensive diet, would pay one guinea; and an upper class, who had their servants with them, would be provided with much better apartments at three guineas. However, taking account of the poor financial position, it was envisaged that initially only the middle class of patients would be admitted, 'although this, perhaps, is not so urgent a charity, as accommodation for the cure of real paupers'. It was 'much to be regretted that this mode of cure cannot be immediately extended to indigent maniacs, who must be supported by their parishes'.

By 1815 the total reached £9100. It had been announced that the Asylum would be a national institution open to patients of all classes, from other districts in Scotland and from all parts of the Empire. The East Indies responded magnificently with contributions exceeding £1300 (237 subscribers from Madras alone), and collections from the churches in and around Edinburgh brought in £1600. The city of Perth was also generous. Preference for the admission of patients was to be given to the parishes that subscribed, and other major contributors.

Fund-raising for the Asylum, however, remained a problem. Lunatics did not have the same appeal as children when it came to charitable giving. Duncan was jealous of the schools founded by generous benefactors such as George Heriot, John Watson and James Gillespie. He felt that a mere fraction of their generosity directed towards the Asylum would have been put to better use. The biggest single benefactor to the Asylum, long after Duncan's death, was his granddaughter Elizabeth Bevan (see page 85).

Laying the foundation

Despite the slow response to fund-raising appeals, by 1809 the trustees considered that there was enough support to commence the building, although 'from want of necessary funds, this commencement will take place under very disadvantageous circumstances'. All the proceeds of the various fund-raising activities went towards the purchase of land and the construction of buildings, but did not even cover these costs.

Land extending to four acres in Morningside was bought for £1420 and Robert Reid, the leading architect in Scotland at that time, drew up plans for the hospital without charge. It was to take the form of a quadrangle, with accommodation varying according to the requirements of the different categories of patients and the levels of fee which they could afford.

First patient admitted

The foundation stone of the Edinburgh Lunatic Asylum [hereafter referred to as the ELA] was laid in June 1809, and by July 1813 work on the east side of the quadrangle was sufficiently advanced to allow the first patient to be admitted on the 19th of that month. Dr Thomas Spens and Dr Andrew

Duncan Jr were appointed visiting physicians, who up to 1816 gave their services gratis. Thereafter they were paid two guineas per patient annually.

The Report of the Managers to the General Meeting of Contributors, held annually on the last Monday of January, in terms of the Royal charter, was presented on 31 January 1814. During 1813 considerable progress had been made in fitting up two wings for the accommodation of patients of the middle and higher classes. Mr John Hughes from London had been appointed Keeper and his sister became Matron. There was space for ten or twelve paying patients, but only six patients had been admitted at one guinea a week. One had had to be removed because his relations could not pay, one had been discharged recovered, and four remained. 'It was a subject of deep regret to the Managers, that they had not been able to extend the blessings of this Institution to the indigent from want of funds and accommodation.' There was no money left over for patient care which had perforce to be self-funding. It proved impossible to admit pauper patients; Fergusson, had he been alive then, would not have gained admission.

Duncan recorded[10] that by 1815, upwards of 20 patients had been admitted. These included three ministers of the Gospel, two children of ministers, and one student of divinity who 'had been partakers of the benefits, and are living witnesses of the blessings already derived from the Edinburgh Lunatic Asylum'. Despite this very modest beginning, Duncan warned that funds were far from sufficient and that it might be necessary to shut the doors for some time, although this threat was never carried out.

The urgent need was for more funding to finish the building of the east side of the quadrangle and to install fittings such as hot and cold baths to bring it up to standard. Fund-raising committees were established to approach the Scottish nobility, the members of the College of Justice, the churches, the Merchant Company, the Deacons of the Incorporations, the medical practitioners, etc. During this period of stagnation, Duncan, who had been put in charge of the medical fund-raising committee, died in 1828. At the time of his death, the ELA was admitting only about 40 fee-paying patients annually. Duncan's ambition to have a facility open to all classes was unfulfilled due to a shortage of funds rather than a lack of will.

The reports during the 1830s emphasise the slow progress towards completion of one side of the quadrangle due to the chronic shortage of money, but this was eventually achieved by 1840 at a total cost of £27,000 – more than the original estimate for the entire quadrangle which was never completed. The Asylum by then proved totally inadequate for its original purpose, having accommodation for only 55 paying patients at most and the design did not allow for the necessary segregation of the paupers from the wealthier inmates. The annual report of 1836 stated that:

... patients of the class hitherto admitted ... who have all received education more or less general, and acquired habits more or less refined, could not have been brought to associate in the public day rooms ... with patients deficient or altogether wanting in these respects; for it is well known how tenacious of their dignity, real or imaginary, and how sensitive in regard to distinctions of rank, such unfortunate beings generally are ... it must not be forgotten, in considering this question, that the whole surplus funds now possessed by the Managers have been accumulated from the savings on the board of those richer patients.

Charitable purpose unfulfilled

The Asylum, which in terms of the Royal charter was a charity, was catering for a small select group of paying patients. The Managers of the ELA were in a difficult situation. Without funds they could not achieve their charitable purpose of admitting pauper lunatics, while paying patients enabled the Asylum to function, albeit at a modest level, and produced a small annual surplus. Meanwhile it was difficult to persuade the public to donate more money to an institution which served only the wealthy.

The managers came in for trenchant criticism from Dr Richard Poole.[11] Dr Poole (*c.*1782-1870) was a physician in Edinburgh with an interest in mental health and a Fellow of the Royal College of Physicians, which he served as a member of council and honorary librarian. Poole conducted a one-man campaign against the ELA. He had studied the history of the Asylum in meticulous detail,[12] finding contradictions and anomalies particularly with regard to the original objective of providing care for poor as well as wealthy lunatics and the realisation that only the wealthy were currently being admitted. The parishes and individuals who had donated money on the understanding that it would help the paupers were being cheated. He highlighted in particular Duncan's writings for their inconsistency, although by then Duncan was long dead and unaware of the criticism. Poole did, however, acknowledge that the inadequacy of funds had been a contributory factor and accepted that the intentions of the managers and of Duncan were honourable. Unusually for his time, Poole did not publish his findings in a pamphlet. His notes remain in manuscript in the library of the Royal College of Physicians.

On 1 November 1834 Poole wrote a letter to the President of the College of Physicians, Dr Joshua Davidson, in which he observed that

... Edinburgh ... has not one Lunatic Asylum of size and accommodation sufficient for public demand. It is absolutely surpassed, in this respect, by some of the minor towns of Scotland, and no less so by others in the sister

Figure 1. Bristo Street in Duncan's day. Wash drawing by W. Geikie *c.*1830. First home of the Duncan family who occupied two floors (later three) of one of the tenement buildings

(BY COURTESY EDINBURGH CITY LIBRARY)

Figure 2. Surgeons' Square. On the left is the old Surgeons' Hall. The central building is Duncan's extra-mural teaching school, later to be used as the anatomy school of John Barclay and Robert Knox. On the right is the Royal Medical Society building towards which Duncan made a major contribution.

(SHEPHERD: *MODERN ATHENS*)

Figure 3. Adam Square. Duncan's second home was the left of the three houses. After Duncan's time the central house accommodated the Watt Institution and School of Arts, the precursor of the present Heriot Watt University. The statue of James Watt shown in this illustration is now sited in the University campus at Riccarton.

(GRANT: *OLD AND NEW EDINBURGH*)

Figure 4.
The old Royal
Infirmary by
John Elphinstone.

Figure 5. Physician's Hall, George Street, 1825, by Thomas Shepherd.

(SHEPHERD: *MODERN ATHENS*)

Figure 6. The Edinburgh Charity Workhouse and Bedlam 1827. Through the port in Telfer's Wall there is a glimpse of the Workhouse. Immediately behind the wall on the right is Bedlam. Despite the high wall the managers of the workhouse had to apologise to the inhabitants of Teviot Row for the annoyance of noise emanating from the Bedlam.

(WATER COLOUR BY JAMES SKENE/
BY COURTESY EDINBURGH CITY LIBRARY)

Figures 7a and **b**. An engraving of the Royal Public Dispensary by J. and H. S. Storer, published in 1820. The coade stone relief of the Good Samaritan, which appears in the pediment of the Dispensary, was preserved following the demolition of the building in 1937 and remains in the possession of the University of Edinburgh.

(WITH PERMISSION EDINBURGH
UNIVERSITY LIBRARY, SPECIAL COLLECTIONS
DEPARTMENT)

8a

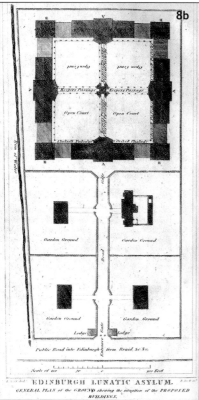

8b

Figures 8a and **b**.
(a) Drawing of the proposed new Asylum.
It was described as a 'grim and grey building'.
(b) A ground plan of the proposed Edinburgh
Asylum. It occupied the site now bounded by
Millar Crescent, Morningside Terrace, Maxwell
Street and Morningside Road, opposite the
present day Volunteer Arms and the Morningside post office.

(BY COURTESY OF THE ROYAL COLLEGE OF PHYSICIANS
OF EDINBURGH)

Figure 9. Elizabeth Bevan. Photograph from
the Annual Report of the Royal Edinburgh
Hospital for 1906.

(WITH PERMISSION LOTHIAN HEALTH SERVICE ARCHIVE,
EDINBURGH UNIVERSITY LIBRARY)

9

Figure 10. Portrait of John Murray by David Allan.
(BY COURTESY OF THE JOHN MURRAY COLLECTION)

Figure 11. William Smellie, engraved by Lizars from *Naturalist's Library* (vol. xxv, frontispiece).
(JARDINE: *NATURALIST'S LIBRARY*)

Figure 12. Engraving of Andrew Duncan Sr by A. Bell, published in 1778 by Charles Elliot.
(BY COURTESY OF THE LIBRARY OF THE ROYAL COLLEGE OF PHYSICIANS OF EDINBURGH)

Figures 13a and **b**. Medallion containing miniature painting, probably of Andrew Duncan Jr. On the obverse is a lock of hair from Dr Andrew Duncan.
(WITH PERMISSION OF LOTHIAN HEALTH SERVICE ARCHIVE, EDINBURGH UNIVERSITY LIBRARY)

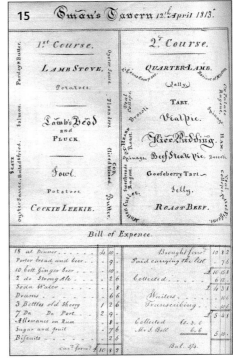

Figure 14. First members of the Aesculapian Club from its Minute Book.

(THE AESCULAPIAN SOCIETY)

Figure 15. Typical Harveian Society menu. In those days different kinds of food tended to be served at the same time. Courses were a later introduction.

(THE HARVEIAN SOCIETY)

Figure 16. Score card (7 April 1786) from Harveian minutes (October 1786).

(THE HARVEIAN SOCIETY)

Figure 17. A golf match taking place at Leith.

(GRANT: *OLD AND NEW EDINBURGH*)

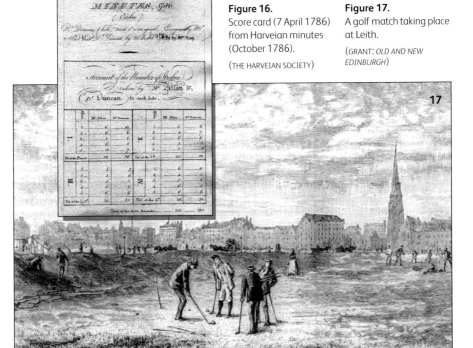

Figure 18. Silver wine label awarded to Mrs Duncan for her currant wine in 1821.

(NATIONAL MUSEUMS SCOTLAND)

Figure 19. The Patrick Neill Medal of the Royal Society of Edinburgh.

(REPRODUCED BY PERMISSION OF THE ROYAL SOCIETY OF EDINBURGH)

Figure 20. The Andrew Duncan Medal of the Caledonian Horticultural Society.

(COPYRIGHT OF THE ROYAL CALEDONIAN HORTICULTURAL SOCIETY)

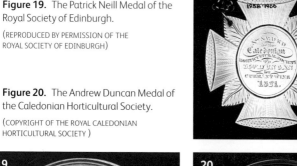

Figure 21. Kay's portrait of John Brown.

Figure 22. Kay's portrait of Andrew Duncan.

Figure 23. Kay's portrait of James Gregory.

Figure 24. Kay's portrait of Alexander Hamilton.

Figure 25. Silhouette of James Hamilton Jr by Auguste Edouart.

Figure 26. Kay's portrait of James Hamilton Sr.

Figure 27. George Watson's portrait of Alexander (Sandy) Wood.

Figure 28. Kay's portrait of Henry Erskine.

Figures 29a and **b.** Archibald Pitcairne's grave in Greyfriars Churchyard. Inset portrait of Pitcairn by Sir John Medina.

(**29a** PHOTOGRAPH BY J. CHALMERS; **29b** BY COURTESY OF THE ROYAL COLLEGE OF SURGEONS OF EDINBURGH)

Figure 30. Headstone of Robert Fergusson in Canongate Churchyard.

(PHOTOGRAPH BY J. CHALMERS)

Figure 31. Plaque in memory of Charles Darwin in the Duncan vault.

(PHOTOGRAPH BY J. CHALMERS)

Figure 32. Bust of Andrew Duncan by Lawrence Macdonald.

(BY COURTESY OF THE ROYAL COLLEGE OF PHYSICIANS OF EDINBURGH)

*Kingdom and on the Continent. I hold this assertion to be uncontestable –
without deprecating the Institution at Morning Side [sic], which is avowedly
imperfect, and probably neither will nor ought to be finished according to
the design of its founders. Passing over that establishment ... however
wide and benevolent the intention of those by whom it was projected and
patronized; the metropolis of our country, is singularly and deplorably in
need of a large asylum both for the insane paupers and for numerous
unhappy individuals among the lower, or even the middle classes of
society.*

In Poole's capacity as Manager of the Charity Workhouse, to which he
had been appointed by the College, he was able to give an account of the
present state of accommodation for pauper lunatics in Edinburgh. On
average 40 inmates, who were supported by £20 per annum, were admitted
to the Bedlam of his Workhouse from the city parishes. The West Kirk
Workhouse of St Cuthbert parish took about 30 inmates. Canongate and
Leith had no building for this purpose and distributed their pauper lunatics
(about 30) to private madhouses, or to his Bedlam if space was available.
The Charity Bedlam rivalled 'any institution whatever in the proportion of
cases recovered to usefulness'.

Poole stated that a threat to demolish the Bedlam in order to widen
Teviot Row had stimulated him to think of alternative solutions to the
problem. His idea was to persuade the managers of the ELA to fulfil the
charitable purpose for which their funding had been obtained, by contributing to the building of a large hospital for pauper lunatics at their site
in Morningside. He proposed that the College of Physicians should establish a committee 'for the purpose of investigating the general condition of
lunatics in and around Edinburgh, more especially those such as are paupers
or from the lower ranks of life, with a view to an extensive and a suitable
establishment for their accommodation'.

The College took Poole's criticisms seriously and set up an investigative
committee with Poole as convener. Meetings were held with the Royal
College of Surgeons, the Edinburgh Town Council and the managers of the
ELA. In November 1836 some 'gentlemen of Edinburgh' (undoubtedly
prompted by Poole) announced their intention of introducing a Bill to erect
a lunatic asylum for paupers belonging to the county and city of Edinburgh.
This Bill was not proceeded with, but the threat, coupled with Poole's
protests, may have hastened the efforts of the managers of the ELA towards
its charitable purpose. In the managers' 1836 Report, the first definite steps
towards provision for the poor were announced. It must be recognised,
however, that this had been the frequently stated intention of the managers
(and Duncan) whenever financial circumstances allowed. Poole himself

81

subsequently became one of the managers of the ELA, but had to retire in 1840 on grounds of ill health.

New initiative: building of the West House

In 1836 the surplus funds accumulated from fee-paying patients amounted to about £10,000 and enabled the governor and trustees to consider plans for the reception of pauper patients. The ordinary managers were instructed to procure plans and estimates for the erection of separate accommodation for this class. Reid's original plan was abandoned.

In 1837 a new architect, William Burn, was engaged. His first plan was to build an extension on the back of Reid's building, but this proved impossible, for it crossed a public right of way and was opposed by the inhabitants of the village of Tipperlinn. A large plot of land further west, extending to 49 acres, was purchased from the George Watson's Hospital[13] and a new free-standing building, designed to accommodate 350 pauper patients, was commenced in 1840 and opened in 1842 – a striking contrast with the time taken to complete the first building. This 'West House' was separated from the original 'East House', which continued to take wealthier patients, by high walls which preserved the right of way, and the two sites were connected by an underground tunnel. In 1840 Queen Victoria, who had contributed to the cost of the West House, agreed to become Patron of the Hospital, and the Edinburgh Lunatic Asylum became the Royal Edinburgh Lunatic Asylum.[14] Ten years later the name was changed again to the Royal Edinburgh Asylum for the Insane.

Inevitably to pay for this new building, which cost £36,000, a further fund-raising appeal was required. A meeting of potential donors was held in the Hopetoun Rooms in Queen Street under the chairmanship of the Duke of Buccleuch (Governor of the Asylum) in December 1840.[15] Many people spoke in support of the cause. His Grace drew attention to the fact that such facilities existed in Dumfries, Aberdeen, Montrose and Dundee. The Earl of Haddington gave a short account of the history of the Asylum, noting that it had been initiated in 1792

> ... and he believed that the person who had originated it was a man whose name needed only to be mentioned to revive all those feelings of respect which he enjoyed so deservedly during life – the late venerable Dr Duncan. (Cheers) The Institution originated with Duncan; and from small beginning, occasionally with partial success, sometimes with scarcely any at all, the Institution at Morningside was at last established.

Richard Huie, President of the College of Surgeons, and Duncan's successor as Aesculapian Secretary, delivered a moving account of the difference between physical and mental illness. The former patient, even at approaching death, 'could whisper his last farewell to his weeping family; or, if the tongue refused to do its office, there was still the darting look of kindness, – the feeble grasp of the cold hand, – to console the survivors'.

With the lunatic on the other hand:

> *The nearest and dearest ... became the objects of suspicion and often the victims of their insane violence. Their affections were seared – their sympathies were dried up, and the only hope of their cure depended upon their immediate removal from that home of which they had been, perhaps, the brightest ornament, or the chief support. (Applause).*
>
> *... Thanks to the march of science, a lunatic asylum was no longer a prison for the insane, but an hospital for their cure. ...*

Mr John Robertson had visited that day the three establishments in the city for the reception of the insane and contrasted the excellence of the Edinburgh Asylum with the City Bedlam and the West Church Bedlam:

> *... the Bedlam in Teviot Row, though defective in every respect for the relief or cure of mental derangement, is a palace indeed compared with the cells provided for the unhappy male inmates of the West Kirk Bedlam. ... He could not adequately describe these miserable receptacles for the most pitiable of all human beings.*
>
> *Lord Jeffrey hoped that everyone would give generously. More was needed than their usual pittances of one, two, or three guineas which they contributed to other charities. Bis dat qui cito dat [he gives twice who gives promptly], said another.*

The response to this lengthy appeal was gratifying. A list of donors accompanied the report, which noted a number of three figure sums. The Duncan family was well represented, with contributions from ten members including three serving with the Honourable East India Company. Eventually £15,000 was raised, leaving a shortfall of £11,700. This deficit was met by a bank loan which was paid off from the annual surpluses provided by the paying patients over many years.

Appointment of a medical superintendent

In 1839 it was decided to appoint a medical superintendent in place of the lay staff hitherto employed. Dr William McKinnon was selected as the first resident medical superintendent. He was an Aberdeen University graduate who had worked in the Aberdeen Lunatic Asylum. He proved an enlightened choice and encouraged many innovations, including musical concerts, excursions to the country, and occupational opportunities of many sorts such as gardening. Indeed, resulting from the activities of the patients, the hospital became a largely self-supporting community. Illiterate patients were taught to read. A printing press was installed and an Asylum magazine, the *Morningside Mirror*, was produced.[16] When McKinnon arrived in 1839 there were 38 patients in residence; and at the time of his retirement in 1846, with the opening of the West House, there were 466. The West House was renamed the McKinnon House in his memory in 1967.

During McKinnon's tenure of office the inmates of the Edinburgh Bedlam were transferred to the West House in the years 1844-45. They were required to be financed at the rate of £15 a year and an initial payment of £2000 was demanded by the managers of the Asylum. These payments had been the subject of a lengthy discussion between the authorities of the Workhouse and the Town Council, but were eventually conceded.[17] The report of the Managers of the Royal Edinburgh Lunatic Asylum for the year 1844 explains that the lump sum payment was necessary, taking account of the deficit in the building costs. 'Indeed the whole arrangement for the transfer of these patients to Morningside was never regarded by the Mangers as one of *pecuniary* character at all ... they were only carrying into effect one of the great objects contemplated by that benevolent and patriotic citizen Dr. Duncan to whose unwearied exertions the community are indebted both for its origin and for much of its early progress.' How sad that Duncan did not live to see the realisation of his dream.

Grant[18] records that a museum of plaster casts from the heads of patients was kept in the East House. This was almost certainly done at the behest of Dr Andrew Combe, who was one of the medical managers of the Hospital. Andrew Combe shared the interest of his brother, George Combe, the leading proponent of the pseudo-science of phrenology in Britain. The Phrenology Society collected head casts of all types of people for their study. The collection, which is now in the custody of the Scottish National Portrait Gallery, contains many examples of individuals with mental abnormality.

A thriving institution

By 1869 there were 711 patients in the Asylum and another wing was being built for pauper patients. A report in the *Scotsman* of 17 June 1869 emphasised the serious overcrowding, with up to five patients being kept in a single room. The pressure to admit pauper patients was so great that a large number of potentially fee-paying private patients had to be turned away.

How things had changed from the early days when only fee-paying patients were admitted.

The mortality rate was high due to the poor condition of many patients on admission. Old age, general paralysis (a consequence of syphilis) and consumption were among the main causes. It was reported that one patient died after giving birth. The child was kept in the Asylum and baptised in the chapel. 'She was a great pet amongst the patients; and in every part of the house, amongst the most violent patients, was nursed and fondled, until she died, at the age of six months, to the general grief of the female community.'[19]

Despite the overcrowding, morale was high. Dr Skae, the medical superintendent, in his Annual Report of 1869, stated that the

> ... work of industrial kind executed by the patients, ... will bear ample testimony to the efficiency of this department. In addition to our ordinary amusements – cricket, bowls, foot-ball, excursions to the country etc, our literary club, and periodical ... we have added theatrical performances ... and readings, interspersed with music. ... We were favoured by a large party of ladies and gentlemen from town with two very fine concerts, which gave great pleasure to the inmates ... the past year may without boasting, but with much gratitude, be regarded as one of great prosperity and usefulness.

In the Report it was recorded that 7144 patients had been admitted since the foundation of the Asylum, and 2740 (38.5%) had been discharged having recovered. This compared with a national average of 21 per cent. Duncan would have been justly proud of the development of his original initiative.

In 1922 the Asylum changed its name for the fourth time to become the Royal Edinburgh Hospital for Nervous and Mental Disorders, or 'Royal Ed' as it is familiarly known. The development of the Royal Edinburgh Hospital as a world famous therapeutic and academic centre is outside the scope of this book, but is loosely covered in Charles Smith's *Historic South Edinburgh* (vol. I) and D. K. Henderson's *The Evolution of Psychiatry in Scotland*. Increasing demand for accommodation for the wealthier private patients resulted in the purchase in 1878 of the historic Old Craighouse and its surrounding land, amounting to 60 acres. Several satellite villas were built around the central mansion, linked by underground passages. In 1886 Mrs Elizabeth Bevan,[20] the daughter of Andrew Duncan Jr, had left a legacy of £13,000 (equivalent to more than £1 million today) 'to supplement the board of patients of the educated class'. Henderson records that approximately 80 patients a year benefited from this fund which, with prudent management, increased to nearly £20,000.[21] One of the Craighouse villas was named the Bevan House in her memory.

The main building, New Craighouse, built in the style of a French chateau, was opened in 1894, and could accommodate several hundred fee-paying patients in great comfort. A panel in the great marble staircase records in Latin the following translation:

> *Citizens mindful of his benevolence desired this asylum which he started long ago to serve as memorial to Andrew Duncan, a man of more goodwill than the rest, who throughout a long life devoted outstanding activity to alleviating human misery and to fostering the science of medicine.*
>
> *His granddaughter Elizabeth Bevan gave noble assistance to her grandfather's plans by endowing the refuge most happily inaugurated by his initiative with all her resources and fortune in her will.*

In the dining hall above one fireplace, there is a reproduction of the plaque of Duncan which is shown on the wall of McKinnon House and the crests of the Royal College of Surgeons, Duncan's family (*fig.* 34) and the City of Edinburgh. It is curious that the crest of his own College is not included.

With the opening of the Craighouse, the original East House became redundant and was demolished in 1896. The Craighouse complex, later renamed the Thomas Clouston Clinic, is now part of the Napier University campus.

Duncan's contribution to the founding of the Hospital is commemorated in the Andrew Duncan Clinic, an acute emergency admission unit, which was opened by Queen Elizabeth, the Queen Mother, on 10 November 1965. Among those present was Mr Duncan Parker, a Suffolk farmer who was a great-great-great-grandson of Andrew Duncan.[22] Duncan is also remembered by a plaque inserted with others on the wall of McKinnon House. A bust of Philipe Pinel is given pride of place at the head of this collection (*fig.* 37) Pinel (1745-1826), a French contemporary of Duncan, is regarded as the founder of humane treatment of lunatics in that country.[23]

The puzzle of the miniature

A final intriguing link with Duncan exists in the form of a locket containing a miniature water colour painting, together with a lock of hair. The origins of this interesting object are unknown. The recent history is given by Sir David Henderson,[24] who records that in 1932, shortly after his appointment as Physician Superintendent of the Royal Edinburgh Hospital, the House Steward showed him the locket which had been lying in a drawer in his desk for a number of years. 'To my astonishment it proved to be Raeburn's miniature portrait of Duncan.' Henderson does not state why he assumed that the artist was Henry Raeburn. The miniature was subsequently put on display in the hospital bearing the legend that it was a Raeburn portrait of Duncan and the lock of hair was that of the poet Robert Fergusson. This belief regarding the identity of the artefact has been held within the hospital until recent times.[25, 26]

The locket is contained in a case in which there is a handwritten note, reading, 'Dr Andrew Duncan Born 1744 Died 1828, Miniature on ivory by Thomson, Longacre London, 1795', and this legend is engraved on the metal frame of the medallion (with Longacre misspelt 'Longaere'). On the reverse side of the medallion is a lock of hair neatly arranged in a bow, under which 'Dr AD' is embroidered on a raised cushion. There is no mention of Raeburn or of Fergusson. If, as the legend states, the miniature was painted in 1795, it is clearly not of Duncan Sr, for it is a portrait of a young man and Duncan Sr would have been over 50 at the time. Andrew Duncan Jr was, however, aged 22 and was studying in London in 1795. It seems possible, therefore, that the portrait is of Duncan Jr, and if so is the only likeness of him that has been discovered.

There is, however, an alternative possibility. The inscription was evidently written after Duncan Sr's death and many years after the portrait was painted. Perhaps the writer's memory may have been at fault and the legend cannot be relied upon. Raeburn did miniature portrait paintings in the 1770s when he was apprenticed to Gilliland (see page 212). Duncan Sr at the time would have been in his early thirties, and therefore just compatible with the apparent age of the subject of the painting. It is also known that he was in contact with Raeburn at that time in connection with Charles Darwin's memorial jewel (see page 212). The miniature portrait also bears a resemblance to another portrait of Duncan Sr engraved in the 1770s (though it is obvious his son may have resembled his father in appearance).

Conflicting opinions of art experts raise further uncertainties. Professor Duncan Macmillan believes it to be the work of Raeburn,[27] whereas Dr Stephen Lloyd, curator at the National Portrait Gallery of Scotland, confirms that the dress and the hairstyle of the subject are typical of the 1790s as is the style of the medallion. He is certain that the painting is not by Raeburn and observes that there were many miniature painters in London at that time.[28]

If the painting is of Andrew Duncan Jr, it is entirely appropriate that it should have come into the keeping of the hospital, for he was one of the first medical officers to be appointed in 1813 and continued to serve until his death in 1832. No record has been found of its acquisition by the hospital. Perhaps his daughter, Elizabeth Bevan, whose generous bequest to the Hospital is recorded above, may have been the source, although this is speculative.

With regard to the source of the lock of hair, it is certain that it is not that of Fergusson. Fergusson had died 21 years before the locket was made and before his reputation had become established. It is most unlikely that anyone would have acquired a lock of his hair at the time of his death and retained it for many years. There seems no reason to doubt that it is, as the medallion indicates, the hair of the subject of the painting.

Notes

1 Houston (2003), pp. 12-20; Comrie (1932), vol. 2, p. 467.

2 Presley (1983), pp. 71-74.

3 Mitchell (1864).

4 Duncan (1818a).

5 Houston (2000), p. 116.

6 In 1803 Duncan sent a letter to the Lord Provost of Edinburgh, Neil Macvicar, seeking his support for an appeal to Parliament to have the bequest of John Watson appropriated for the asylum. In 1762 Watson had bequeathed £4,721 to the city of Edinburgh for 'such pious and charitable purposes as the trustees decided'. The trustees had favoured a foundling hospital, but no action had been taken and Duncan regarded this idea as pernicious. By careful management the fund had grown substantially. The Lord Provost refused to back Duncan's request and eventually the bequest was used to found the John Watson Hospital for destitute children which later became the John Watson School (now the Scottish National Gallery of Modern Art).

7 Duncan (and others) (1807).

8 Duncan (and others) (1809).

9 Duncan (and others) (1812).

10 Letter to the Lord Provost, 1815.

11 Short accounts of Dr Richard Poole are given by Pitman (1988), pp. 300-305 and Craig (1976), pp. 443-46. Poole's detailed manuscript records of the failings of the Edinburgh Lunatic Asylum are kept in box files in the library of the Royal College of Physicians. Box 17, file 124 is the most relevant. Poole was proud of his obsessional record-keeping: '… no functionary, paid or unpaid, ever did or could surpass me in a disposition to be faithful as their historian' (Pitman, p. 302).

12 Papers of Richard Poole.

13 Details of the land purchases in connection with the various stages of development of the Hospital are given in Bryce (1917/8), pp. 206-10.

14 Smith (1978), vol. I, pp. 183-204 gives a good account of the development of the Hospital.

15 Anon (1840).

16 Smith (1988), pp. 171-73.

17 Anon (1843b).

18 Grant (1881), vol. III, p. 39.

19 Dr Skae's annual report, The Scotsman, 23 February 1869.

20 Elizabeth Duncan, married surgeon William Bevan in 1838. They had no children. Her total estate at her death in 1886 amounted to £24,300 – a huge sum for those days. Presumably her husband, who predeceased her, must have had a successful practice.

21 Henderson (1964), p. 60.

22 The Scotsman, 11 November 1965.

23 Henderson (1964), p. 19 gives the history of Pinel's bust. It was originally placed in the hospital entrance by Dr Andrew Combe and Sir Robert Christison, both medical managers of the Board of Management of the Hospital, who had studied under Pinel in France. The stone bust was removed during the course of reconstruction and this bronze replica was unveiled in its present location by the French Ambassador in 1930. The other plaques were added five years later.

24 Henderson (1964), p. 22.

25 Smith (1978), pp. 198-99.

26 Personal communication from Professor Henry Walton.

27 Macmillan (1990), p. 151.

28 Dr Stephen Lloyd, in personal communication. The locket is now in the custody of the Archivist of Lothian Health Board.

CHAPTER V

Duncan's Therapeutics

JOHN CHALMERS

The advancement of the sciences has been much retarded by the credulity of those who have cultivated them. This credulity discovers itself by an easy acquiescence in what are asserted to be facts, although not properly authenticated, ... by bigoted attachment to some great names, or by a superstitious veneration for antiquity.   John Gregory 1772[1]

Much more than 99 parts in the 100 of all that has been written on the Theory and Practice of Physic for more than 2000 years, is absolutely useless.   James Gregory 1800[2]

The enormous advances in medicine since Duncan's day enable us to look with critical hindsight at the therapies in use then. Almost without exception they would be regarded at best as ineffectual and at worst as being positively harmful. Duncan was well aware of the natural healing potential of many disorders given time and favourable living conditions, but nevertheless was obliged, by the prevailing medical teaching and traditions, to follow the practice of his colleagues. Medicine in those days was not a science, but an uncritical acceptance of the untested theories and beliefs of men of influence of the past.

Information about Duncan's management of patients and the drugs he used can be found in surviving case notes kept by his students[3] in the three published volumes of medical cases selected from the records of the Public Dispensary,[4] and from his textbooks *Elements of Therapeutics*[5] and *Observations on the Operation and use of Mercury in the Venereal Disease.*[6] The 98 volumes of *Practical Observations in Medicine,* which consist of his case records used in teaching, handwritten mostly by Duncan, represent a virtually untapped resource which exists in the library of the Royal College of Physicians of Edinburgh (RCPE).

Duncan's first book, *Elements of Therapeutics,* published in 1770 just one year after he obtained his MD degree, is largely based on the teachings

Emetics – excite vomiting	Antacids – destroy acids
Cathartics – evacuants	Antalkalins – neutralise alkalinity
Diaphoretics – promote sweating	Attenuants – thin the blood
Epispastics – increase local blood flow	Inspissants – thicken the blood
Diuretics – increase urine	Antiseptics – prevent putrifaction
Expectorants – increase sputum	Astringents – condense fibre
Errhines – increase nasal secretion	Emollients – soften fibre
Sialogogues – increase saliva	Corrosives – remove morbid excrescences
Blood-letting	Demulcants – diminish local sensitivity
Emmenagogues – increase menstruation	Stimulants – quicken the senses
Anthelmintics – treat worm infestation	Sedatives – diminish animal energy
Lithontriptics – dissolve urinary calculi	Antispasmodics – allay involuntary spasms

Table 1: Duncan's 24 categories of drugs or therapeutic procedures

of William Cullen. It is in two parts, the first detailing at length the difficulties encountered from the errors and inadequacies of previous publications, the variable presentation of disease and its response to treatment. He recognised that therapeutics was not an exact science and in the preface he writes:

> *The author is well aware, that, … many things here assumed as facts, and laid down as general principles, many rules and observations pointed at as meriting attention, will frequently appear to his readers to be chimerical, ill-founded, or even absurd. … every remedy has been celebrated for properties much more considerable than it really possesses.* (p. 16)

The second part consists of his classification of drugs into 24 categories (see Table above)

Duncan lists the drugs used in each category and describes their effects, clinical indications and contraindications. For example, diuretics occasion a discharge of urine in greater quantity without endangering the life of the patient. The drugs used included *apium, genista, scilla, colchicum, acetosa, berberis, acetum sal diureticus, aqua, aquosa* and *serum lactis*. Diuretics remove superabundant ferocity from the blood, remove morbid acrimony from the blood, diminish the quantity of circulating fluids when too great for the state of the system, and remove obstructions in the urinary passages. They were employed in cases of ascites, icterus and nephritis. They were contraindicated in cases of a high degree of morbid sensibility in the kidney, and fixed obstruction in the urinary passages.

It seems anomalous to include bloodletting among his categories of drugs, but its uses were described as follows:

> *Blood letting removes part of the circulating fluids and causes a temporary increase of the celerity of the pulse, diminishes animal heat and changes the mode of circulation. Generally carried out by venesection or arteriotomy, by topical scarification,* curcurbitulae cruentae [wet cupping] *and by* hirudidum [leech] *application.*

It was indicated in cases of angina, pleurisy, phthisis pulmonalis, rheumatism and fever. Care was required in infancy and old age.

Duncan's use of these drugs is described in detailed case records of Duncan's patients kept by an anonymous student of his patients in the professorial wards of the Royal Infirmary between 1 February and 25 April 1795. The patients were selected from the general admissions to the hospital as being most suitable for teaching purposes. There were 65 patients (30 men and 35 women) who spent on average 40 days in hospital. Each report starts with a case history and clinical findings, on which Duncan makes a commentary and discusses the possible diagnosis and treatment. Follow-up notes are kept on the patient's progress and response to treatment.

The diagnoses made are listed in the records. (Several patients had multiple conditions, hence the number of diagnoses exceeds the number of cases.)

Dyspepsia	4	Amenorrhoea	1	Cephalgia	2
Hydrothorax	3	Nephralgia	1	Paralysis	4
Catarrhus	3	Ophthalmia	3	Ascitis	1
Anasarca	2	Pertussis	1	Epilepsia	1
Quartiana	1	Menorrhagia	1	Hypochondriasis	1
Tertiana	1	Pemphigus	1	Hydrocephalus	1
Atrophia Cligo	1	Enteritis	1	Syphilis	2
Apoplexia mentalis	1	Rheumatismus	3	Haemoptysis	1
Phthisis	4	Dysenteria	1	Erysipelas	1
Icterus	1	Herpes	2	Caligo	1
Leucorrhoea	2	Asthma	1	Colic pictonum	1

A detailed analysis of these cases was made by J. Worth Estes.[7] Ninety-four drugs were used, the most commonly prescribed being opium. Blistering by means of *cantharides* (an irritant composed of crushed insects) was used in half the patients, and a third received *cinchona* and mercurial preparations. Nearly all received cathartics and a third were given enemas. Bleeding by venesection was performed in only 3%, although more were bled by leeches and wet cupping. Duncan tended to be more conservative than his colleagues with regard to venesection. Francis Home at one time bled 41% of his patients and James Gregory 17%.[8] Static electricity was applied to 10%. Most patients received multiple changes of therapy during their admission – sometimes ten or more being tried, according to the response or lack of it. Cures or partial cures were obtained in 60% of patients, of whom Duncan thought that nearly a quarter would probably have recovered without treatment. Two of these cases are given as examples:

CASE 1: John Menthe, age 46, *Hypochondriasis*

According to the account of this Patient, his complaints are very numerous and if as he describes them very distressing, but I apprehend that more depends on his imagination than on any particular disease. Since he came in we have had no flatulence, tremor, tinnitus aurium as he mentioned in his case and if a strict inquiry was made we should probably find that they never existed, for those symptoms which he particularly noticed, as dejection of spirits have disappeared. It is not unlikely that the causes to which he attributes his disease, as cold and want of proper nourishment, are those which constitute, the principle if not the whole of his disease. He is a poor indigent man without house or family and to him the accommodations of an [*sic*] Hospital are luxuries and may possibly overcome all his diseases. If this is true it will supersede all observations and if he dislikes his medicine he will probably leave us.

There are however strong symptoms of hypochondriasis, as passing blood in his stools which with the haemorrhoids is a common symptom. The hypochondriasis is commonly a disease of the indolent but it sometimes exists in the poor man. A melancholic temperament (that is a person with black eyes and hair, rough skin and large superficial vessels) is particularly subject to this disease and such we observe in our patient. As long therefore as he remains with us this disease must be kept in view. He is certainly subjected to another disease not mentioned in his case, an inguinal hernia of many years standing. Of this the cure or rather alleviation is a steel bandage, a remedy not afforded by the Hospital. It is however no object of practice. I have therefore advised for his other complaints, give him full diet and pills of camphira, assa foetida and soap which may correct the bound state of his body connected with the hernia and remove the flatulence and other symptoms if they exist. This practise I shall continue.

Some weeks later Duncan is recorded as saying:

What he seemed most to want was shelter and protection during the severe wintry months and wholesome diet which he had no opportunity of obtaining by his labour. I concluded that there would be no opportunity of doing anything and little was indeed done. At his admission, to correct flatulence and to relieve his depression of spirits, which last perhaps was the most obvious complaint, I ordered pills composed of camphor, assa foetida, and soap, and on these he continued for some weeks. They had the effect of supporting a regular discharge. The only uneasiness he felt was, as far as we could discover from the hernia and this was merely temporary, allowing him therefore to continue longer than we could have wished and perhaps longer than it was proper.

Several points in this case might be commented on such as the acceptance of blood in the stool as a symptom of hypochondriasis and the curious characteristics ascribed to the melancholic. The diagnosis of hypochondriasis, however, seems reasonable even by modern standards, and Duncan appears to have dealt with it in a kindly and appropriate manner with minimal use of drugs.

CASE 2: James Glen, aged 53, *Epilepsia occasionalis.*
The symptoms of this Patient as entered in our register are all characteristic of epilepsia.
I have no doubt of the nature of his affection and there is nothing uncommon in his case except the regular return of his fits at an interval of 11 days. If this is true, I have not met with a similar instance, in my own practice. The returns are generally periodical but I never heard of their being fixed to particular days. Our practice is in this disease much regulated by the cause. It may arise from smallpox, teething or it may in some instances be more obscure. In most it is attended with an affection of the brain or of the cranium. We have grounds for forming a conjecture with respect to the cause in this instance, as he bears the evident marks of a blow. From that blow there was incontestible proof of a wounded cranium, by his having pieces of bone extracted. He enjoyed good health however for some time after the cure. He recovered in about six months without any symptoms of this complaint with which he has only been attacked about 5 months before his admission. I do not however consider the time between the cure and the attack as sufficient proof against the blow being the cause. The circumstances of the long interval only serves to shew that it was not from the immediate consequences of the injury, but from a morbid growth of the bone or exostosis so that there has been more irritation to the brain than the original fracture. Of this we have no proof but it seems the most probable cause of his complaints.

… I had recourse to the cuprum ammoniacum but it would certainly be much better to remove the cause and if the hint I have given be well founded it perhaps cannot be done without it. This if other practices should fail must be done by the trepan, but we may try less dangerous practices first.

After several weeks it became apparent that medical treatment had failed. The fits became more numerous despite trial of *lineum praecipitatum* and precipitate from the sulphate of lime, as well as the *cuprum ammoniacum*.

> ... *I formerly suggested my suspicion of the disease arising from a blow he had received on the head from which fragments had been extracted and as there was still a depression I hinted that it seemed not impossible that a cure might be effected by removing the part with the trepan, but upon consulting the surgeons many arguments were urged against it because the cure was not certain and because from the extent of the bone to be removed, the operation must have been hazardous. It is certainly better to die of disease than from the operation. They thought that it should only be performed at the particular request of the patient.*

This case shows that Duncan had a good understanding of some of the causes of epilepsy and a realistic awareness of the inadequacy of the available drug therapies at that time. He realised that surgical removal of the cause of cerebral irritation was the best option, but although trepanation had been practised for centuries, one can understand the hesitation of the surgeons.

The Edinburgh Pharmacopoeia and the Edinburgh New Dispensatory

The drugs used by Duncan were mostly those detailed in the *Edinburgh Pharmacopoeia*, a publication started by the Royal College of Physicians in 1699 with subsequent editions and revisions until 1841. Each edition was produced by a committee of Fellows of the College under the chairmanship of the president. Andrew Duncan Sr was one of the eight committee members responsible for the seventh (1783) edition, and during his first term as president he was much involved in the eighth edition. The *Pharmacopoeia* was written in Latin until the 1839 edition, but a number of English translations had been produced, including an *Edinburgh New Dispensatory* by William Lewis in 1753 and several subsequent editions. Andrew Duncan Sr produced further updated editions in English of the *Edinburgh New Dispensatory* between 1789 and 1801, and Andrew Duncan Jr continued the publication, producing eleven further editions between 1803 and 1830, the last being a massive volume of 960 pages. It was inscribed to his father, as were his others, 'most dutifully and affectionately by his son'. The Duncan family editions were very popular, being reprinted 50 times in six translations and American editions.[9]

Duncan Sr had used William Creech as his publisher. Duncan Jr, however, changed publisher to Bell and Bradfute, which must have provoked an angry reaction from Creech. In the library of the Royal College of Physicians of Edinburgh (RCPE) there is a copy of a letter from Duncan Jr to Creech which vividly recalls the angry correspondence between his father and John Murray (recounted in chapter II).

> *Andrew Duncan Jr to William Creech, Edinburgh 17 Nov 1803*
>
> *... in place of being the much injured person you represent yourself, your conduct in this transaction, has been most unjustifiable, and even for the sake of argument, supposing that the Edinburgh New Dispensatory is your property, and that it has been invaded, still your conduct has been highly blameable. ... In the private circles of your friends, ... you endeavored to awaken their partial sympathy; by unfounded complaints of injurious treatment; ... and finally when these clandestine attacks upon my reputation as an author, and my character as a man, fortunately came to my knowledge, instead of the explanation required, you returned an evasive answer, in which ingenious sophistry is substituted for plain matters of fact. Who now, Sir, has a right to complain? You, of an imaginary infringement of your property, which a few guineas could repair, or, I, of a real defamation of my character, for which no reparation can be made.*

The resolution of this dispute is not recorded, but how similar are the reactions of the son to those of his father.

Duncan's 1789 *Dispensatory*, which was largely derived from the college *Pharmacopoeia*, records all the drugs in current usage in Edinburgh derived from plants, animals and minerals. Herbal remedies were by far the most numerous, a vast range of plants being listed as having medicinal properties, although exactly what these properties were and the indications for their use were not always well defined. Very few are still in use today, notable exceptions being opium, cinchona bark (*quinine*) and foxglove (*digitalis*) which William Withering (1741-85) had recently found to be good for dropsy and a powerful diuretic (although Boerhaave had dismissed it as poisonous).[10] Curiously there is no mention of the remedy for scurvy (the juice of citrus fruits) discovered by James Lind (1716-94) in a pioneering clinical trial[11] which he had reported in 1753, or of saur kraut which was reported as being effective in Duncan's own journal.[12] He does however, in his section on 'Medicine' in the *Encyclopaedia Britannica*, give due prominence to Lind's work of which he was well aware. By 1824 Duncan was teaching his students the result of 'interesting improvements, in the way of prevention [that] have lately been made. ... Sea-scurvy is now almost banished from the British Navy'.

Drugs derived from animal sources were listed, but without enthusiasm. These included preparations derived from antlers (hartshorn), oyster shells, millipedes, crabs claws and eyes. Bezoars (balls formed of hair and other materials accumulated in the stomach), and ants and their eggs, were no longer used in Edinburgh. Sponge prepared by heating and grinding to a powder was regarded as superior to bees and earthworms prepared in the same way. Bizarre though these seem to us today, they do represent the residual survivors of a much stranger range of animal preparations used a century earlier, such as dog's dung and *Cranium hominis violenta morte extincta* (the skull of a murdered man). Archibald Pitcairne's prescription for juvenile epilepsy included broth of earthworms, pigeon's dung, powder of human skull and shavings of elk's hooves.

One animal product which was overlooked in the *Dispensatory* was the use of fish liver oil in the treatment of rickets. This method of curing rickets was used in the Western Isles and was communicated to Duncan by an 'ingenious gentleman' and published in *Medical Commentaries*.[13] Skate liver oil was rubbed into the skin of the limbs and trunk and the children wore a flannel shirt impregnated with the oil. Cure was achieved in a short time. Rather patronisingly Duncan says in relation to this report, which presumably came from a non-qualified person, 'We are indebted to the most uncultivated part of mankind for many useful discoveries ... and however inexplicable they may be by our theories, yet even the most unpromising of them deserves attention and trial'. He does, however, mention this therapy *inter alia* in his entry in the *Encyclopaedia Britannica*.[14] What an opportunity he missed by not following up his own advice to carry out a trial. He might have anticipated, by more than a century, Sir Edward Mellanby's discovery of the antirachitic properties of cod liver oil in 1921.

Drugs derived from metallic elements were recorded in profusion. Mercurial preparations, for example, were used for a wide range of disorders often in doses which would now be regarded as highly toxic.

Clinical trial or testing of any sort was singularly lacking in the accounts of drugs included in the *Dispensatory*. James Gregory was positively against clinical trials, which were done to 'gratify our own curiosity or zeal for science'.[15] Duncan, however, recognised the need for clinical trials. He gave an account of a drug, which he manufactured from lettuce juice, which, being white like the poppy juice from which opium was obtained, he thought might have similar properties.[16] He tried it out on himself and others and believed that it had a soporific effect and proposed a clinical trial. There is no evidence that this was undertaken, although later he did report its clinical use by which time his drug, which he called *lactucarium,* had been produced in commercial amounts and was included in the *Pharmacopoeia* of the Royal College of Physicians.[17] The case which he reported happened to be his grandson who had developed croup, the condition from which his own son, Henry Francis, had died 15 years previously. His grandson survived, having been bled and blistered as well as receiving lozenges of *lactucarium* – hardly a clinical trial by modern standards![18] Duncan Jr includes this drug in his editions of the *Dispensatory*, in which he refers to trials in man and frog which tended to confirm its similarity of action with that of laudanum.

Reading Duncan's case reports and his writings on therapeutics leaves today's reader to conclude that patients mostly recovered by virtue of their natural healing powers, despite the treatment offered. Duncan had considerable insight into this possibility. 'In every case where medicines are not actually indicated their use is undoubtedly to be avoided.'[19] He was aware of the value of placebos. 'Where the only intention of prescription is to satisfy a patient, it is easy to order something which, although it may be found in a list of materia medica, does not deserve to be esteemed a medicine.'[20] He also recognised the therapeutic effects of laughter, exercise and the passage of time, especially if accompanied by good wine and good fellowship:

> *See Nature's bounty, all her children share,*
> *She gives profusely, yet has more to spare,*
> *With careful hand remove the noxious weeds,*
> *And richest crops will spring from fertile seeds.*
> *Thus man; though placed in hot beds of disease,*
> *Gets health from action and a mind at ease.*
> *Thus by due culture root out every ill,*
> *And trust the rest to Providence's will.*[21]

The age of scientific medicine was at its threshold. Duncan and his contemporaries were labouring under the heritage of traditional teaching, based largely on custom and usage. It cannot be claimed that he made any significant advance in the field of therapeutics; his contributions were in other areas. The great advances in medicine during the 19th century were just beginning. Duncan anticipated some of these developments. In a letter to the Presidents of the Royal Colleges of Physicians in London, Dublin and Edinburgh, 1 October 1826, he advocated that a common pharmacopoeia should be produced by the three Colleges under an act of legislature, which would regulate the practice of pharmacy throughout the Empire. He also recommended that a decimal system of weights should replace the use of grains, scruples and drachms.[22] The inter-collegiate rivalry, however, was too great to allow these sensible suggestions to progress. It was not until 1864 that the *British Pharmacopoeia* was introduced, not by the Colleges, but by the General Medical Council under the terms of the Medical Act of

1858, and it was to be more that a century before the introduction of a metric system in medical prescription in Britain.

Notes

1   Gregory (1772), p. 159.
2   Gregory (1800), p. 218.
3   Anon (1795).
4   Duncan (1778).
5   Duncan (1770).
6   Duncan (1772).
7   J. W. Estes, Appendix D, 'Drug usage at the infirmary: the example of Dr Andrew Duncan Sr', in Risse (1986).
8   Risse (1986), p. 207
9   Cowan (1957), pp. 123-39.
10 William Withering received a letter from Edinburgh in 1779 which reported that 'Dr Hope … has tried the Foxglove in the Infirmary with success. I am assured by my worthy friend Dr Duncan that Dr Hamilton … has employed it very frequently in the Hospital …', quoted by Roddis (1936), pp. 107-108.
11 Lind (1772).
12 *Medical Commentaries* (1776), 4, pp. 237-78.
13 *Medical Commentaries* (1779), 6, pp. 95-96.
14 'Medicine' in *Encyclopaedia Britannica*, 4th edition (1809), p. 421.
15 Gregory (1800), pp. 139-41.
16 Duncan (1810).
17 On 4 December 1823 the gold medal of the Caledonian Horticultural Society was awarded to Mr Francis G. Probost for his method of preparing *lactucarium* or lettuce opium.
18 Duncan (1820).
19 Duncan (1770), vol. 1, p. 190.
20 Duncan (1770), vol. 2, pp. 64-71.
21 Duncan 'Poems on various occasions written either by myself or by intimate friends' (RCPE Library Ab 3.72).
22 The British system of weights at that time was extraordinarily awkward: 1 pound = 12 ounces = 94 drachms = 188 scruples = 5760 grains.

CHAPTER VI

Medical Jurisprudence and Public Health

The Role of Andrew Duncan Junior

JOHN CHALMERS

... it is useful to regard the Duncans, father and son, as being involved in a single economic enterprise, with the elder Duncan concerned, not just to provide for his son, but to train and equip him to take his place in the Duncan family business of physicking, university teaching, journal editing and medical power broking. ...[1]

Andrew Duncan Junior

Before embarking on the main subject of this chapter, it is appropriate to give some of the details of the life of Andrew Duncan Junior (1773-1832) who was much involved in the establishment of Medical Jurisprudence and Public Health in Edinburgh.

Andrew Duncan Jr (hereafter to be referred to as Andrew to distinguish him from his father) was born on 10 August 1773, the second of the Duncan children and the only one to follow in his father's profession. He was educated at the High School in Edinburgh and at the age of 14 was apprenticed to the surgeons Alexander and George Wood, the sons of Duncan's great friend Sandy Wood. Andrew regarded this as an unprofitable experience.[2] He matriculated at the Medical School of the University of Edinburgh from 1788-93, graduating AM in 1793 and MD in 1794. His MD thesis was entitled '*Tentamen inaugurale, de Swietenia soymida*'.[3] He became President of the Royal Medical Society during his last year at university.

With the encouragement and financial support of his father, Andrew extended his medical education with visits, first to London accompanied by his father, and then to continental centres. While in London he lodged as a paying guest at the home of John Barclay, the eminent Edinburgh anatomist, then based in the capital. The winter of 1794 was one of the coldest on record, with people skating on the Serpentine and fogs so thick that visibility was reduced to three feet; carriages had to carry lit flambeaux. Andrew's main occupation was dissection, which he carried out at the Great Windmill Street Anatomy School which had been established by William Hunter. The conditions were not entirely favourable, as there was a shortage of bodies. In a letter to his father (3 November 1794), Andrew wrote: 'Dr Baillie[4] says there is no managing the resurrection men, one of them called some time ago to see if anything was wanted and atho' several were commissioned, yet nothing has come in.' Subjects did not keep well due to wetness and warmth, and at other times it was too cold to hold the scalpels. Fortunately he avoided the fate of some of his fellow dissectors who suffered severe infections and even died from contamination acquired during their work.

Andrew was well entertained in London by his father's friends and kept a note of the dinner menus of his hosts. On Sunday 5 October at Dr Lettsom's, he had boiled beef, roasted veal, ham, pigeon pye [sic], damson pye, apple pye, tarts, greens, potatoes and salad. On Christmas day at Mr Wilson's the meal consisted of soup, skate, boiled beef, roasted fowls, veal cutlets, damson pye, greens, potatoes, etc.[5]

In 1795 Andrew left for the continent and spent the next three years (with a short return home during the winter of 1796/97) visiting medical centres in Germany, Austria and Italy. The unrest of the French Revolution ruled out a visit to Paris. His father had instructed him to keep him informed of medical developments and gossip, as well as medical and national politics, and this he did most conscientiously with long and regular letters which are preserved in Edinburgh University Library.[6]

In a letter to his father from Göttingen, 12 August 1795, Andrew wrote:

> *I have not yet by any means acquired so much of the language that I could trust my accuracy of translation, … I flatter myself with the hopes that a good knowledge of German and a great deal of industry will enable me to repay my whole journey. I still go on with Frank, not quickly but with increasing pleasure and the great length of 3140 pages does not in the least damp my ardour. But I have already informed you that a mere English translation will not do in my country and the plan I have proposed to myself is this; After translating completely one of the sections, to study … to consult those authors who have written of the subject … and then model the whole so as to have England in place of Germany in view. I don't know if you are acquainted with Frank's works.*

'Frank' was Johan Peter Frank (1745-1821), a German professor of medicine, a contemporary of Duncan, and similar in that he continued teaching until his death at 76. An English visitor wrote, 'He is now above seventy years of age, is perfectly firm and upright and in all his faculties and dispositions, possesses the force and energy of youth, tempered by the mildness of advancing years'.[7] At that time he was based in Vienna, where Andrew was to meet him in June 1796.[8] Frank's work, which Andrew proposed to translate, was the *System Einer Vollstandigen Medicinischen Polizey* [*Complete System of Medical Police*], published in six volumes (6262 pages) between 1779 and 1819. This monumental and influential work detailed Frank's views on public health – a subject taught in the medical schools of Germany and France at that time, but not in Britain. The term 'Medical Police' sounds rather sinister, but Frank meant public health administration in which the state played a large part. Duncan Sr was to adopt this term in his teaching, but did not accept the concept of state control, preferring a less regulated management at a more local level.

Throughout his continental tour, Andrew made a particular study of forensic medicine and medical police, no doubt with thoughts for his future. In a letter from Leghorn, 18 April 1796, he said:

> ... *I shall collect the most essential works on medical policy and juris-prudence. I hope that you are preparing to assist me in my labours, which I am impatient to commence and I trust if they should end only in an abridged translation of Frank, they will be of use not only to me, but to my country.*

Andrew never achieved his object of producing an English version of Frank's work, but he studied it in depth and was influenced by it. Duncan Sr did not have the opportunity to learn German and would not have been able to read it himself, but Andrew in his letter of 12 August 1795 gives a brief outline, and his father referred to Frank's work in *Memorial to the Patrons of the University of Edinburgh* in 1798.

In his letters, Andrew makes occasional reference to the family. In April 1796 he wrote: 'I am happy to hear of the addition to the family and of my mother's and sister's health, whom I am quite impatient to see.' What a surprisingly laconic comment on the birth of his sister Ann – the last of the twelve Duncan children to be born. He ruminates about his other siblings:

> *I hope that Betsy and Sandy do not forget their French ... Margaret I suppose continues her music. ... John is like other boys trifling away his time at the Latin grammar and Henry and Ann busy about nothing. Bless me Catherine was so busy sewing in the corner that I did not see her.*

In another letter from Göttingen, dated 1 September 1795, Andrew seems to regret his life of all work and no play. He comments that he thought it more useful to perfect his knowledge of German rather than improving his Greek and Latin, and adds the rather plaintive note:

> *The less necessary accomplishments, which I wish I possessed, are to draw well, to play tolerably various games at cards, and to ride well. ... if you*

will permit me to offer you any advice, do not let your other sons be defective in that art, for the sake of a few half crowns.

After nearly three years of travelling, Andrew was clearly depressed and longing to return home, as this letter from Florence (10 November 1797) suggests:

… once returned I hardly expect that any offer will be made sufficient to tempt me abroad again. On the contrary it is time to determine in some measure upon my future plans. Whether it will be better for me to fix at Edinb. or elsewhere. My profession is of the kind that for years yet I must rely upon your support, for altho' by writing I might earn something yet it is but uncertain and interferes much with laying the basis for a more certain income. … I want memory and energy, neither of which I am afraid it is now in my power to acquire. But perhaps my present desire to become independent, in some measure, of you, may excite me to greater activity. I am anxious for this not only that I may cease to remain a burden to you, but that I may be entitled to seek for happiness where I trust it will be found.

Two months later he wrote from Leghorn: 'I am very tired of Italy or rather being from home.' He regretted the frivolous society in which he was immersed. 'I mean to make up for lost time when I get home, tho' I am afraid to tell you what I mean, I so seldom execute my intentions. As however I have great favors [*sic*] to beg of you, I must make great exertions in order to obtain them.'

Andrew must have received instructions from his father to return home urgently, for in a letter from Bremen, 6 June 1798, he wrote: 'As you wish my immediate return and on so important a business, I shall not postpone it unnecessarily a day and with the next packet … I set out for England.'

It is not difficult to guess what this urgent matter was. Duncan Sr had introduced lectures on medical jurisprudence and medical police into his course since becoming Professor of Institutes of Medicine in 1790. In June 1798 he proposed in his *Memorial to the Town Council* that a professorship in these subjects should be established, emphasising what an important aspect of medical teaching this had become on the continent. Andrew, who had been studying these matters during his travels, was clearly a strong candidate for the chair.

The Chair of Medical Jurisprudence and Medical Police

As was the case with the establishment of the Public Dispensary, Duncan's purpose in trying to have this chair established was not entirely altruistic.

Alexander Grant in his *Story of the University*[9] wrote: 'This move, which in itself was a very proper one, was made by Dr Duncan in the interest of his son who afterwards became a distinguished Professor.' In the event, the founding of the chair was thwarted by Duncan's colleagues in the University Senate from which Edinburgh Town Council had sought advice. The Senate condemned it on the ground that 'the multiplying of Professorships, especially on new subjects of education, does not promise to advance the prosperity or dignity of the University'; and felt that the subject might be covered by existing professors. As was the case over the Chair of Midwifery (see chapter XIII), the hidden reason for rejection was probably the potential dilution of earnings by the established professors.

Having been temporarily frustrated in his ambitions for Andrew, Duncan Sr had to help him to obtain a livelihood. Andrew quickly became a licentiate and then Fellow of the Royal College of Physicians of Edinburgh, of which he was to be elected president in 1822. He was appointed a physician to the Royal Public Dispensary and temporarily to the fever hospital at Queensberry House. His father engaged him as co-editor of the *Annals of Medicine*, and in 1805 he became principal editor of its successor, the *Edinburgh Medical and Surgical Journal*, which, for a time, was the leading British medical periodical with a circulation of nearly 3000 copies quarterly. In 1803 Andrew published his first edition of the *New Edinburgh Dispensatory* following the example of his father (see chapter V). In the son's hands the *Dispensatory* flourished and ran to eleven further editions with translations into German and French and republication in America. No doubt he also established a private practice, but there was intense competition and his earnings from this source would have been slight.

In 1807 Duncan renewed his efforts to create a Chair of Medical Jurisprudence, this time bypassing the Town Council. The coalition government at that time created an opportunity, and with the assistance of his friend Henry Erskine, as Lord Advocate, they were successful in obtaining a Royal warrant from George III for a Regius Chair of Medical Jurisprudence and Medical Police 'as taught in every university of reputation on the Continent of Europe'. The reluctant Senate had no choice but to accept this, but stipulated that the occupant of the chair 'shall not on any pretence ... interfere with any of the courses of lectures now delivered in the said university'. At last Duncan achieved his ambition on behalf of his son who was appointed first professor, without opposition, on a salary of £100 per annum. The chair was at first established within the Faculty of Law until its transfer to the Faculty of Medicine in 1819 as an optional subject in the medical curriculum. In 1833 it became compulsory.

The nature of the subject

From a modern perspective it seems strange to couple together two subjects as disparate as forensic medicine and public health under the heading of 'Medical Jurisprudence and Medical Police'. Nevertheless these subjects remained linked in Edinburgh until the University created a separate Chair of Public Health in 1898. Duncan Sr, who introduced these subjects into his lectures in 1790, was a pioneer in this field in Britain, although it had been established in the medical schools of Germany and France as *Medicinae Forensis* for some years.

Duncan acknowledged his debt to the work of Frank, which has been well reviewed by Baumgartner and Ramsey,[10] and in a recent paper by J. H. Baron.[11] The first of Frank's six volumes was concerned with matters surrounding marriage and child-bearing. Fertility was to be enhanced by physical education of young women. Pregnancy should be supervised by professional midwives. Children should be cherished and breast-feeding was encouraged. Corsets should be banned because 'the thoracic cavity was not created by the Creator to the taste of us Europeans'.[12] With regard to eugenics, 'it is ... a distinct duty of the officials of the community to allow no one ... who is afflicted with severely disadvantageous or hereditary disease to marry'. On the other hand, healthy people should be encouraged to have as many children as they could afford to maintain. Pregnant women should avoid riding in fast carriages, climbing stairs, attending overlong church services, indulging in inappropriate or excessive eating, drinking and frivolity, wearing improper clothes and doing too much or too little work. Frank was in favour of public amusements, but plays should avoid murders. Forty pages were devoted to the history of celibacy of the clergy. He believed in the harmful effects of continence.

The second volume discussed illegitimacy, venereal disease, abortion and prostitution; the upbringing and education of children; schools and the importance of gymnastics. The third volume considered air pollution; nutrition and the regulation of food, water and alcohol; road-paving and cleansing; unhealthy and dangerous trades; clothing, housing, drainage and latrines. In volume four, he proposed laws on public safety to prevent people being crushed by crowds or injured by unsafe buildings, fire, water, road accidents and horrible natural phenomena. Carts and hackney carriages should be subject to police inspection. Volume five was concerned with resuscitation, death and disposal of the dead; and volume six with medical and veterinary education and the examination and certification of physicians. A supplementary volume, published posthumously in 1827, covers hospitals, epidemics and infectious diseases.

State regulation of public health matters has been documented since biblical and Roman times and remains today a matter of controversy. Frank's view was that 'it is incomprehensible to me how anyone can hope to retain natural freedom in political life without curbs. ... I understand the objections well, people want fewer laws, and with the few laws they want to retain their complete freedom – but is this not a complete contradiction?'[13]

Duncan was against rigid state control and argued that:

Public medical institutions and laws, must be adapted to the country for which they are intended. Many local circumstances, national character, habits of life, prevalent customs and professions, situation, climate, etc., make considerable varieties necessary. And many institutions, many a law, which would be highly beneficial to the public health, in some circumstances, would be useless, impracticable, and even hurtful, in others.

He pointed out that in Britain, matters relating to public health were ill organised, but 'the prevention of diseases among the great body of the people is one of the most important duties of the magistracy ... [and it] was incumbent on a medical practitioner to suggest the cause of particular disease to the magistrate'.[14] Where regulations existed, they were poorly codified and observed. Even as late as 1851, *The Times* reported that 'we prefer to take our chance of cholera and the rest than be bullied into health'.

McCrae has reviewed the social and political background to the development of public health measures in Duncan's time.[15] Social awareness of these matters had developed slowly and sporadically in this country, often due to the work of a few philanthropic individuals. Duncan paid tribute to John Howard (1726-90) for his contributions towards prison and hospital reform, and to (Count) Benjamin Rumford (1753-1814), an American immigrant to Britain, who had researched means of reducing smoke pollution and improvements in lighting. Duncan hoped that making public health an academic subject would improve matters and, by pointing out areas of need, encourage further philanthropic endeavour.

Medical Jurisprudence

In his *Heads of Lectures on Medical Jurisprudence* (Edinburgh, 1795) and in his *Memorial to the Town Council* (1798), Duncan Sr outlined his course which was conducted every Saturday at 2pm during the winter months and was open to law students as well as medical students. He considered only medical matters on which doctors might be called to give evidence in Courts of Law.

Many a doctor appearing as an expert witness today can empathise with Duncan's comment:

... while he is delivering his sentiments, his own reputation is before the bar of the public. The acuteness of the gentlemen of the law is universally acknowledged, the versatility of their genius, and the quickness of their apprehension, are rendered almost inconceivable, by constant exercise. It is their duty to make every possible exertion for the interest of their client, and they seldom leave unnoticed any inaccurate or contradictory [sic] evidence. How cautious must then a medical practitioner be, when examined before such men, when it is their duty to expose his errors, and to magnify his uncertainties till his evidence seem contradictory and absurd? How often must he expose himself to such severe criticism, if he be not master of the subject on which he is giving evidence, and have not arranged his thoughts on it according to just principles?

Duncan detailed the type of cases on which the doctor might be called to give evidence. In Criminal Courts these were the cause of death, the nature of wounds (whether accidental or intended), abortion (spontaneous or induced), and rape, etc. In Civil Courts the common questions related to the state of mind, the circumstances surrounding pregnancy and parturition, and the age and expectation of life of an individual. Matters concerning Consistorial Courts might be impotence, sterility, and diseases such as venereal disease and leprosy preventing cohabitation.

Medical Police (Public Health)

In his *Heads of Lectures on Medical Police* (Edinburgh, 1801), Duncan stated that it was concerned not merely with the welfare of the individual, but with the prosperity and security of the nation. He defined it as the 'application of the principles deduced from the different branches of medical knowledge, for the promotion, preservation and restoration of general health'. He regarded this as being of incomparably greater consequence than Jurisprudence.

His list of subjects followed closely the teachings of Frank, whose writings he recommended to his students. They were:

- *Insalubritas Aeris* – temperature, humidity and foreign impregnations of the air;
- *Insalubritas Aquae* – purity, smell, temperature and supply of water;
- *Insalubritas victus et potus* – price, quality and preparation of food and drink;
- *Consuetudines Salutare et Noxiae* – exercise conducive or adverse to health;
- *Morbi Contagiosi* – prevention of infectious diseases;

- *Carceres* – abuses and defects of jails;
- *Nosocomia* – regulation of hospitals;
- *Seultura adaveum* – proper burial of the dead.

The benefits of exercise – a favourite theme of Duncan's – had to take account of three circumstances: first, it should leave the individual to the exposure of pure air; second, it should afford a variety of bodily motion so as to exercise every muscle; and third, it should be of such a nature as to interest the mind as well as the body. Walking and riding fulfilled the first two criteria, but did not engage the mind. Hunting, fishing and fowling were acceptable, except that they were seasonal. Tennis, cricket, archery, bowling and swimming were good, but best of all was golf which could be played at any age and at any time. Cards served only for relaxation of the mind.[16] It was the duty of the 'police' to provide suitable recreational facilities adjacent to large towns, and clubs could also help.

The contagious diseases to be prevented included jail fever, dysentery, syphilis, smallpox and canine madness (rabies). Prevention of accidents also came under this heading. In relation to deaths, he discussed the importance of obtaining statistics relating to death and its causes (bills of mortality), another of his pet topics which he strived, without success, to introduce in his lifetime. For the medical practitioner, Duncan acknowledged, attention to these subjects would be expensive rather than lucrative, but he would enjoy the luxury of doing good.

> *Can medical knowledge be more usefully employed than in pointing out the means of improving and of preserving health? – of supplying proper nourishment to the indigent, especially in times of scarcity? – of securing to the diseased, the advantages intended by their benefactors? – of rearing the orphan to be the support of the nation, by whom he has been adopted? – of alleviating the miseries attendant to the lamentable situation of the unfortunate maniac? – and of diminishing the horrors of confinement, not only to the unfortunate prisoners of war, but even to the guilty criminal?*

Vaccination for smallpox

One public health measure with which Duncan became increasingly preoccupied was vaccination for smallpox. Edward Jenner had introduced the use of cowpox vaccination[17] for immunising against smallpox in 1798.[18] Prior to this, the only preventive measure had been the inoculation (variolation) of children with lymph from the vesicles of active cases of smallpox, a measure which carried a risk of inducing a serious case of the disease and even death, albeit at a much lower incidence than the 20% mortality of the unprotected patient.[19] Duncan had encouraged the wider use of inoculation during his first presidency of the College in 1790 and advocated the involvement of the clergy in encouraging the public to accept this risky procedure. After Jenner's discovery, he enthusiastically promoted this safer technique in his Public Dispensary, to which the title 'Vaccine Institute' was added. In 1822 nearly 17,000 individuals were vaccinated at the Dispensary.

Inevitably there was a dispute about this pioneering treatment which was to involve Duncan in a public debate. In 1802 one of the Public Dispensary staff, James Bryce, had published a pamphlet in favour of vaccination. This was challenged in a book by a Dr Thomas Brown of Musselburgh,[20] who maintained that vaccination in his experience had no lasting benefit. An angry exchange of letters took place between Bryce and Brown during 1809. On 8 July 1809, Duncan entered the fray by asking Brown for the statistics of his experience which would justify his opinion. Brown, who had been one of Duncan's pupils, answered with a lengthy, but courteous, account, but with vague and unconvincing figures; his follow up had been very incomplete. Duncan replied that from information which he had received from practitioners in and around Edinburgh, 'I am convinced, that it [vaccination] affords as strong protection against *variola* [smallpox] at the end of five years as at the end of five days; and I have no doubt, that posterity will find vaccination as complete a protection against smallpox as variola inoculation, even to the end of a long life'.[21]

Perhaps unwisely, Duncan followed up this letter with a copy of an advertisement for the Dispensary accompanied by a sermon by John Lee, who was both doctor and cleric, in which he advocated the adoption of vaccination. Brown responded by publishing a letter to Duncan in the *Courant* in which, *inter alia*, he said, 'I have so much respect, *even for Dr Lee's medical abilities*, that I must suppose he has been both coaxed and goaded, before he allowed his otherwise respectable sermon to become the defence and prop of vaccination …'.[22] John Lee, in a letter to Brown of 21 August 1809, stated that he had not been pressurised into writing his sermon. 'I cannot sufficiently regret your precipitation in publishing that letter to Dr Duncan which subjects me to the necessity of saying publicly that several of your conclusions are both hasty and incorrect.'[23]

Duncan responded to Brown (2 September 1809), 'I have ever been of opinion that newspapers are a very improper channel for communicating medical disputes to the public and I am sincerely sorry that you should have provoked a newspaper controversy, which I think was totally unnecessary …'.[24] Brown replied with a published 96-page letter with an appendix of 23 pages containing copies of all the correspondence,[25] addressed to the Surgeons of the Vaccine Institution of Edinburgh, in which he attacked the opposition at length and defended his position. He concluded with a strong recommendation for the old fashioned inoculation. 'It is a practice possessing the most satisfactory characters; it is propagated from the same disease it means to combat; produces an affection in all respects similar; its progress and effects are certain and uniform; it is in general mild and safe, and its consequences are complete and satisfactory.'[26]

Time was to prove that Duncan's belief in the effectiveness of vaccination was correct, although it was not until 1864 that the Vaccination Bill made it compulsory in Scotland. The correspondence indicates the differences of opinion prevailing at that time and the intensity of feeling that seemed to characterise medical disputes then.

There is no record of the content of Andrew Jr's course as Professor of Medical Jurisprudence and Medical Police. Copies of his lectures may have been in circulation, for on 8 June 1812 Benjamin Rush wrote to his son James, then a medical student in Edinburgh, regretting that he had not instructed him to obtain a copy of young Dr Duncan's lectures upon Medical Jurisprudence, for he anticipated that the subject would soon be taught at the University of Pennsylvania. No doubt Andrew covered much of the same ground as his father had done, enriched by the knowledge acquired during his travels and from his experience as medical adviser to the Scottish Widows' Fund and Life Assurance Society. He occupied the chair from 1807 until 1819, when he resigned to become conjoint Professor of Institutes of Medicine with his father. Two years later he became Professor of Materia Medica. In 1809, in addition to his other responsibilities, he was appointed to the salaried position of University Librarian[27] and Secretary to the Senate, in which capacity he was much involved in the rebuilding of the University quadrangle. It is said the overwork contributed to his early death in 1832 aged 58, only four years after his father's death.

He was a very conscientious teacher, often working until 3am to prepare his lectures. An obituary, cut from an unidentified newspaper, stated:

> He was not so successful as a lecturer as might have been expected. By some of the students he was always intensely beloved, but the greater part thought his lectures tedious. This was in no degree owing to any want of exertion on his part; but his intense anxiety to do justice to every subject, led him to dwell longer on many than was consistent with the limits of a six months course ... his error was too great a zeal.

Charles Darwin was one of those who did not enjoy Andrew's lectures. He recalled in a letter to J. D. Hooker (18 April 1847): 'I shall ever hate the name of Materia Medica, since hearing Duncan's lectures at 8 o[']clock in a winter's morning – a whole, cold, breakfastless hour on the properties of rhubarb!'[28]

Andrew is buried in vault 16[29] in St John's Church, Edinburgh, where his wife Mary McFarquhar and his unmarried daughter Jane are also buried. His other daughter Elizabeth married William Bevan, a surgeon, on 21 August 1838 and is remembered for her generous bequest to her grandfather's lunatic asylum (see page 85).

After Andrew's retiral from the Chair of Medical Jurisprudence, a succession of individuals added distinction to the chair and to the reputation of the Edinburgh Medical School,[30] fully justifying Duncan Sr's efforts to found it, whatever his motives may have been. Edinburgh's example was followed by Glasgow University in 1839, but it was not until 1878 that the subject was introduced to the English medical schools. Andrew's successor was William Pultney Allison (1790-1859), a son-in-law of James Gregory. He held the post only for a year, after which he succeeded Andrew again to the Chair of Institutes of Medicine, but he continued his interest in public health, publishing the important *Observations on the management of the poor in Scotland* (Edinburgh, 1840). [Sir] Robert Christison (1797-1882) held the chair from 1822-32. He describes his surprise at being appointed at the age of 24, with little experience in the subject. His early lectures were ill prepared and the number of students declined from twelve in the first year to one in the third, but he learned on the job by studying French and German literature, and by his last session 90 students attended, although it was still not a required subject on the curriculum.[31] He became noted for his expertise as a medical and scientific witness in numerous trials, including that of William Burke. He also made a particular study of toxicology and post-mortem examination. Of the others who followed, three were knighted for their contributions. Sir Henry Littlejohn was appointed Edinburgh's first Medical Officer of Health in 1862; and, as mentioned above, in 1898 the importance of Public Health in the prevention of disease led to it become a separate chair.

Macrae, in his book *Physicians and Society*,[32] wrote:

> *When he was first elected* [to the Presidency of the College] *in 1790 there was no government body in Scotland charged with a responsibility for health policy. In the absence of such a body Andrew Duncan led the College to become an agency through which otherwise neglected health concerns in Scotland were brought to the attention of the British Government in London.*

Duncan's initiative in this area of medicine was arguably his most important achievement.

Notes

1 Nicolson (2000), p. 91. He gives an excellent review of Duncan's travels based on Andrew Duncan Jr's letters of 1794-98.

2 This must have been an informal arrangement, for it is not listed in the Record of Apprentices held by the RCSE.

3 'Preliminary trial of Swietenia soymida', a tree of the mahogany family, whose fruits are still used for medicinal purposes. Named after Gerard von Swieten, physician to Maria Theresa of Austria.

4 Matthew Baillie (1761-1823) was William Hunter's nephew, who inherited the Academy after his uncle's death in 1783.

5 From a list of his London meals in the Duncan Archive.

6 The letters of Andrew Duncan Jr to his father, 1794-98 (EUL, Mss. Dc.1.90).

7 Richard Bright, cited in Baumgartner and Ramsey, in *Annals Medical History* (1933), 5, p. 531.

8 Andrew's letter from Vienna on 1 June 1796: 'In the morning at eight, Frank goes round the clinical ward and at nine gives his practical lecture. … He speaks a great deal at the bedside of the patient, generally in Latin, but sometimes in German. …' In his next letter he criticises medical practice in Italy and Germany, but 'I must, however make an exception from this remark the Franks, whose practice is extremely plain and simple.'

9 Grant (1884), p. 291.

10 Baumgartner and Ramsey (1933/4), 5, pp. 525-32; 6, pp. 259-77.

11 Baron (2006), pp. 708-15.

12 William Buchan in his popular *Domestic Medicine* had much wholesome advice regarding diet and exercise and many other matters. Like Frank, he was concerned about suitable clothing. His advice regarding the dress of young people has resonance today if one substituted diet for corsets. 'Another thing very hurtful to females about this period of life is strait cloaths [*sic*]. They are fond of fine shape, and foolishly imagine that this can be acquired by strait cloaths. Hence by squeezing their stomach and bowels they hurt digestion and occasion many incurable maladies. Human invention could not possibly have devised a practice more destructive to health.'

13 Baron (2006), p. 710.

14 Duncan's course of lectures was recorded almost verbatim by his student David Pollock in two beautifully presented manuscript volumes entitled *Observations on Medical Jurisprudence*. This quotation comes from vol. 2, p. 105. (1797/8)(CRC, EUL)

15 McCrae (2003), pp. 2-11.

16 Frank's favourite exercises were fencing, military drill, ballroom dancing and tree climbing. Neither Frank nor Duncan mentioned football.

17 Jenner had coined the name 'vaccination' (after the Latin name for a cow, *vacca*), in order to distinguish his procedure from 'inoculation'. The two terms have since tended to become used interchangeably.

18 Jenner (1798).

19 Inoculation was introduced into Britain in 1717 by Lady Mary Wortley Montague who had encountered this procedure while living in Constantinople. It became widely adopted following the endorsement of the Royal College of Physicians in London in 1754, but remained controversial because of its complication rate.

20 Brown (1809).

21 Duncan Sr had never carried out a vaccination himself. This being a practical procedure was in the province of the surgeon-apothecary.

22 Thomas Brown's letters and associated correspondence are contained in a pamphlet in the RCSE Library.

23 *Ibid.*

24 *Ibid.*

25 *Ibid.*

26 *Ibid.*

27 Minor disagreement arose in 1815 between the University and Edinburgh Town Council involving Andrew Duncan Jr who, as librarian to the University, was awarded by the Council an increase in his annual stipend from £30 to £70 to be paid out of the matriculation fund which the Senate regarded as being under its control. In order to avoid a confrontation, Duncan generously declined to accept the

award, whereupon the Senate increased his stipend to £100 from the same fund!

28   The Correspondence of Charles Darwin, vol. 4, 1847-50 (Cambridge University Press).

29   Presently the One World Shop.

30   For a history of the Chair of Medical Jurisprudence up to the present day, read Kaufman (2007), pp. 121-30.

31   Christison (1885), vol. I, p. 275.

32   McCrae (2007), p. 131.

ANDREW DUNCAN JUNIOR

From the medallion containing a miniature portrait believed to be of Andrew (see page 87 and *fig.* 13a).

CHAPTER VII

Medical Clubs and Societies founded by Andrew Duncan

JOHN CHALMERS

... although the Medical Practitioners in Edinburgh, have not been exempted from quarrels, highly disgraceful to the profession, yet that many of them have lived, so now live, and I trust will continue to live, on the most social and friendly term with each other.

From Duncan's Harveian oration on Alexander Monro *secundus*

The 18th century was characterised by the development of a host of clubs and societies which flourished in the liberated environment of the Enlightenment. Some existed solely to give opportunity for overindulgence and debauchery, such as the Spendthrift Club, the Hell-fire Club, the Bonnet Lairds, the Sweating Club, the Dirty Club, the Boar Club, etc. Others had a more serious purpose, such as the Speculative and Dialectic Societies. The Poker Club, whose members included Thomas Carlyle, David Hume, William Robertson, Joseph Black and Adam Smith, must surely have been one of the most intellectual gatherings of all times. The Friday Club, which had among its members the cleric Sydney Smith, and the eminent lawyers Francis Jeffrey and Henry Cockburn – the latter two destined to become judges and all noted for their wit and wisdom – must also have been a lively gathering.

These clubs offered the menfolk an escape from the cramped and squalid domestic conditions that prevailed in Edinburgh until the development of the New Town, and they thrived in the stimulating atmosphere of the Scottish Enlightenment. They offered a meeting ground for a wide cross-section of society where the aristocracy, intellectuals and *literati* caroused with lesser mortals. Most of the clubs met in the taverns off the High Street, where much of the daily business of the city was conducted, there being no other suitable meeting places except in the University which allowed access to a few of the more intellectual societies. Most of the myriad of 18th-century clubs declined in the 19th century as living conditions improved, allowing more home entertainment, but some of the more intellectual have survived to this day, including the Speculative and Dialectic Societies.

Duncan was an inveterate joiner of such societies, being a member of at least 17. If one did not exist to meet his requirements, he would create it. Thus he founded the four societies listed below (the terms club and society tend to be used interchangeably).[1]

Aesculapian Society*
Harveian Society*
Gymnastic Society
Royal Caledonian Horticultural Society*   *still surviving*

The Aesculapian Club

The Aesculapian Club was founded on 2 April 1773 by Duncan, and he remained its secretary for 54 years, resigning one year before his death in 1828. The name derives from the Greek god of medicine, the son of Apollo. From this club two others were generated – the Harveian Society and the Gymnastic Club. All three in their early stages had virtually the same membership but different objectives.

The early activities of the Aesculapian Club are recorded in nine minute books held in the Royal College of Physicians on behalf of the club. The first three volumes of minutes have been transcribed in beautiful calligraphy, for which the scribe, a Mr Tennoch, was rewarded with one guinea as a Christmas gift in 1799.

The first entry reads: 'The Aesculapian Club was conceived in a happy moment, and in due time brought forth. Drs Duncan and Hamilton, Messrs Hay, Bell, McLure and Dewar assisted at the birth on the first Friday of April 1773.' The club was to meet each month at a tavern of the members' choice for the purpose of wining and dining under the peculiar care and patronage of Apollo as the god of poetry and music, Bacchus as the god of wine, and Venus because the club at first met on Friday – *die Veneris*. Later Duncan was to say that the purpose of the club was to promote goodwill and fellowship between physicians and surgeons who, up to that time, did not always live in close harmony, surgeons being regarded as of a lower status than physicians. Surgeons were not allowed to become full members of the medical faculty or to act as examiners. Thomas Young, Professor of Midwifery, for example, was obliged to resign from the Incorporation of Surgeons and become a Fellow of the Royal College of Physicians to enable him to occupy his chair. Surgeon apothecaries, on the other hand, were allowed to dispense and sell drugs, a privilege denied to Fellows of the Royal College of Physicians – a cause of bitter resentment.

Members and guests

The founding members were Dr Andrew Duncan, Mr William Chalmer, Mr Alexander Wood, Dr James Lind,[2] Dr James Hamilton Sr, Mr Benjamin Bell, Mr Thomas Hay and Mr Forrest Dewar. At first membership was limited to 15 members, elected by ballot, from Fellows of the Royal College of Physicians or the Incorporation of Surgeons. By 1828 the number had increased to 22, and by tradition rather than by rule, eleven have since been elected from each of the Colleges of Physicians and Surgeons. No explanation for this curious figure is known, but it was clearly a subject of discussion. Richard Huie, the secretary who succeeded Duncan, wrote a lengthy poem about it beginning '*Some think the Club contains too few, Because we are only twenty two*', and ending

> *Then why an untried course pursue,*
> *And pass away from twenty two?*
> *No let us all be members true*
> *We're quite enough at twenty two*
> *And thus the best that we can do*
> *Is just to stop at twenty two.*

and so it remains to this day.

Huie, like Duncan, enjoyed writing doggerel and was appointed poet laureate of the Harveian Society. The minutes following Duncan's death contain two poems in his memory by Huie.

Chairmanship of the meeting rotated between members, but the secretary controlled the affairs of the club. The secretaries are notable for their longevity, for there have been only 14 in the 233 years since its foundation. In 1857 [Sir] Douglas Maclagan designed the secretary's medal which is worn at the dinners. Maclagan was a remarkable man. Starting his career as a surgeon, he became Professor of Medical Jurisprudence and President of both the Royal Colleges of Surgeons and Physicians, as had his father before him. He was a member of the Aesculapian and Harveian Clubs for more than 50 years. A Latin scholar and a poet, he had a fine tenor voice, being given the title of the Aesculapian Bard. Guests were initially restricted to members of one of the Colleges who lived outside Edinburgh, but over the years this restriction has been relaxed and guests from all walks of life have been welcomed.

At first the meetings were held monthly and took the form of a supper club, implying presumably a fairly simple meal. This, however, did not appear to have much appeal, as attendance began to drop off in the early years of the 19th century, sometimes as few as two turning up. In 1810 it was decided to change the format to a more formal dining club, with meetings held quarterly, starting at 4pm with a medical discussion. Dinner commenced at 5 pm to give time for the gargantuan feast. One menu is recorded as consisting of roast fowl, rice, fish, curried chickens, crabs, sallad [*sic*], cold lamb, apple pye [*sic*], mock turtle, potatoes, eggs and gravie [*sic*], lobster, spinage [*sic*], minced pies, roast lamb, and ham. Beverages included wine, brandy, gin, whisky, port and sherry. The total cost of the meal was less than £2 for the entire company.

Business

In 1777 the club decided 'to bestow annually a gold medal for promoting experimental enquiry among the students of Medicine at Edinburgh'. The first medal was awarded to Charles Darwin, uncle of the more famous namesake, for his essay on 'The Best Criteria for distinguishing Matter from Mucus as Discharged Expectoration'. Before he could receive his award, Darwin suffered a severe illness, probably septicaemia, following the dissection of the brain of a child who had died of hydrocephalus. Despite the best attentions of Professors William Cullen and Joseph Black, he rapidly went downhill and died.[3] A year later the club decided to discontinue the award, possibly because the cost, five guineas – equivalent to about £520 today, was too great for the small membership at a time when the annual subscription was only six shillings. Duncan offered to resign as secretary in protest, but on further consideration decided that a new club with a larger membership might spread the cost. Thus the Harveian Society was conceived.

The early minutes of the Aesculapian Society record only the names of those present and absent, and the visitors. No business matters are included, apart from the recording of wagers, the purpose of which appears to have been the provision of wine at the dinner. The bets were placed on very varied topics such as 'Lord North shall be out before the end of the present session of Parliament', or, in 1796, 'that there will be no French invasion of Britain for six months'. Golf matches were frequently the subject of bets. On 5 June 1801, Mr Bryce bet a magnum against Dr Duncan that he 'shall shoot a candle through a half inch board if allowed 12 trials at a distance of three yards'. He won his bet and the board was deposited with the Royal College of Physicians for its museum. The nature of the weapon used to propel the candle is not stated. The wagers were usually limited to a magnum of wine or occasionally melons, which must have been a rare delicacy at that time. The last bet recorded was in December 1914 – 'that the war would end by July 1915'. During the two World Wars, the club meetings were suspended.

The minute books after 1839 are written in normal handwriting by the secretary himself and become progressively more informative and lengthy, some recording in great detail the events of the evening – the topics discussed such as current political events and the progress of the Crimean War. The songs sung are recorded – some familiar ballads and others written for the occasion. Jokes feature quite often and were of a Christmas cracker standard:

> *Why did Mr X swallow his watch?*
> *So that he could experience the passage of time!*
>   or
> *What were your father's last remarks?*
> *He made none; my mother was with him to the end!*

In 1845 the availability of American Ice was recorded, which enabled a new drink called sherry-cobblers to be drunk with gusto. On 5 September 1846 three Indian doctors from Bengal were guests. At that dinner a hookah was passed round the table.

Venues

The club had a peripatetic existence, meeting first in Sommer's Tavern in the Old Town and in 1792 moving with the tavern to new premises in West Regent Street in the New Town, and later to Oman's Hotel in Waterloo Place. In 1830 the club transferred to Barry's Hotel at 9 Princes Street and held summer meetings at the Granton Hotel. The minutes record the excitement of the members when they were first conveyed by train to Granton, through the Scotland Street tunnel, by the newly opened railway. Their enthusiasm was dampened by the realisation that the Defiance coach which they observed waiting on the pier, with its four prancing bays and scarlet-robed guard and coachman, would soon cease to operate with the advent of the railway. Their enjoyment of the evening was even further spoiled by having to wait an hour for the return train. Complaints by club members to the Edinburgh Granton Railway Company were ignored because they were not submitted in writing! The next move was to the Douglas Hotel where the food was good but the wine a deplorable 'combination of flatness, coarseness, astringency, and thinness as to make the addition of the corked flavour rather an improvement'. Later venues included the Palace Hotel, the Caledonian Station Hotel, the University Club and the North British Hotel. In 1924 the Royal College of Physicians gave permission for the meetings to be held in the New Library at 9 Queen Street, and this elegant room has remained its venue to this day.

Mergers and offshoots

In 1796, Sandy Wood proposed that the Dissipation Club be absorbed into the Aesculapian. The origins and purpose of the Dissipation Club can only be guessed at, for no records remain. Its numbers, however, must have been small, as the limits of the Aesculapian membership were scarcely exceeded by the union. Its membership must have been similar to that of the Aesculapian Club, for the constitution of the Harveian Society stated that 'those wishing to become members must be proposed at the April meeting of the Aesculapian Club or at the Dissipation Club in March'.

At the meeting of the Aesculapian Society on 4 June 1836 it was announced that in consequence of the demise of many of the senior members of the Gymnastic Club, and more especially of Dr James Hamilton Sr, who had for many years filled the office of secretary, the surviving members had resolved to dissolve it. Certain articles of plate in their possession were handed over to the Aesculapian Club as both clubs had originated with the same founder, Dr Duncan. The plate consisted of three drinking cups with medals attached, bearing the names and arms of the victors in the *Ludi Apollinares* (Games of Apollo). Sir George Ballingall was appointed *Custos Poculorum* (Guardian of the Cup), with the responsibility of ensuring that the cups were produced and filled at each meeting. The cups remain in the possession of the Aesculapian Club, but one is currently displayed in the National Museum of Scotland.

Landmarks

In the early years of the Aesculapian Club, a 'Convivial Meeting' or *Lustrum* was convened every five years to which wives, family and friends were invited. These meetings involved dancing and card games and were occasions of 'innocent mirth and social happiness'. This agreeable custom has long since been abandoned and the exclusion of ladies from the club's activities has been a source of contention in recent times.

Special commemoration dinners have been held from time to time to mark notable occasions such as the club's centennials or Queen Victoria's Jubilees. At these celebrations a number of distinguished male guests were invited and the lengthy speeches were deemed worthy of publication. At the centenary dinner in 1873, the chairman, Sir Douglas Maclagan, gave an account of the founding members. Of Andrew Duncan he said, '... many of us are old enough to remember ... him going about the streets of Edinburgh as an old man, with, what my colleague the Professor of Botany would call his specific character of an umbrella with a hooked ivory handle ...'.[4] At the bicentenary meeting held on 13 October 1973 the principal speaker for the club was Sir Derrick Dunlop, Professor of Therapeutics, who was renowned for his oratory, as many of his past students can still recall. His speeches on this occasion confirmed his brilliance. Dunlop briefly reviewed the history of the club and mentioned some of the distinguished members from the past, paying particular tribute to the founder, Andrew Duncan. Lord Kilbrandon, Senator of the College of Justice, replied for the guests with similar felicity.[5]

The pattern of the meetings of the club has changed little over the past 200 years. The membership remains at 22. Photographic portraits of members have been kept since the early 20th century. The dining hour has become progressively later, in keeping with custom, and the gargantuan meals of the past have been replaced with more modest collations, although the food and wine remain of high quality. Since the meetings were resumed after the Second World War, their frequency has been reduced to two a year on the second Saturday of March and October. The venue remains the New Library of the Royal College of Physicians. Derrick Dunlop noted that the practice of singing popular ballads and improvised songs had been discontinued after the war, and the wearing of white ties and tails was abandoned 'because the smell of moth balls had became intolerable'. Smoking was permitted, the club providing the cigarettes. At a meeting on 10 March 1934, it was noted that Struthers averred that the Virginian cigarettes were the worst he had ever smoked. All others, members and guests, said that they were magnificent and it was decided to continue to buy them from the same supplier. Needless to say, smoking has long since been disallowed.

The table is decorated with mementos and trophies accumulated over the years. In addition to the cups given by the Gymnastic Club, a handsome silver loving cup was presented by the London Aesculapian Club at its demise in 1925, and various other artefacts have been donated by members over the years. Traditional rituals and statutory toasts are observed and the secretary reads a whimsical account of the previous meeting which rarely bears any resemblance to reality. The chairman toasts the guests and the senior guest replies. These toasts and responses are usually of the highest quality. The chairman concludes the occasion with a short talk on a subject of his choosing and gives the toast *Floreat Res Medica*.

This account of the club reads as if its activities are purely self-indulgent and hedonistic, yet it is clearly a formula which has worked well for more than 230 years, and is probably the oldest surviving dining club in Scotland. The list of past members contains nearly all of Edinburgh's eminent medical men of the period, including James Syme, one of the greatest surgeons of his day, his son-in-law Lord Lister, discoverer of antisepsis, and Sir James Young Simpson, discoverer of the anaesthetic properties of chloroform. Today's members feel privileged to follow such a distinguished lineage. The light-hearted atmosphere established by the founder remains the characteristic of

these occasions, and his purpose of creating goodwill and friendship between different branches of the profession is worthily fulfilled. Sir Douglas
Maclagan, in his chairman's speech during the centenary dinner of 1873,
said:

> *Viewed apart from the social entertainments, which are merely accessories,*
> *the principles of the Aesculapian are neither more nor less than these: to*
> *promote in our own circle, and, so far as our example goes, beyond our*
> *circle, peace on earth, by cultivating good-will between man and man.*

Harveian Society

The early history of the Harveian Society is contained in a minute book held
in the Royal College of Physicians. It covers the period from its inauguration
in 1782 to 1832. Just as is in the first minute books of the Aesculapian Club,
it is written in painstaking calligraphy.

In 1782 Duncan founded the Harveian Society or Circulation Club, as it
was also known until 1829, in honour of William Harvey (1578-1657) who
demonstrated the circulation of the blood. The society met annually on 12
April to celebrate Harvey's birthday and 'to commemorate the discovery of
the circulation of the blood by circulation of the glass'. It has been suggested
that Duncan's primary reason for creating the Harveian Society was to
spread the cost of providing the prize for best student essay, initiated by the
Aesculapian Club, by having a larger membership.

A revision of laws in 1839 detailed the purpose of the society:

> *The objects of the Society shall be threefold, to commemorate the discovery*
> *of the circulation of the blood, to cherish a kindly feeling among members*
> *of the medical profession, and to foster a spirit of experimental enquiry*
> *among the students of the School of Medicine. The Society shall endeavour*
> *to accomplish the first and second of these objects by dining together on the*
> *12 April – the birthday of the illustrious Harvey; and the third by bestowing*
> *an Annual Prize on the author of the best essay on a subject announced by*
> *the Society which subject shall be ... of an experimental nature.*

The president, who served for one meeting only, appointed his successor.
Andrew Duncan was the first president. Two secretaries were appointed,
senior and junior. Duncan served as the first senior secretary for 46 years. At
first, membership was limited to 30 Fellows of either of the Colleges of
Physicians or Surgeons resident in Edinburgh. New members had to be proposed at meetings of either the Aesculapian Club or the Dissipation Club,
and were elected by ballot. From the early membership list, almost the entire

Aesculapian Club appears to have become members of the Harveian Society, although others made up the numbers. In 1832 the numerical limit was abolished and membership was opened to all Fellows of the Royal Colleges provided that they pass the ordeal of the ballot box, two black balls excluding a candidate. Members from adjacent counties were eligible, as were medical officers from the army and navy. The election meetings took place in March and were no longer under the aegis of the Aesculapian Club.

Honorary membership was offered to selected non-medical friends who were characterised by their joviality and good companionship. Among these were John Wilson, Professor of Moral Philosophy and chief contributor to *Blackwood's Magazine* under the pen name of Christopher North, Sir Henry Raeburn the artist, and Robert McNair the Collector of Customs at Leith who was given the title of *Collector Pecuniae*. Sir Alexander Boswell, eldest son of James Boswell (biographer of Samuel Johnson), was appointed poet laureate of the society in 1810. Several of his poems are recorded including this extract from his Harveian hymn, which was his last work, read at the society after his death:

Hail! To immortal Harvey hail!
Thine inspiration breathed upon his soul,
And to his ken the hidden truth unfurled;
That as the seasons change, the planets roll,
As from the eastern wave to western flood,
Thy course revolving animates the world,
So circling moves the current of the blood.

In 1822 Boswell was killed in a duel by James Stuart the Younger of Dunearn, whom Boswell had insulted in a poem. Boswell had deliberately missed, but Stuart did not show the same courtesy. The bullet entered at the base of his neck fracturing the right clavicle. He was attended on site by his surgeon George Wood (son of Duncan's friend Sandy Wood) and by Stuart's surgeon, Robert Liston. Both surgeons removed some fragments of bone and tried without success to locate the bullet which had lodged near the spine. Boswell was carried to nearby Balmuto Castle, home of his distant cousin, Claud Irvine Boswell, Lord Balmuto. John Thomson, Professor of Military Surgery, was summoned from Edinburgh and arrived later that evening. Boswell told Thomson he felt like '... a man with a living head and a *dead* body mysteriously joined together'. Despite the attentions of three of Edinburgh's most eminent surgeons, Boswell died the following day. At the subsequent trial Stuart, who was represented by no less than six advocates including Francis Jeffrey and Henry Cockburn, was acquitted.[6]

Duncan recorded in the society minutes:

They have been deprived of their truly amiable Poet-Laureate, ... His astonishing convivial powers have, on different occasions, added to their innocent mirth, by obliging them to laugh at themselves. But he was equally capable of gratifying the finest feelings of the human heart by serious strains. ...

Another honorary member was Gilbert Innes, Deputy Governor of the Royal Bank of Scotland and a great friend of Duncan, who said that Innes 'found it not incompatible with the important duties of his office to derive both health and pleasure from being a Member of the Harveian Society'. He and Duncan had been elected to the Royal Company of Archers in the same year and both engaged in golf matches at the *Ludi Apollinares* (see below). Innes was Duncan's 'companion in Youth, his coadjutor in Manhood and his compatriot in Old Age'.

Since 1803, clergymen, chosen principally for their conviviality, have been invited to serve as chaplain with the title of *Pontifex Maximus*, the first being the Rev. Dr Moodie. Dr James Grant was chaplain at 56 festivals until his death aged 97. Since 1912 the Dean of the Thistle has been the honorary chaplain and he and the two honorary secretaries are the only officers of the society. The society, for a time, also awarded a Diploma of Mirth which took the form of a poem. Alexander Wood was the first recipient in 1803. His Diploma, composed by Duncan, starts:

Evectus nunc, sit Sandy Wood,
Honestus vir, both wise and good,
Doctor of Mirth, nos hunc creamus,
And to you all, nunc commendamus.

and ends:

Mirth proves there's more in man than sluggish clay;
Long may it cheer our hearts on Harvey's day!
I speak of mirth that's innocent and good;
Such mirth be ever thus, dear Sandy Wood.

Other holders of the Diploma of Mirth included Duncan himself, Douglas Maclagan, and Dr Moodie, the *Pontifex Maximus*. These awards were discontinued after 1855.

The subject for the students' prize essay was advertised and the essay had to be lodged by 1 January. The successful candidate had the choice of a copy of Harvey's works or a silver medal and was invited to the next Festival to receive his award. The list of award winners, kept by the Harveian Society, includes those awarded by the Aesculapian Club before the foundation of the Harveian Society, indicating the common origins of the two societies. In the early days the prize was keenly contested and the early winners included students from England, the Continent and the Americas. A Scot, Ralph Irvine, won the prize twice for his essays on Peruvian Bark and Ipecacuanha. Benjamin Smith Barton (1776-1815) of Philadelphia won with an essay on *Hyosciamus niger*. Barton later became a distinguished Professor of Botany at the University of Philadelphia. Gradually interest declined due to the increasing number of prizes which had become available in the Medical School. Perhaps also the selected topics lacked inspiration, for the subjects chosen for the years 1796-1800 were the therapeutic effects of the cold bath, the tepid bath, the hot bath, the vapour bath, and the medicated vapour bath![7] The selected topic for 1849 was 'The physiological and pathological effects of alcoholic liquors on the human body', and the prize fund was increased from five guineas to ten, but still there were no takers. The last prize to be awarded was in 1856, and the offer of the award, one of the main reasons for founding the society, was discontinued after 1864.

Other charitable activities of the society included a contribution towards the restoration of Archibald Pitcairne's gravestone (see pages 221-22), and in 1873 a donation of £10 was sent to the Vicar of Folkestone towards the cost of a window commemorating William Harvey which was being installed in the parish church. The society also bought a bust of Alexander Monro *primus* for £60, which the members presented to the University.

At first the pattern of the dinners was very similar to those of the Aesculapian Club, even to the extent of having bets and challenges to supplement the liquid refreshment. For example, 'on the motion of Dr Home, Dr Duncan Sr was directed to produce his Diploma as a Knight of the Beggar's Benison, under the penalty of a bottle of rum. The rum to be paid by Dr Home if Dr D. does produce his Diploma.' The following year, 'in compliance with the order of last meeting, Dr Duncan Sr having produced his Diploma and Medal as a Knight of the Beggar's Benison, Dr Home was sentenced to treat the society with a bottle of his best Rum at the next annual meeting'. The wagers were generally a magnum of punch or claret. The last record of a wager in the minutes was in 1812. The meetings were held in the same range of taverns and hotels as the Aesculapians: initially in Sommer's Tavern in West Register Street, next Oman's Tavern in Waterloo Place, then Barry's Hotel in Queen Street. As the numbers increased, finding suitable venues became more difficult. The meeting in 1856 in the Royal Hotel was a disaster because there was not enough to eat! The early menus by modern standards were as gross as those of the Aesculapian Club.

In 1884 the dinner was held in the Royal College of Physicians during the Festival to commemorate the tercentenary of the founding of the University of Edinburgh. Rudolph Virchov, the eminent German pathologist, and the Lord Mayor of London, were among the guests. Louis Pasteur sent his apologies. Dr Keiller delivered the address. Since 1889 the dinners have been held in the hall of the Royal College of Physicians.

By this time the pattern of the dinners, or 'festivals' as they were sometimes called, had evolved their unique character. Numbers attending frequently exceeded 100. A bust of William Harvey was displayed and a small terracotta figurine of Harvey holding a heart in his hand was placed before the president of the day. Music was played throughout the meal. Ox heart was one of the dishes and neophytes had to stand and be scrutinised with regard to their standard of mastication, deglutition and assimilation to the background music of 'Hearts of Oak'. In the early days the meal commenced at 3 pm, but later the company met at 7.15 to listen to the president's oration before dining at eight. The date of the meeting was changed to June, April having proved awkward because of conflicting pressures of examinations and holidays. Membership since 1963 has been limited to 240, drawn from all over Scotland. By custom the president on alternate years is now appointed from outside Edinburgh. The presidential badge of office was presented by Dr Douglas Guthrie, the medical historian, in 1956. Until 1966 full evening dress was worn for the festival. James Innes describes the assembly as being 'like a resplendent host of emperor penguins. The merry popping of studs from starched shirt fronts was a familiar sound during the Oration and ... [the] later stages of the feast'.[8] Since then dinner jackets have been the accepted dress, after some initial resistance from the older members.

The custom of the presidential oration was established in 1799, although occasional orations had been delivered earlier. On the bicentenary of Harvey's birth in 1778, Duncan had delivered to the Aesculapian Club, in Latin, the 'De laudibus Gulielmi Harvei oratio', and Harvey and his works remained a recurrent theme in many of the subsequent orations. Increasingly other topics were introduced, such as obituaries commemorating distinguished individuals. Duncan contributed nine orations between 1778 and 1825, several of which are in print, and are chiefly of interest for the insight which they give on Duncan himself. He dedicated his published Harveian oration on Alexander Monro *secundus*, delivered in 1818, to the dissolute Prince Regent, with the following rather unctuous effusion:

May it please your Royal Highness, to permit an old and faithful Member of your Household, who has, by your gracious favour, enjoyed the honourable title of Physician to the Prince of Scotland, more than thirty years, to express his sincere gratitude for the much valued distinctions which have been conferred upon him by one of the best of Kings and a Son, on whose character it will reflect immortal honour that he has followed the footsteps of one of the best of fathers.

In the introduction to this oration Duncan said that, since the founding of the society, 'it has been my good fortune to enjoy such good health, as to enable me to be present at every one of these meetings. Once more, I meet you here for the 40th time, and in the seventy fourth year of my age.' (Actually it was the 36th meeting.) He concludes his lengthy account of Monro's life and achievements with comments on his social side: 'Of his talents as an agreeable companion, over a social glass, we had incontestable proof at our convivial meetings. Without transgressing the bounds of the most strict sobriety, he afforded us demonstrative evidence of the exhilarating power of wine.'

In his oration, Duncan mentions their shared passion for gardening. Monro had bought the large estate of Craiglockhart on the outskirts of Edinburgh, which he converted into a garden. He had no house there, but entertained in a cottage: 'The melons and grapes could not be excelled.' Duncan adds that 'two of the most eminent Practitioners in Edinburgh, and of my most intimate friends, Dr Monro, and Mr Alexander Wood, had excellent gardens within an easy walk of the City. ... [they] were companions of my youth as well as friends of old age.'

In the printed version of the Monro memorial, Duncan 'subjoined a few *poetical effusions*, which have occasionally added to the hilarity of the convivial meetings of medical men at Edinburgh. ... they will at least serve to demonstrate to the world, that although the Medical Practitioners in Edinburgh have not been exempted from quarrels, highly disgraceful to the profession, yet that many of them have lived, so now live, and I trust will continue to live, on the most social and friendly term with each other.' (Monro's family requested that these '*poetical effusions*' should be deleted from further printings.)

Duncan published *Miscellaneous Poems extracted from the records of the Circulation Club at Edinburgh* in 1818,[9] including those composed by himself and various members of the society. Some are in dog Latin and many now seem very puerile, but they do reveal the prevailing sense of humour and the interrelationships between members. Dr Barclay's poem on 'Duncan's Grand Panacea' points out in many verses that time is a great healer:

Let Duncan be honour'd, whose wonderful skill
Cures every complaint without potion or pill.
With all kinds of drugs henceforth dispense,
The cure of all cures is – THE HUNDRED YEARS HENCE.

Another song composed and sung by Alexander Boswell at the Harveian Anniversary on 12 March 1816 is a word-play on the names of some of the members.

If on WOOD I but think,
From deal coffin I shrink;
If on BELL I hear a bell tolling'
For nothing can save
From that dead HOME the grave,
The HOPE, smiling Hope, sits cajoling.

If Murder and Death
Chill our blood in Macbeth,
Talk of DUNCAN, we hear ravens croaking,
But the Duncan that's here,
Is th'assassin, I fear,
Who kills us, remorseless, with joking.

Duncan was awarded an honorary diploma by the society five days before *Ides Aprilis* 1816, which was written as a poem in dog Latin. The first verse reads:

With all the rites of due decorum
Nunc ad altissimum honorem   [Now let him be carried up
Evectus sit, Andreas Duncan   the highest honour]
Honestus vir, if e'er there was one.   [Honourable man]

The 17 members who signed the diploma gave Latin versions of their signatures. Sandy Wood's was *Andreas Lignum*.

Following Duncan's death on 5 July 1828, Richard Huie, who succeeded Duncan as Secretary of the Harveian as well as the Aesculapian Societies, delivered the Harveian Oration in his memory. In this he details with great warmth Duncan's life and achievements in so many different spheres. One passage in particular describes Duncan's purpose with regard to the societies which he founded:

He knew that asperities did and would occur in practice, when rival inter-
ests came into collision, ... He delighted, therefore, to assemble us around
the social board; and to make us feel, amidst the harmless festivities of the
unbending hour, that, if we had many points of difference, we had also
many things in common; and that neither our comfort as men, nor our
respectability as practitioners, was to be enhanced by standing aloof from

each other's society, or exchanging the sullen scowl of individual dislike.
For these ends he established the Aesculapian and Gymnastic clubs; and
last, not least, the Harveian Society.

That the society continues to thrive to this day is a tribute to the man and
his vision.

Gymnastic Club or *Ludi Apollinares*

At a meeting of the Aesculapian Club on 5 September 1846, the chairman
produced the records of the Gymnastic Club in two quarto volumes which
had turned up in a private collection. These elusive records, which were
thought to have been lost, have once more disappeared, so details of the
club's origins cannot be confirmed. R. Omond, Secretary of the Harveian
Society, who seems to have had access to the minute books in 1871,[10] states
that it was founded in 1786 by members of the Aesculapian and Harveian
Clubs together (the membership of the two clubs at that time being virtually
identical), with the purpose of providing healthy exercise to counteract the
effects of dietary indulgence. The founder was inevitably Andrew Duncan,
but no doubt encouraged by his good friends Sandy Wood, James Hamilton
Sr and William Inglis, 'the chief restorer of the Ludi Apollinares' who
remained among its most constant supporters. Hamilton Sr served as secretary throughout its existence. Henry Raeburn was given the title of
Quaester (magistrate or treasurer). In its early days it was so popular that
attendance at the meetings of the Aesculapian and Harveian Societies suffered in favour of the Gymnastic Club. No new members were recruited after
its early days, and at its prime it had probably no more than 50 members.

Duncan said that the club provided the 'admirable combination of
healthful exercise with social mirth'. The principal activity was an annual
competition, held at Leith during the second week of August, to engage in
the *Ludi Apollinares* (the athletic games established by the Romans in the
3rd century BC), during which bowling, gowfing (golfing) and swimming
contests were undertaken. During its first 20 years the victor in each sport
was awarded a silver medal suitably inscribed. No one else matched Duncan's total of four medals for golf, two for bowling and four for swimming.
Several of Duncan's medals have the family crest engraved on the obverse.
One of the medals records (in Latin) that Alexander Duncan, medical
student aged 19, was victor in the swimming contest on 6 August 1832,
beating 'Andre' Duncan aged 79. Alexander was Duncan's grandson who
lived with his grandparents (see page 30). A medal of 1824 records that
Andrew Duncan Sr was *iterum iterumque victor lauream Apollinarem,* i.e.
again and again winner of the laurel [wreath] of the club. The contests seem

to have been undertaken in a light-hearted manner: one medal was awarded to Gulielmus Cheyne because, as was recorded in Latin, he swam so far as to disappear from sight. Apparently a thick mist allowed his disappearance after a few yards.

After the matches the members repaired to the Gowf House adjacent to the Leith Links for dinner. Poetry and song, as ever, were features at these occasions.

Duncan, always ready with a poem, produced one of his better ones at a Gymnastic Club dinner which may indicate the tenor of these meetings.

> Here lies Sandy Wood, a good honest fellow,
> Very wise when sober, but wiser when mellow;
> At sensible nonsense by no man excell'd.
> With wit and good humour dull care he repell'd.
>
> In the cure of diseases, his talents long shone;
> As a good operator he was second to none:
> A friend and a bottle were long his delight;
> He could toil all the day, and yet laugh all the night.
>
> But though now he's laid low, we must not complain,
> For, after a sleep, he'll be with us again:
> Shed no tears my good friends, wear no garments of sable,
> SANDY WOOD is not dead, but laid under the table.

Sandy Wood, one of the founders and most enthusiastic members of the club for more than half a century, was given the title of *Gymnaciarchus Magnificus*.

Golf and medicine

The association between golf and medicine has a long history which continues to the present day. Sir Robert Sibbald, founder of the College of Physicians, is said to have been injured by the back swing of his partner in 1690. The Honourable Company of Edinburgh Golfers was founded in 1744, with the surgeon John Rattray (1707-71) as the first captain. Rattray is credited with drawing up the first rules of golf which were formulated during his captaincy. He was also the winner of the Silver Club – the trophy of the first Open Championship in 1744. The Honourable Company was based at Leith Links until it moved to Musselburgh in 1836 and in 1891 to its present location at Muirfield. Another surgeon, William Inglis (1712-92), was captain between 1782-84 and also a winner of the Silver Club.

There have been many other celebrated medical golfers since that time, including the eye surgeon Douglas Argyll Robertson (1837-1909) who founded the Royal Colleges Golf Club, open to members of the Colleges of Physicians and Surgeons, which is still enthusiastically supported by the medical fraternity of all ages and abilities. Duncan represented golf as one of the most healthful exercises. Benjamin Rush (1745-1813), an American contemporary of Duncan, who studied medicine in Edinburgh at the same time and may well have been introduced to the sport by Duncan, reckoned that a man who played golf 'would live ten years longer for using this exercise once or twice a week', and he hoped to introduce it to America. Rush appears to have been much influenced by Duncan, for he was instrumental in introducing psychiatric medicine in Philadelphia, just as Duncan was to do in Edinburgh, and commenced a journal modelled on Duncan's *Medical Commentaries*.

The golf course on Leith Links consisted of five holes, starting at the Golf House and extending around the periphery of the Links. The holes were named as follows:

1 Sawmill 325 yards   4 South Mid Hole 495 yards
2 North Midhole 407 yards   5 Thorntree hole 435 yards
3 East Hole 426 yards

Seven strokes a hole was about average. The balls in Duncan's day were 'featheries' which consisted of enough feathers to fill a top hat compressed into a tight ball encased in leather. In dry conditions they could be driven 150 yards, but if wet they were useless.

Bets were taken on the outcome of matches at both the Aesculapian and Harveian dinners. One of the golfing wagers was recorded in 1797: 'Mr Duncan offers to bet a Magnum of punch against Mr Alex Wood that in the Match of golf to be played to-morrow – Mr Alex^r Wood aet 70 & Master Alex^r Wood aet 7 against Dr Duncan aet 50 & Master H. Duncan aet 5 the Duncans shall be victorious. Mr Wood accepts.' The match between the two men and Wood's grandson and Duncan's son ended in a draw.

To celebrate the centenary of the union with England, the Gymnastic Club held a gowf match on 12 May 1807. A later dinner consisted entirely of fish dishes at which upwards of 20 different kinds of fish were served. Inevitably this inspired Duncan, an uncritical monarchist and patriot, to poesy:

The oysters now are past their prime,
But Crab will fill their place:
Yet in our jolly company

You'll see no crabbed face.

With merry glee we'll spend our hour,
We'll pun and laugh and sing,
And drink a bumper of good wine
To George our virtuous King.

The Union next shall claim a toast,
Which Britons ties together:
Long may their sons live social friends!
May Union last for ever!

Another match is recorded in an anonymous letter (almost certainly by Duncan himself) from a medical practitioner in Edinburgh to a brother doctor in London.

On 6th August 1823 at the Commemoration of the Ludi Apollinares ... the Scottish Game of Golf, which has occurred for many years, excited no inconsiderable admiration among numerous spectators. Dr Andrew Duncan Sr, Father of the Royal College of Physicians Edinburgh, now in his 79th year of age, appeared on the links as Champion for the ancient City of St Andrews, and Gilbert Innes, Deputy Governor of the Royal Bank of Scotland, not many years younger ... appeared as Champion for the City of Edinburgh. These two squires have the reputation of being, at present, two of the best Golfers in Scotland. ... This contest ... was carried on with all the fire of youth, the strength of manhood, and the wisdom of old age. After a keen match, the parties came off perfectly equal.

On a visit to St Andrews on 25 September 1823, Duncan, aged 80, 'played golf on those links where he had amused himself aged eight. After a very interesting contest, the Octogenarian came off victorious by one hole, and the cadet who carried his clubs emphatically declared that he played astonishingly.'

In Duncan's later years the athletic activities of the Gymnastic Club were held less regularly than the dinner, and after his death in 1828, despite its motto '*Esto Perpetua*', the meetings virtually ceased. It was finally wound up in 1836 and its memorabilia handed over to the Aesculapian Club.

Perhaps inevitably Duncan's rival James Gregory did not share his liking for medical clubs, although he was a member of other societies including the Royal Company of Archers and the Canongate Kilwinning Lodge of Freemasons (Duncan was also a member). Duncan wrote that Gregory declared 'that he belonged to no medical club, whether Aesculapian, Harveian, or

Gymnastic, holding the exhilarating power of Wine in great contempt, yet these medical clubs, which have long subsisted, and still continue to subsist, with uninterrupted harmony, include at least a very respectable minority'. Gregory's account was that he declined joining any of these clubs, 'though often invited', because he did not want to become involved with the disputes which he had heard took place frequently among members and 'other reasons' not specified.[11] He stated, 'We are certainly a most amiable brotherhood ... [but] we are not all perfect angels. The consequence is that ... [when] obliged to scramble for fame, and fortune, and daily bread, we are apt to get into rivalships, and disputes and altercations, which sometimes end in open quarrels and implacable animosities ...'.[12] Nothing in the minutes of these societies supports Gregory's suggestion of such disputes. Perhaps among Gregory's other reasons were the rivalry which existed between him and Duncan, and their differing attitude to alcohol. Gregory, who was known for his abstemious habits, declared that 'though much has been said, and with some truth, of the good effects of wine in producing rapidity and vivacity of thought, it has scarcely ever been pretended that it favoured the exercise of discrimination and judgement. But some Physicians, who should be supposed to know themselves best, ... have boasted that they prescribed as well drunk as sober. ...'[13]

Duncan quotes a verse suggesting that Gregory had modified his views since he wrote the above 20 years earlier:

> If the Patient be ailing, and knows not of what,
> Take DUNCAN's restorative, Laugh and be Fat;
> Even GREGORY, I'm told is not now so rude,
> As to starve his poor patient whose appetite's good;
> Nay, I hear he has even discovered a plan,
> Tho' an ass drinks no wine, to allow some to Man.

Certainly Duncan's therapeutic advice probably did less harm than the Gregorian Physic of free bloodletting, the cold affusion, brisk purging, frequent blisters, and the nauseating action of tartar-emetic.

Notes

1   Duncan also created a society of one. In the introduction to the first issue of *Medical and Philosophical Commentaries*, he refers to himself, with unusual modesty, as secretary to the society responsible for the journal, but there is no evidence of such a society; Duncan was the sole founder and editor.

2   James Lind was a second cousin of his namesake, famous for the discovery of the cure for scurvy, who, by that time had left Edinburgh to become chief physician at the Royal Naval Hospital at Haslar. The Aesculapian Lind graduated MD in 1768 and became a Fellow of the Royal College of Physicians of Edinburgh in 1770. 'The year following' wrote Duncan, 'I obtained the same honour, and became his immediate junior in the College ... and we lived on terms of the most intimate and cordial friendship.' Lind accompanied Joseph Banks on his Icelandic expedition in 1772. They visited islands on the west coast of Scotland, where they discovered the columnar stratifications of Staffa, which until then, had been unobserved and unknown to naturalists. He subsequently moved to London where he prospered, becoming Physician to King George III and a Fellow of the Royal Society.

3   *Medical Commentaries* (1777), 5, pp. 329-36.

4   Maclagan (1873), pp. 563-72.

5   Dunlop (1974), pp. 197-201.

6   Full accounts of the circumstances surrounding this duel are given in Cockburn (1909), pp. 368-74, and Smith (1871), pp. xlix-liv and *The Trial of James Stuart Esq* (1822) (Edinburgh: Archibald Constable and Co.).

7   Duncan had an obsession with baths. One of his first acts as President of the Royal College of Physicians was to appoint committees to consider vapour baths and cold bathing.

8   Innes (1983), pp. 285-89.

9   The copy of *Miscellaneous* Poems in the National Library of Scotland is inscribed by Duncan, 'To Mary Hill Duncan the wife of John Duncan from her matrimonial Father, Andrew Duncan, who is still able although now in the 80th year of his age to compose poetical effusions on the top of Arthur's Seat.'

10 Omond (1874), pp. 97-104.

11 Gregory (1803), p. 456.

12 Gregory (1800), p. 193.

13 James Gregory is expressing the views of his father, who wrote, 'I have heard it said of some eminent physicians, that they prescribed as well when drunk as when sober. If there was any truth in this report, it contained a severe reflection against their abilities in their profession.' See Gregory (1772), p. 25.

CHAPTER VIII

The Royal Medical and
Medico-Chirurgical Societies

JAMES A. GRAY

*Dr Duncan became the most active and judicious Patron of the Society,
and whatever dignity and importance it may since have attained to, must
mainly be ascribed to the wise and permanent organization which it received
under his friendly surveillance. ...*

From a letter from the Royal Medical Society
to Andrew Duncan Jr, on the death of his father

Andrew Duncan and the Royal Medical Society

The Royal Medical Society is the oldest existing medical society, with a continuous record of activity going back to 1737. It is also unique, being the only medical society boasting a Royal charter, which was founded by, and still run by, medical students, albeit with guidance from more senior members of the profession. Its Royal charter was granted by King George III in 1778.

That a large, full-length, oil portrait of Dr Andrew Duncan has hung in the society's meeting halls and in its different homes over many decades, recognises the enormous contribution he made to the society's growth and welfare throughout his life. Sadly this fine portrait, attributed to Sir John Watson Gordon, is no longer on public view. It was lent to the Scottish National Portrait Gallery and is presently in store.

Without Andrew Duncan's enthusiasm and drive, the society's first purpose-built rooms might never have been constructed; without his successful petition for the Royal charter, the society might still be called the Medical Society of Edinburgh and not the Royal Medical Society. After Duncan was elected a member in 1765, he faithfully attended the society's meetings and was later elected, on six occasions, to be one of its four annual presidents. His deep and continuing interest in the society reflected his love of clubs and fraternal meeting places. It also reflected his great devotion to medical education.

The Royal Medical Society can date its beginnings to August 1734 when

James Russell, one of a group of six medical students, was offered 'for a pecuniary gratification' the body of a young woman, a stranger, who had died of fever ten days before. James Gray's *History of the Royal Medical Society 1737-1937* (from which much of this chapter is derived), goes on to describe the sequence of events, quoting from letters written 48 and 49 years later by William Cumming, one of the group of students involved with James Russell at the time. By kind permission of Alexander Monro *primus*, Professor of Anatomy and a founder of the Edinburgh Medical School, the students used the University's anatomical theatre in which to dissect the woman's body over the next month. William Cumming later developed a fever, probably as a result of the unhygienic conditions prevailing in the theatre. After the dissection the six students spent a social evening at a tavern. There they resolved to meet every fortnight in each other's lodgings to discourse, either in Latin or English, on a medical topic. Reflecting the students' interests at the time, the titles of the first papers they read to each other included subjects like rabies, gonorrhoea, epilepsy and menstruation.

After several of the original six students left Edinburgh to study under the great teacher Hermann Boerhaave in the University of Leiden, the Edinburgh meetings ceased temporarily. In 1737, however, they were resumed on a more formal basis, now with ten members, who called themselves the Medical Society. One of the founding signatories of the new society was James Russell, who had received the body for dissection in 1734. Russell was awarded the Chair of Natural Philosophy in Edinburgh in 1764.

Early in the society's history, the members agreed a constitution. All members were required to sign a Promissary Obligation to agree to obey the laws of the society. A membership fee of five guineas restricted membership to the wealthier students and exclusiveness in the choice of members resulted in membership being regarded as an honour. Later election procedures ensured a more democratic membership. Regular attendance was required at meetings and fines levied on absentees. Choosing to watch a play rather than attend the society's meeting was especially frowned upon.

Initially a single negative vote excluded a prospective member from being admitted to the society. In this way it was hoped that amity would prevail among the members. Later, only a three-fourths majority was required. To begin with the members elected a president for the week, and later also elected a secretary and treasurer for a month, to keep the business of the society running smoothly. In the 19th century the office bearers were given Latin names, which have continued to be used – *Praeses* and *Olim Praeses* for president and former president, *Scriba* for secretary, *Quaestor* for treasurer and *Socius* for Fellow, an ordinary member being a *Socius ordinarius*. By 1764 it was agreed that four presidents should be elected to serve annually, a system that prevails in the society today.

Although the society's business can sometimes be conducted in a light-hearted manner, its serious, primary intention has always been, and still is, to promote medical education among its members. Originally each member was obliged to write and speak to a dissertation. When there were relatively few members in the early days, the dissertations were circulated before each meeting, individual members being allowed no more than six hours in which to read the papers. A porter was assigned to carry the documents, but, with the increase in membership and the distance some members now lived from the society's hall, this practice had to be discontinued.

In his inaugural address to the society in 1912, Sir Robert Hutchison Bart, himself a former senior president of the society, spoke on 'The Function of the Royal Medical Society in Medical Education'. He warmly commended the society's excellent library, which had become a valuable resource of modern and historical medical books; the continuing opportunity that the members had to prepare, write and deliver dissertations and to defend and be challenged on their content in debate; and, finally, what he regarded as even more precious than any of these – the friendships made in the society which would afterwards help to sustain happy co-operation within the medical profession.

There were many famous men associated with the society from its earliest days. A particularly colourful founder member in 1737 was Sir Stuart Threipland. His father, Sir David, had supported the Jacobites in 1715, had been captured, escaped and then lived in exile abroad, so forfeiting the family estates in Perthshire. Sir Stuart had therefore to make his own way in life. He studied medicine, graduated in Edinburgh in 1742, and two years later became a Fellow of the Royal College of Physicians of Edinburgh. Following their father's tradition, Sir Stuart and his brother David both enlisted with the rebels in 1745. David was killed in action. Stuart, however, was a medical advisor to Prince Charles Edward throughout the campaign, escaping with the Prince after the defeat at Culloden in April 1746, although they soon became separated. With Dr Archibald Cameron, Stuart had assisted the wounded Jacobite, Cameron of Locheil, who was hiding in a cave on Ben Alder. Dr Cameron was later tried, convicted and executed at Tyburn for his part in the 1745 rebellion, despite the pleadings of his former teacher, Alexander Monro *primus*, himself a Hanoverian. Sir Stuart was luckier and, using various disguises, managed to escape to France. He returned to Edinburgh under an amnesty in 1747 and practised medicine in the city. In 1775 he was one of the subscribers to the fund for the society's new hall. Although he remained a covert Jacobite all his days, he was eventually allowed to buy back the family estates in 1783.

Another eminent member of the society was Francis Home, who joined as a student in 1740. After studying in Leiden, he was appointed as a surgeon to the Dragoons then serving in Flanders. His orders to the troops to drink only boiled water must have saved many lives from dysentery, which was rife in the armies of the time. Home graduated in Edinburgh in 1750 and later became the University's first Professor of Materia Medica.

Dr John Hope joined the society in 1745. Qualifying in medicine in Glasgow, he was appointed to the Chair of Botany and Materia Medica in Edinburgh in 1761, elected a Fellow of the Royal College of Physicians of Edinburgh in 1762, and in 1768 became Regius Professor of Botany and the King's Botanist in Scotland. In this capacity he was responsible for relocating Edinburgh's second botanic garden (which occupied a site now covered by Waverley Station) to a better position off Leith Walk, where it remained until finally moving to its present location in Inverleith in 1822. Dr Hope, being both botanist and physician, exemplified the multi-talented brilliance of so many of these men of the Scottish Enlightenment. He died in 1786 during his second year as President of the Royal College of Physicians of Edinburgh.

Dr John Roebuck was elected a member of the society in either 1741 or 1742. After studying medicine in Edinburgh, he graduated in Leiden, like so many other students. He practised for a while in Edinburgh but, by 1749, had become deeply interested in experimental chemistry and perfected the lead chamber technique to manufacture oil of vitriol (sulphuric acid). In Prestonpans, to the east of Edinburgh, Roebuck, with John Garbet and William Cadell, was involved in the production of ceramics at the Auld Kirk Pottery. In 1770 Roebuck and William Cadell started the Carron Iron Company, near Falkirk, and numbered James Watt among their engineers. The company became famous for making naval guns, or 'carronades' as they came to be called. Even into the later 20th century, the Carron Iron Company continued to produce kitchen grates and ranges, and metal telephone kiosks.

In 1742 John Gregory joined the society. He graduated in Aberdeen and became Professor of Medicine there before being appointed to the Chair of the Practice of Physic in Edinburgh in 1776. In his address to the society in 1771, Andrew Duncan Sr quoted John Gregory as being among those doctors in the early days of the society who, with every respect to the great master, would not slavishly adhere to the teachings of Boerhaave. This suggests from the outset that the society's members were willing to challenge established dogma and make up their own minds about medical matters.

Dr William Cullen became Professor of Medicine in Glasgow in 1751, then Edinburgh's joint Professor of Chemistry in 1755, and later Professor of the Institutes of Medicine. Finally, in 1773, as Edinburgh's Professor of Medicine, Cullen was criticised for not promoting experimental medicine. He was, however, a brilliant teacher who championed independent thought among his students. It is inconceivable that he did not discuss with the members of the Medical Society the merits and faults of Boerhaave's teaching. Cullen, who staunchly supported the fledgling society, was granted honorary membership in 1764.

Among Cullen's students, who subsequently became eminent in the profession, was Gilbert Blane. He was a president of the society in 1775 when he gave an address on the nature of antiseptics. Blane was later Surgeon to the Fleet under Admiral Rodney and enforced James Lind's recommendation on the use of lemon juice to prevent scurvy at sea. Other notable pupils of Cullen were William Withering, famous for using digitalis, obtained from foxgloves leaves, to treat dropsy, and John Rogerson who became Physician to the Empress of Russia.

One of the most eccentric characters in the society in the mid-18th century was the novelist and playwright, Oliver Goldsmith, who became a member in 1753 while studying medicine in Edinburgh. Always sociable and over-generous, though he could not afford to be so, he was constantly in debt, and once had to pawn his expensive, flamboyant clothes to pay for theatre tickets promised to friends. Once he nearly fled the country to avoid imprisonment for debt, but was generously bailed out by friends in Edinburgh, one of them being a member of the Medical Society. Although his literary skills were considerable, his medical skills left something to be desired. It is reputed that he hastened his own early death from a fever in 1774 by too vigorously self-medicating with powders containing antimony.

Among medical students in the middle of the 18th century, there were those who, like Sir Stuart Threipland, were ardent supporters of the Stuart cause. There were also anti-monarchists. Sylas Neville regularly commemorated the anniversary of the execution of King Charles I and, along with several colleagues, sympathised with the American colonists, whom they felt were being unfairly treated by the British government. Dr William Cullen actively encouraged American students to study in Edinburgh and they were attracted to do so because of his reputation as a teacher. The society also became involved in these transatlantic associations.

John Moultrie from South Carolina became a member of the society in 1747. He graduated from Edinburgh two years later with a thesis on malignant fevers. According to Gray's history of the society, Moultrie was the first American student to graduate in medicine abroad. Gray also mentions several others who followed in Moultrie's footsteps. Thus Americans qualifying in Edinburgh included Peter Middleton of New York, who joined the society in 1749 and later wrote the earliest American history of medicine, Samuel Bard, also of New York, and John Morgan of Philadelphia, a co-founder with William Shippen of the medical department of the University of Pennsylvania.

Adam Kuhn of Pennsylvania joined the society in 1766 and later became Professor of Botany in the College of Philadelphia. Together with William Shippen and Benjamin Rush, Kuhn was associated with the foundation of the American Philosophical Society, of which Benjamin Franklin was the first president. The American Philosophical Society is the oldest and among the most prestigious scientific societies in the United States. It could be argued that it is indirectly an offspring of the Edinburgh Medical Society. Andrew Duncan Sr was elected a member of the American Philosophical Society in 1774.

Shippen graduated in medicine in Edinburgh in 1761 and was elected an honorary member of the Royal Medical Society in 1787, in the same year as Benjamin Franklin. Benjamin Rush from Pennsylvania became an ordinary member of the society in 1767 and graduated in medicine in Edinburgh the next year. He was also active in the early years of the College of Philadelphia and the University of Pennsylvania, holding chairs in both institutions. In 1776, with Benjamin Franklin, Rush was one of the representatives of the famous Thirteen Colonies who signed the Declaration of Independence. Caspar Wistar (or Wister) from Philadelphia was 23 when he joined the Royal Medical Society in 1784. He graduated MD in Edinburgh in 1785, later becoming Professor of Anatomy in Pennsylvania. He gave his name to the climbing plant wisteria. Such were the interesting connections between medicine in Edinburgh and that developing in the young America.

The close relationship between students and their teachers is frequently recorded in *The Diary of Sylas Neville 1767-1788*, which will often be quoted here. Sylas Neville joined the Medical Society in April 1773 after some misgivings and became junior president two years later. When he was a student of Dr Home, Neville developed an eye infection and consulted Drs Home and Alexander Monro *secundus*, both of whom were happy to give free advice. The hypochondriac Neville recovered quickly after applying a leech to his temple. He next developed ill-defined symptoms – probably gastric – and again consulted Dr Monro, who did not think him as unwell as he thought himself to be. Nonetheless Dr Monro prescribed 'a gentle course of mercury', after which Neville recovered completely.

The students reciprocated with concern for their teachers. In May 1774, when Dr William Cullen's health was failing, the students of the Medical Society sent him a touching letter urging him immediately to 'end his course of practice, if he thought it inconsistent with his health to go on with it'. The society tactfully added that they had 'the highest esteem for his labours'. After his next lecture, Cullen replied that, although not completely well, he was somewhat better and that 'he should go on as well as he could & thanked the Gentlemen for this mark of their attention and indulgence to him'. Their beloved professor lived on for another 25 years, dying aged 79.

Many of Edinburgh's 18th-century clubs and societies, like the Royal Medical Society, started by meeting convivially in taverns and some continued to do so. By 1771, however, the society's membership had grown too big even to be accommodated in the rooms that the managers of the Royal Infirmary had lent to them. In particular the society's library, which had already accumulated a fine collection of books, was too cramped. A committee consisting of Drs William Cullen, John Gregory and Andrew Duncan, together with the four annual presidents, was set up to ask for donations to fund the building of a hall for the society. Duncan was particularly successful in fund-raising, both in this country and abroad. Several donations came from doctors from the American Colonies, who had trained in Edinburgh and were former members of the society. Peter Middleton and John Morgan, both sent their contributions personally to Duncan, who had always taken a special interest in his overseas students.

By 1775 sufficient money had been collected to build a hall for the society. The Royal College of Surgeons of Edinburgh generously made ground available on the west side of Surgeons' Square near the Royal High School, close to the old Surgeons' Hall. Professor Kaufman describes the handsome building, with its portico mounted on four classical columns, as comprising three spacious rooms, one for the weekly meeting, one for the library and collections, and one to be set up as a chemistry laboratory (*fig. 2*).

On 21 April 1775 the senior president, Gilbert Blane, later to be the Fleet's Surgeon, made an eloquent speech in Surgeons' Hall outlining the purpose and aspirations of the society, thanking the fund-raisers, including Duncan, and acknowledging the generosity of the many contributors. Next Dr William Cullen, then President of the Royal College of Physicians of Edinburgh, performed the opening ceremony by laying the foundation stone, which is still preserved in the society's rooms. Dr Cullen was accompanied by the four annual presidents, the whole society, and all the professors, except Alexander Monro *secundus* who excused himself because of the death of a relative.

After the opening ceremony, the professors and the whole company, which must have included Andrew Duncan, sat down to a convivial supper. Neville wrote that 'Old Cullen was very merry and gave us one toast which ought not to be forgotten: May the Professors and Students always live in amity together, and sometimes drink wine together.' Neville and some of his fellow students 'made a snug party at a side table, where we enjoyed ourselves more than we should have done at the great table'. He stayed on till about 2am. Duncan would have been in his element there, on an occasion that nicely combined the serious and the sociable sides of life.

The society held its first meeting in its new home on 26 April 1776, when the senior president, Mr Freer, addressed the professors, subscribers to the building, the members and their visitors. This time the much more confident Sylas Neville, now a junior president, hoped that the building 'would be attended with the success and advantages the utility of the Institution deserves'. At the convivial meeting held afterwards, the students were again honoured by the company of their professors, who were 'very merry'. Neville mentions his great surprise when Professor Joseph Black 'gave us a song'. The jolly party broke up at 5am, with tea and coffee, after which Neville and another gentleman admired the sunrise over Berwick Law from the top of Calton Hill.

Andrew Duncan was elected a junior president of the society in 1767, 1769, 1770 and 1771, and senior president in 1772 and 1773. He was most active in the public and private business, posing medical questions to which the replies might be given in English or Latin. Aphorisms of Hippocrates were popular at the time. After one case report Duncan had set in the 1774-75 session, the unnamed respondent gave a graphic account of the suffering of an unfortunate six month-old child, who developed fever and convulsions after variolation – the scarification with smallpox – containing material, in the days before Jennerian vaccination, which used the milder cowpox. The student's clinical description of post-variolation disease, and his hypotheses regarding its causation and the spread of the infecting agent, would still be acceptable today.

Duncan did not confine his activities in the society to medical matters alone. As president, he was anxious to safeguard the society's property, particularly its library, and to ensure it would always remain in the society's hands. Backed by the professors and many doctors, Duncan presented a charter to the Edinburgh Town Council asking for security of tenure. Unfortunately the University, arguing on rather tenuous grounds, blocked the application. Not one to be easily deterred, Duncan formulated a new plan. He asked the Royal College of Surgeons of Edinburgh, who had feued to the society the ground on which their meetings were held, to grant a disposition of this ground in favour of the presidents of the society in perpetuity, and to obtain for the society the rights and privileges of an incorporated body.

Fortunately one of the two senior lawyers consulted by the society was the Hon. Henry Erskine, Duncan's old friend. Besides, Henry Erskine's elder brother, the 11th Earl of Buchan, just happened to be a regular correspondent of the King. After approval of counsel, a petition was drawn up, agreed by the members of the society, and then lodged with the Secretary of State. Happily this was successfully received, and in 1778 the Medical Society was granted a Charter of Incorporation by George III, so becoming the *Royal Medical Society*. The following year the Royal seal was affixed in Edinburgh and the precious document remains in the society's possession.

Not all the society's affairs were plain sailing. A certain John Brown joined in 1761 and became a junior president in 1773. He promoted the eponymous Brunonian Theory, which suggested that all diseases were caused by an imbalance of excitability and irritability, as opposed to asthenia, atony or exhaustion from over-stimulation. Although the theory was popular for a time, especially in Germany, Cullen warned his students against it. Nonetheless, feelings about the theory ran so high that the society felt obliged to forbid its members from challenging each other to a duel over it! Ultimately the Brunonian theory fell out of favour and Brown died in London aged 52, either over-excited by, or over-exhausted by, whisky and laudanum. Brown's contretemps with Duncan is detailed in chapter XI.

Other contentious issues involved the irresponsible publication of the society's proceedings in the lay press, leaving it open to disrepute and ridicule. Laws were then passed forbidding members or their guests from revealing any of the society's business. In 1779 Duncan, with the society's approval, tried unsuccessfully to get the communications officially published, together with medical and philosophical contributions from around the world. Even when revived in 1814, the idea never really caught on. Perhaps Duncan's own, very popular, *Medical and Philosophical Commentaries* had already stolen the limelight, and any additional contributions from the Royal Medical Society would have been seen as superfluous.

In 1789 an event took place which did not reflect well on the society. The senior president, a Dubliner called Francis Foulke, quarrelled with a Lieutenant Charles Grant, who was stationed in Edinburgh Castle, over a seemingly trivial incident with a dog. Although the army officer would have let the matter pass, Foulke persisted, and unwisely challenged the reluctant Grant to a duel. Foulke did not give Grant time to consult his fellow officers and, seeing no other honourable way out, Grant met Foulke on the beach at Leith, together with their seconds and a surgeon. Two shots were exchanged but missed. Then, after reloading, a third shot was fired. Foulke was mortally wounded, dying a few minutes later 'with a ball in his heart'. Andrew Duncan allowed Foulke's body to be buried in the Duncan family family vault.

By 1818-19 the membership of the society had risen to 84 and the meeting hall in Surgeons' Square was no longer adequate. Initially Duncan, a keen promoter of this building project, objected to any suggestion that the old hall should be demolished or sold to provide funds for a new one. He claimed that the subscriptions raised for the old hall were given with the express purpose of its construction, and that the society's property could not be alienated in this way.

A committee of senior doctors and professors, including the presidents of the two Royal Colleges and, indeed, Duncan himself, then took advice from counsel about the society's building. It concluded that, as there was no longer any written evidence as to the way in which the original subscriptions were to be used, the society was within its rights to dispose of the original hall as it thought fit. Ultimately it decided against an extension of its current building, which was later bought for a generous sum by the Royal College of Surgeons of Edinburgh. In the meantime, the College kindly supported the society by providing temporary accommodation.

Probably Duncan's last significant contribution the society was in 1822, six years before he died. On behalf of the society he drafted a Loyal Address for King George IV, whose famous visit to the capital was stage-managed by Sir Walter Scott. The address was afterwards acknowledged in a letter sent to the senior president from the Home Secretary, Sir Robert Peel.

Following Duncan's death in 1828 the society sent a letter of appreciation to Andrew Duncan Jr, which contained the following:

The Members of this Society have indeed strong and peculiar reason for addressing you on the present occasion, for in him, they are sensible, they have lost their warmest friend and one of their most distinguished associates, accustomed from the commencement of his career to contemplate and earnestly to pursue whatever could conduce to the honor and interests of the University and his Profession. Dr Duncan became the most active and judicious Patron of the Society, and whatever dignity and importance it may since have attained to, must mainly be ascribed to the wise and permanent organization which it received under his friendly surveillance. ...

Much more could be written about the progress of the Royal Medical Society after Duncan's death. The society eventually moved in 1851 to new premises on Melbourne Place (a continuation of George IV Bridge to where it meets the High Street). The elegant rooms there were refurnished and made in the style of a comfortable gentleman's club, with the society's logo embossed on the walls and the framed Royal charter displayed in a glass case. The full-length portrait of Duncan hung at one end of the hall.

One important change, which would have surprised the original 18th-century founders, took place in the early 1960s, when the stuffy, all-male image of the society was at long last transformed by the introduction of women students. On 15 January 1965 the hall was packed with University staff and students of both genders, who heard Professor Dame Sheila Sherlock, doyenne of the study of liver disease, deliver a memorable address on the subject of jaundice. Also, in 1966, the society had to move from Melbourne Place under a compulsory purchase order. It went into temporary accommodation in Hill Square, once again by courtesy of the Royal College of Surgeons of Edinburgh.

The society's library in the early days had been one of its most useful assets to its members. The resources of the Edinburgh University Library were limited and the professorial staff had priority of access. Andrew Duncan Jr, while studying in London in 1794, wrote to his father: 'There is nothing in the way of literature which I miss so much as the library of the Medical Society. Students here have no access to books of value and are therefore, in general, extremely illiterate.' However, by the 20th century, access to current medical literature was readily available in the University and elsewhere, so the society's library was no longer required. Largely now because of lack of space, but also because of the deteriorating condition of the books and the cost of their insurance, it was reluctantly decided, after much consultation, to sell the bulk of the collection. With the assistance of the medical historian and retired paediatrician Dr Douglas Guthrie, the society selected the works which were to be kept, particularly those relating to its early history and also all the bound dissertations. This left a mass of valuable historical medical books, which was sold over six days at Sotheby's in 1969 realising £145,000 (in today's money well in excess of £1.5 million).

The society remained in Hill Square for about ten years. After a successful appeal for funds, led by Professor Sir Derrick Dunlop (*Olim Praeses*, 1926-27), together with the proceeds from the sale of the books, it moved to its present home in the Students' Centre, Bristo Square. There it holds its weekly meetings on Fridays in the winter and spring terms, and continues to maintain the same twin traditions of medical education and friendship that united its founders in 1734.

At the society's annual dinner in 1907, the senior guest Sir William Osler commented on the great number of eminent men who had added lustre to the society since 1737. He said he had not expected to find quite such 'a list of extraordinary distinction'. He went on to say, 'I doubt if there is any other society in the world, except, perhaps, the Royal Society of London, with such a roll of honour'.

A random, but certainly not exhaustive, list of luminaries, not so far mentioned in this chapter, is perhaps invidious, but must include the following men who were members, Fellows, honorary members, office bearers, or otherwise closely associated with the society: Peter Roget of the Thesaurus, Sir Charles Bell of Bell's facial palsy, Richard Bright of Bright's disease of the kidneys, Thomas Addison of Addison's disease of the adrenal glands and Addisonian pernicious anaemia, Sir Robert Christison the expert on poisons, Thomas Hodgkin of Hodgkin's lymphoma, James Syme of Syme's amputation, Sir James Young Simpson of anaesthesia, Lord Lister of antisepsis fame, Joseph Bell astute clinician and prototype for Sherlock Holmes, Sir James Paget of Paget's disease of the bones, Louis Pasteur, honorary member in 1875, Theodor Billroth of gastric surgery and Spencer

Wells of the eponymous surgical forceps, both honorary members in 1880, and James Haig Ferguson who developed the famous obstetrical forceps. In the 20th century, Harvey Cushing, of Cushing's disease of the adrenal glands, was made an honorary member. And on the list might go.

Andrew Duncan Sr assuredly deserves his place in this roll of honour for his work with the Royal Public Dispensary, for his pioneering improvements in mental health, for his devotion to medical education and for his unwavering support for the Royal Medical Society over so many years. He continued to attend the society's meetings at least once a year into his eighties. Duncan's deep interest and concern for the society is demonstrated by his willingness to allow members, who died while students, to be buried in his family vault. Duncan would have been surprised to find innovations such as the admission ladies and the reduced formality of meetings, yet delighted to know that the society, whose Royal charter he promoted and whose rooms he was instrumental in having built, still flourishes today.

Andrew Duncan and the Medico-Chirurgical Society of Edinburgh

The Medico-Chirurgical Society of Edinburgh originated in early May 1821, largely due to the enthusiasm of an ophthalmologist, Dr Robert Hamilton. At a gathering of 53 doctors and surgeons, the following proposal was drawn up and circulated:

> *By subscribing our names to this paper we testify our approval of the objects and Constitution of the Medico-Chirurgical Society of London, and our willingness to co-operate in the formation of a similar Institution in Edinburgh.*

The Medical and Chirurgical Society of London, upon which the Edinburgh society was to be based, had been founded in 1805 by a group of professional gentlemen. They had become dissatisfied with the Medical Society of London (founded 1773 by John Coakley Lettsom) because of the allegedly high-handed tactics of its president. In 1834 the Medico-Chirurgical Society of London became incorporated as the Royal Medical and Chirurgical Society of London. In 1907 it merged with various other societies to become the Royal Society of Medicine.

Notable among the 53 gentlemen who subscribed to the proposal to form an Edinburgh Medico-Chirurgical Society in May 1821, were Robert Hamilton, ophthalmologist, Robert Knox, anatomist (of the Burke and Hare scandal), Joseph Bell and William Wood, both eminent surgeons, William Pulteney Alison, physician, social and public health reformer and later a member of the Edinburgh Cholera Board of Health, both Andrew

Duncan Sr and Jr, John Abercrombie, physician and prolific writer on pathology even before this speciality was recognised, and Alexander Monro *tertius*, anatomist.

All the signatories to the proposal to form the Edinburgh Society were requested to attend a meeting at Oman's Hotel the following Wednesday. Oman's Hotel was to be the venue for meetings of the fledgling society's council for some time to come. At this gathering of the whole of the proposed society, Dr James Buchan, President of the Royal College of Physicians of Edinburgh, was asked to take the chair. The constitution and laws for the society were drawn up and decided upon in May 1821.

On 25 July 1821, Andrew Duncan Sr proposed that office bearers be elected at the next meeting, which was scheduled for 2 August 1821, now regarded as the starting date of the society. Robert Hamilton was graciously thanked 'for the trouble he has taken in framing the laws and promoting the formation of the society'. When the signatories next met on 2 August in Oman's Hotel, Dr Buchan again took the chair. After signing the laws and taking their seats, the gentlemen present elected the following office bearers:

President:	Dr Andrew Duncan Sr
Vice Presidents:	Dr James Home, James Russell Esq.
	Dr John Thomson
Secretaries:	Dr Robert Hamilton
	Dr W. P. Alison
Treasurer:	James Bryce Esq.

Three physicians, including Drs Andrew Duncan Jr and John Abercrombie, and five surgeons, were elected to the council. Dr James Buchan was thanked both for chairing the previous sessions and for allowing the new society to hold some of its meetings in the Physicians' Hall. The influence of Andrew Duncan Sr in securing that venue for the future was also apparent in the council meeting held on 5 September 1821, when he instructed the secretary to request the Royal College of Physicians of Edinburgh 'to have the kindness to grant their Hall for the use of the society at its meetings'.

The constitution and laws were thus drawn up very early on in the society's existence. Its name was confirmed as the Medico-Chirurgical Society of Edinburgh. Its objects were 'to receive communications on Medicine and Surgery, and subjects connected therewith: to converse on medical topics, but without the form of debate or disputation'. (Here it differed from the Royal Medical Society, which rather encouraged scientific argument.) Next, the new society was 'to publish such of the papers submitted to it that were judged to be worthy of public notice'. (Here again it differed from the Royal

Medical Society, which, despite the previous efforts of Andrew Duncan Sr, had decided not to publish its communications.) Finally the new society was 'to promote professional improvement by any other means that may, from time to time, be approved by the society'.

The Medico-Chirurgical Society of Edinburgh was to consist of three grades of member – ordinary members, corresponding members and honorary members. Prospective ordinary members could only be recommended by existing ordinary members. Their names were to be approved by council, then exhibited at two further society meetings and, at the next meeting after that, they were to be balloted upon. A three-quarter majority was required. They must subscribe to the society's laws and pay two guineas on election and one guinea annually thereafter. Corresponding members, most of whom lived out of Edinburgh or even abroad, had to fulfil the above obligations, but were not charged an admission fee. This, therefore, became a very popular category of membership. A meeting of council on 6 April 1824 noted that the number of corresponding members had become so great that it included 'individuals, altogether strangers', and it was suggested that admission to the corresponding membership should be much restricted, 'confining it to men of known eminence'. The honorary members, who required a four-fifths majority at ballot, were to be selected from among those 'gentlemen eminently distinguished for their professional abilities or for their attainments in general science and literature'. The office bearers, as previously described, were to be elected by ballot at the first meeting in December.

The serious purpose of the society

Unlike the other medical societies of which Duncan was a founding member, the Medico-Chirurgical Society of Edinburgh had a much more serious political and academic purpose. From an early stage in its history the Medico-Chirurgical Society of Edinburgh took an interest in medical politics. On 21 May 1821 one of the members, Dr William Brown, later to be a secretary and vice president, produced a pamphlet 'Remarks on the Expediency and Practicability of a Union of the Royal Colleges of Physicians and Surgeons in Edinburgh'. This idea was promptly rebutted by a physician, Dr Henry Dewar, who said that the time was not yet ripe for such a union. Had Dr Brown's recommendation been implemented, it could have resulted in joining the two Edinburgh Colleges together into a body more like the Royal College of Physicians and Surgeons of Glasgow is today.

At the council meeting on 5 September 1821, Andrew Duncan proposed that the meetings should comprise, *seriatim*, minutes of the last meeting, remarkable cases in Edinburgh, medical news, new publications, communications, and, finally, private business, including the election of new members. This last item was later advanced to an earlier stage in the meetings because, by the end of the evening, many members had already left to go home. Later the election of new members was streamlined. Instead of a separate vote being taken on each individual, a list of prospective applicants was given to each of the members present, who simply deleted the name of any candidate to whom he objected, and then returned the completed paper.

At the same council meeting in September 1821 Duncan proposed that, according to the custom of the London Society, 'a Gold Medal be given annually to the Gentleman, who shall communicate to the society, the most important discovery for the improvement of the healing art'. In addition, transactions of the new society's communications were published. In this connection there was probably a major influence by the society's first president, who remained keen to see the transactions printed.

In 1824 the first volume of *Transactions* appeared. It ran to 725 pages and covered the first two sessions of the society's existence. Adam Black of Edinburgh printed 750 copies at a cost of 18 shillings each. The frontispiece contains the words: 'Printed for Adam Black & Thos. Ireland & Co.; and Longman, Hurst, Rees, Orme, Brown & Green, and T. & G. Underwood, London'. With publishers both in Edinburgh and London, an extensive circulation must have been anticipated. The first volume of *Transactions* contained a list of members – two honorary members, 85 ordinary members and 107 corresponding members – showing how rapidly the society had grown in its first three years. The second volume of *Transactions*, covering the third and fourth sessions in 435 pages, had a print run of 500 copies and appeared in 1826. In 1829 the third and last volume came out, covering the communications of the fifth and sixth sessions in 676 pages. This time Adam Black produced only 300 copies, and the price per copy had risen to £2-16/-. Subsequently the society's reports were published in the *Monthly Journal of Medical Sciences*, the *Edinburgh Medical and Surgical Journal* and its successor the *Edinburgh Medical Journal* until 1880. Thereafter the society resumed publication of a *New Series* of *Transactions* in 20 volumes up to 1901.

The contents of the early volumes of *Transactions* give a fascinating insight into the interests of the medical profession at the 'cutting edge' of its activities during the first quarter of the 19th century. The scrutineers of material submitted to the society for publication certainly insisted that the papers be of a satisfactory standard. A minute of the council meeting of 23 October 1824 commented on the quality of some of the papers submitted, noting that some had to be returned as unsuitable, or with a request that they be shortened. Indeed, two such papers criticised were by Andrew Duncan Jr.

One of the notable early papers published was 'Contributions to the Pathology of the Heart' by John Abercrombie. This covered aspects of inflammation, organic affections, rupture and displacement of the heart, all delivered at a time when the University did not yet have a chair in pathology. Abercrombie's case reports included children and adults with acute rheumatic heart disease, with or without pericarditis, and one patient with probable tubercular pericarditis. He also described cysts of the left auricle, lesions suggesting rheumatic valvular nodules and vegetations, an infant with a ventricular septal defect, an adult with aortic dissection and ventricular rupture, and another with right heart enlargement or displacement due to a lung abscess. Most reports were supported by autopsy evidence. Besides, John Abercrombie later contributed work on tuberculosis, as did William P. Alison and the surgeon William Wood.

George Ballingall, Regius Professor of Military Surgery, delivered a paper on 'Remarks on the Cranium of a man who died of Syphilis'. During his time as the society's vice president, James Russell, Professor of Clinical Surgery of the University of Edinburgh, also reported on disease of the cranial bones.

Other contributors described yet more cases of carditis and possible valvular disease of the heart, again with descriptions of post-mortem specimens; diseases of the oesophagus, trachea and lungs, all strangely lumped together in the same section; gastrointestinal maladies, including those of children; and disorders of the central nervous system. This last group included a description of a 'native assistant' suffering from phrenitis and congestion of the brain, whose life was reputedly saved by the prompt action of a cavalry surgeon in the service of the Honourable East India Company, who venesected first the temporal veins and then the radial vein.

Among the medical papers, Robert Hamilton reported on a hysterical 'fever' among the inmates of the Magdalene Asylum. A description of Yellow Fever in Barbados, and another discussing fevers among British troops in the Burma Campaign, were both submitted by military surgeons. There were two reports on syphilis and five on therapeutics. One of those in the therapeutics section was by Thomas Anderson, Inspector of Shipping and a member of the Medical Board, Port of Spain, Trinidad, who described the application of boiled tobacco leaves to relieve the muscle spasms of tetanus.

Three interesting papers on poisoning included one on arsenic, which was used at the time by certain criminals to dispatch their victims. The author, Sir Robert Christison, was then the undisputed authority on the forensic investigation of poisoning.

Andrew Duncan Jr, then Professor of Materia Medica at the University and also president of both the Royal College of Physicians of Edinburgh and the Royal Society of Edinburgh, wrote at length on a fatal 'Case of Diffuse

Inflammation of the Cellular Substance ...' in a woman who presumably suffered from cellulitis of her side with abscess formation. This was accompanied, as usual, by a post-mortem report. In an equally lengthy sequel to this paper, Andrew Duncan Jr described several patients with sepsis following venesection and other puncture injuries, including one inflicted by a meat hook.

Surgical contributions covered a wide field. A surgeon from Hull reported successfully using silkworm gut to suture together the ends of divided arteries. Military surgeons described gunshot wounds and the frequent occurrence of gangrene in their hospitals during the Peninsular War. Other contributions covered subjects as disparate as disease and injury to the cranial bones, lingual tumours, aspects of ophthalmic surgery, the emergency treatment of hernias, particularly one strangulated umbilical hernia, the removal of bladder calculi, dislocation of the hip, and a case of a loose cartilage in the knee, beautifully illustrated by Dr Robert Knox the anatomist.

The entries in the 'Physiology' section included two by Dr John Davy, one on the effect of the sun's rays on the human body, and a second, curiously, on the apparent acquisition of weight by the body when immersed in a water bath. Dr J. C. B. Williams, in a paper on respiration and animal heat, correctly postulated that 'the change effected on the blood in the lungs consists in the acquisition of oxygen and the loss of carbonic acid'. Professor J. W. Turner attempted to explain in his presentation the cause of the first and second heart sounds heard on auscultation of the chest.

Among the papers in the 'Pathology' section were a further two by Dr John Davy, the first describing his observations on the loss of heat from the body after death and a second recommending the use of sulphurous acid as an antiseptic. Dr George Kelly of Leith quaintly reported to the society 'On the appearances observed on the dissection of two out of three individuals found dead in the immediate vicinity of Leith on Sunday morning of 4 November last, supposed to have perished in the severe storm of the preceding night, with some reflections on the Pathology of the Brain'.

Early in the society's history, both the *Edinburgh Medical and Surgical Journal* and the *Edinburgh Medical Journal* published material other than case histories. In the first volume of the former, in 1805, there appeared under 'Medical Intelligence', accounts of the Surgical Academy in Berlin, the Fever Institution in London, the anti-variolous power of vaccination, and regulations for improving the situation of medical officers in the Navy and Army. Under the military regulations were reported the rates of pay and pensions for medical officers, the number of surgical assistants required for ships of the line and in hospital ships, and the qualifications recommended for surgeons' mates.

Reports on Public Health matters also appeared in the early publications. In 1821 the redoubtable health pioneer Dr William P. Alison produced interesting statistical material: 'Two Tables; to be continued Quarterly: the one containing a list of Diseases of the Patients admitted to the New Town Dispensary in the last quarter; the other, a list of the Deaths in Practice of that Institution, with the Ages and Diseases of the Dead: accompanied with a short Statement of the purposes to be served by such a Register, if accurately kept for some time together.'

A later contribution published by Dr Alison was 'Observations, with Tables, on the Probabilities of Life'. Inevitably this type of research was enthusiastically pursued by the burgeoning life assurance societies of the period. During the 1840s a Dr Begbie published his 'Observations on the Mortality of the Scottish Widows' Fund and Life-Assurance Society from 1815 till 1845'. That particular society was founded initially to make provision for the widows of military men killed in the Napoleonic Wars. Dr Begbie continued to produce and publish life insurance statistics up to 1860. In 1853, the aforementioned Dr Christison had published similar material from the Standard Assurance Company.

Reports from institutions, often with health recommendations, were featured early on in the *Transactions*. For example, in 1824 the *Edinburgh Medical and Surgical Journal* printed in full a report from the Select Committee of the House of Commons on the State Penitentiary at Milbank, which included a discussion on the use of lemon juice in the prevention of scurvy among the inmates.

From 1847 and even into the 1880s, the society continued to debate the relative merits of ether and chloroform, and the dangers inherent in both forms of anaesthesia. In no. 52 Queen Street, Edinburgh, on the evening of 4 November 1847, James Young Simpson had famously demonstrated to his family and some friends the effects of the inhalation of chloroform on himself and his two assistants, George Keith and Matthews Duncan. Only six days later, on 10 November 1847, Simpson addressed the Medico-Chirurgical Society of Edinburgh with the news of his ground-breaking discovery of the anaesthetic effects of chloroform and an account of it as a substitute for sulphuric ether in surgery and midwifery. In his valedictory address to the society in 1921, on the centenary of the society's inauguration, the president, Dr F. M. Caird, wrote of this event: '... there was never a more epoch making night in our annals than in November 1847 when Simpson produced his historic paper amidst the applause and wonder of a crowded audience.'

Of course such innovations were not without their critics, and in 1847 Dr James Pickford of Brighton wrote to the *Edinburgh Medical and Surgical Journal* about ether anaesthesia:

Pain during operations is, in the majority of cases, even desirable: its prevention or annihilation is, for the most part, hazardous to the patient. In the lying-in chamber nothing is more true than this: pain is the mother's safety, its absence her destruction. Yet are there those bold enough to administer the vapour of aether even at this critical juncture, forgetting it has been ordered that 'in sorrow shall she bring forth'. ...

In 1847 the society held another debate on anaesthesia, largely triggered by a paper entitled 'A note on a case of death during the administration of chloroform', read to the society by Mr Chiene. Problems had often occurred in patients under anaesthesia and it had been noted frequently that the pulse could still be felt despite the cessation of respiration. Some of these patients had been successfully resuscitated either by Sylvester's or Howard's method of artificial respiration. Much of the debate then correctly centred on the fundamental importance of maintaining a free airway in the unconscious patient by tongue retraction, and keeping the air passages free of 'copious mucus, inhaled vomitus, false teeth and sweetmeats'. In his summing up of the debate, and obviously keeping an open mind about this novel anaesthetic, the president expressed satisfaction that the title of Mr Chiene's paper had been '... death during the administration of chloroform', rather than, as it might have been, '... another death from chloroform'.

Dr Andrew Duncan Sr, who had been such a leading light in the formation of the society, held the office of president until late in 1823. On 3 December 1823 he was warmly thanked by the newly-elected president of the 4th Session, Dr James Russell, for his 'valuable services' to the society. The new vice president of the society for the 1824-25 session was Andrew Duncan Jr.

The society was peripatetic in its earlier years. The minutes record that meetings were held in 19 and 91 Princes Street, 65 George Street, and 18 Hill Street. Indeed, in his valedictory address to the society in 1874, Dr P. D. Handyside quotes no less than 13 different venues over those 50 years. These included two addresses in Hill Street, the committee room of the Antiquarian Society in the Royal Institution (later the Royal Scottish Academy), various hotels and private houses in the New Town, Cay & Black's Saloon at 45 George Street, Freemasons' Hall at 98 George Street, Smith & Philpot's Saloon, also on George Street, and a photographer's saloon at 60 Princes Street. The Royal College of Physicians of Edinburgh was also a frequent venue, thanks to the efforts of Andrew Duncan Sr as the society's president and the generosity of the College's president, James Buchan. After selling the George Street Hall, and before moving into no. 9 Queen Street, the College was itself homeless from 1843-46. During this time the society wandered from one address to another until the College again came to the rescue by granting the society temporary accommodation in the apartments it rented at 119 George Street.

Besides its academic and teaching activities, the society continued to play its part in medical politics. In the 1850s Scottish-trained and qualified doctors, including those who were members or Fellows of the Scottish Royal Medical Colleges, were still being denied the right to practise in other parts of the United Kingdom, '... except under the condition of additional examinations and expenses ...'. This seemed particularly unfair because there was no reciprocal bar to English-trained doctors practising in Scotland. Indeed doctors qualified in Scotland regarded themselves as better trained than some of those from other parts of the United Kingdom. In May 1853 the Medico-Chirurgical Society of Edinburgh laid a petition before both Houses of Parliament expressing their view that the training and qualifications received by them in Scotland, 'which are considered a sufficient legal security for their fitness to practise in Edinburgh, ought also to be considered in London and Dublin'.

In the Medical Act 1858 many of the grievances of the Scottish doctors evaporated, with the firm establishment of the General Medical Council as the regulatory body. Improperly trained men were barred from practising medicine, the large number of licensing bodies was reduced, and there was greater equality accorded between the English, Scottish and Irish systems of licensing to practice. Doubtless the input of the Scottish universities, the Scottish Royal medical colleges, and societies like the Medico-Chirurgical Society of Edinburgh, all played their part in bringing about these welcome changes.

Fifty years after the society's inauguration, the then president, Dr Handyside, in his valedictory address of 1874, remarked, 'The objects and characteristic features of our society have undergone since its foundation no change; and time-honoured, these testify to the sagacity and far-sightedness of its Founders'. Doubtless Dr Handyside would be delighted to know that the society still exists, albeit in a rather different format.

The late Dr J. J. C. (Jack) Cormack, a fondly remembered Edinburgh general practitioner, gave an amusing after-dinner speech to the Medico-Chirurgical Society of Edinburgh in 1997 when he spoke of the way the society's business was conducted in the 1960s and 70s. He had been a secretary and later president of the society, which he had joined in 1964. Then the meetings consisted of formal medical lectures, discussions and symposia. The president, speaker and the president's guests at the traditional pre-meeting dinner, all wore formal dress. Not infrequently the president's party, dinner-jacketed and obviously well dined and wined, would delay the advertised start of the meeting by arriving late. Dr Cormack caused some consternation among the senior members of the society, who thought he was a rather 'dangerous radical', by suggesting that this degree of formality should be abandoned. Happily a more relaxed form of meeting now prevails.

Dr Cormack also recalled the difficulties that beset the society in the early 1970s when, after a rise in the annual subscription rate, there followed such a spate of resignations that the very existence of the society seemed endangered. A working party was set up and consideration given to a previous suggestion that there should be an amalgamation of all the Edinburgh medical societies. Happily, however, with better publicity and less formality, the society's fortunes were revived.

A decade later, when Dr Cormack was president (1980-82), less formal and more general topics were inserted into the programme. Titles of the papers then included 'Medicine in Uganda', 'Health Care in Europe', 'Nelson's Eye' and 'Hypnosis and Acupuncture'. Dr Cormack's own very personal contribution at that time was entitled 'Medical Misadventures', and he recalled, self-deprecatingly, that the society's minutes recorded that 'Dr Cormack gave a beautifully illustrated account of his various medical problems in such far flung corners of the world as Labrador, Nyasaland and Corstorphine!'

The society now meets on six Friday evenings a year, starting in October, when a paper is read on a medical or non-medical topic, either by one of its own members or by an invited speaker. One joint meeting, combining a talk and a dinner, takes place every year, either in Edinburgh or Glasgow, with the Medico-Chirurgical Society of Glasgow. The Edinburgh Clinical Club also joins forces annually for a meeting with the society. Dr Handyside would have been surprised to find that female doctors are now admitted as members. Indeed, the more recent introduction of the spouses or partners of members was very controversial, but they are now welcomed to the meetings, which often include a popular social content. For instance, an annual dinner, a Burns Supper, and an outing, regularly form part of the society's programme during the year.

Despite these changes and innovations to suit 21st-century needs, Dr Andrew Duncan Sr, and his son too, both of whom played such an important role in the early days of the society, would surely be pleased to know that their infant society continues to flourish today.

Main sources

Caird (1921-22), pp. 4-6.
Cameron (1971), p. 1.
Chalmers and Tröhler (2000), pp. 238-42.
Comrie (1932).
Cormack (1997).
Council Minute Book of the Medico-Chirurgical Society of Edinburgh (1821), pp. 1-59.
Cozens-Hardy, B. (ed.) (1950).
Craig (1883-84), pp. 38-49.
Craig (1976).
Grant (1883), p. 266.
Gray (1952).
Handyside (1874), pp. 769-87, 895-912, 1004-1020, 1092-1105.
Hutchison (1913), pp 20-30.
Jenkinson (1993), pp. 12-13 and pp. 142-43.
Kaufman (1997), pp. 119-29.
Kaufman (2003b), pp. 56-63.

Laws and List of Members, Medico-Chirurgical Society of Edinburgh, (1821).
McCrae (2003), pp. 2-11.
McElroy (1951).
Minute Book of the Medico-Chirurgical Society of Edinburgh (1821-24).
Passmore (2001).
Risse (2005), ch. 2, 'Debate and Experiments. The Royal Medical Society of Edinburgh', pp. 67-104, and ch. 3, 'The Royal Medical Society v. Campbell Denovan: Brunonianism, the press, and the medical establishment', pp. 105-32.
Royal Medical Society, Bound Dissertations, 4, (1774-75).
Transactions of the Medico-Chirurgical Society of Edinburgh (1824), p. 1, *et seq.*

COAT OF ARMS OF THE
MEDICO-CHIRURGICAL SOCIETY
(COURTESY OF MEDICO-CHIRURGICAL SOCIETY)

CHAPTER IX

The Royal Caledonian Horticultural Society

CONNIE BYROM AND JOHN CHALMERS

The nineteenth century promises greatly to increase the reputation of
Scotland for gardeners and gardening ... from the stimulus of the
Caledonian Horticultural Society which, by well devised competitory
exhibition and premiums has excited a most laudable emulation among
practical gardeners of every class.

John Claudius Loudon,
Encyclopaedia of Gardening (1826, 4th edition)

The founding of the society

Reference has been made in chapter I to Andrew Duncan's life-long interest
in gardening. In 1809, inspired by the establishment of the Horticultural
Society of London five years earlier by Sir Joseph Banks and other enthusiastic horticulturists, Duncan directed his energies to establishing a similar
society in Edinburgh.[1] By then he was a veteran campaigner for good causes
and had a wide circle of influential friends and associates who could be
relied upon for support, many of whom had large estates and legions of
gardeners – vital ingredients to the success of this project.

The Caledonian Horticultural Society minutes record that on 25 November 1809, a meeting took place at the home of Thomas Dickson, nursery-
man, to discuss the formation of a Horticultural Society in Scotland. Among
those present were Duncan and his friend Patrick Neill. It was agreed to
circulate various 'skilful professional gardeners and zealous amateurs',
telling of the proposals, and inviting those interested to attend the hall of the
Royal College of Physicians in George Street. The meeting duly took place
on the 5 December, chaired by Duncan, when the 17 present 'unanimously
resolved to constitute themselves into a society for encouraging and improving the cultivation of the best fruits, of the most choice flowers, and of the
most useful culinary vegetables'.[2]

Dr Duncan told the meeting that 'he had received letters, from several
noblemen and gentlemen, and from a considerable number of professional

gardeners, accepting offers made to them to become honorary, ordinary, or corresponding members' – proof that a lot of preparatory work had already taken place. A council was formed with Walter Nicol and Patrick Neill (1776-1851) agreeing to become joint secretaries. Nicol died soon after and Neill became the principal secretary for the first 40 years of the society's existence. The Earl of Dalkeith was elected president and the first vice presidents were Sir James Hall MP,[3] Dr Rutherford (Professor of Botany), Dr Coventry (Professor of Agriculture) and Mr Alexander Dickson Hunter of Blackness. Twelve council members, consisting of an equal number of professional and amateur gardeners, were elected.

Sir James Hall said 'the thanks of the Meeting were unanimously voted to Dr Duncan Sr for the zeal and activity displayed by him in promoting this institution, and for the very suitable manner in which he had conducted the business of the day'.

The purpose of the society was 'the improvement of horticulture in all its branches'. Noblemen or gentlemen were invited to be honorary members; they were exempted from paying a subscription. Candidates for ordinary or corresponding membership had to be proposed by two members and then elected by ballot. The annual subscription was one guinea or ten guineas for life membership.

From the outset the society flourished. By 1818 there were 42 honorary members, 227 ordinary members and 148 corresponding members. By 1829 this had increased to 66 honorary, 700 ordinary and 270 corresponding members. By then King George IV was patron, and his two brothers, the Dukes of York and Clarence, were among the honorary members, as were many aristocrats from elsewhere in Britain and Europe. (After 1815 honorary membership was restricted to individuals living outwith Scotland.)

Among the ordinary members were many whose names have appeared elsewhere in this book, including James Hamilton Jr, Henry Cockburn, Francis Jeffrey, Sir Robert Preston, Henry Erskine, Gilbert Innes and Henry Raeburn. Andrew Duncan Jr became a member in 1813 and was rapidly involved in committee work. The corresponding members included Duncan's other sons, Alexander and John, who were then serving officers with the Native Infantry in Bengal. One of the honorary members was Duncan's physician friend in London, John Coakley Lettsom, who, like Duncan himself, was a keen horticulturist and apiarist. In a diary entry in April 1814 he wrote: 'On the 20th, sent a letter to Dr Duncan, of Edinburgh, with thanks to the Horticultural Society for my admission as an honorary member of that society. My letter contained various horticultural remarks, particularly on mangold [sic] wurzel, turnips and seakale.'[4] Lettsom, who had an absorbing interest in spreading the cultivation of mangel wurzel, requested seeds from an associate. 'The reason I ask you for seed is on account of my friend Professor Duncan of Edinburgh having required seed of me, as he means to cultivate it freely.'[5]

The links with the Royal College of Physicians

The society met quarterly on a Tuesday. In its early days it met in the hall of the Royal College of Physicians in George Street (now The Dome), no doubt due to the influence of Duncan. In 1811 the secretary was directed to thank the Royal College of Physicians for permitting meetings to be held in the hall of the College, and at the same time to offer to keep the garden at the back of the hall in good order without expense to the College.

The appreciation was expressed again in a letter which exists in the College library, from Patrick Neill to the president of the Royal College of Physicians, Dr James Buchan, on 5 December 1821.

> *Sir*
>
> *I am directed by the Council of the Caledonian Horticultural Society to beg that you will accept the sincere thanks of the Society for the permission of holding their most numerous meetings in the Hall of the Royal College of Physicians.*
>
> *They also desire me to request that the College will accept of a few apples and pears which accompany this letter, and which have been this day produced in competition for prizes.*
>
> *They have given directions to their Treasurer to keep the ground around the Hall in the best possible order. They are sorry, however, to say, that all their attempts to get beautiful exotic shrubs to grow in a situation necessarily so much exposed to smoke, have been fruitless.*
>
> *They have given directions for a plentiful supply of crocuses, sea pinks etc. and if any of the gentlemen belonging to the College will have the goodness to point out articles which they think will beautify the ground they may rest assured that due attention will be paid to their recommendations.*

The last meeting in the Royal College of Physicians was held in 1831, its rooms by then being too small for the society which moved to rented rooms in the Waterloo Hotel on Regent Bridge (now the Balmoral Hotel).

Andrew Duncan's role in the society

Duncan's leadership lasted 19 years until his death. He started as an ordinary member of the council, but was almost immediately elected vice president. One of the four vice presidents retired annually in rotation, but in Duncan's case an exception was made and he was appointed permanent vice president. In this capacity he chaired most of the meetings until a few months before his death. From the outset he took an active part in the affairs of the society, presenting a number of papers which were published in the *Memoirs of the Caledonian Society* which appeared in four volumes between 1814 and 1829. Among Duncan's subjects were 'Observations on the preparation of Soporific Medicines from common garden lettuce'[6] (see page 97) and several follow-up papers on the same subject.

His most interesting paper was 'Observations on the propagation by cuttings of the Original, the Mother, the Oslin or the Bur-knot Apple tree'.[7] In this he attributes the introduction of fruit trees into Scotland to the ecclesiastics of St Andrews. The bur-knot tree was one of several names by which it was known. It was characterised by multiple burs on its branches which Duncan demonstrated were potential roots. If a branch containing a bur was planted in soil, it readily took root and reproduced the tree. If planted in the spring it blossomed the same year and produced fruit in the autumn. He had confirmed this in his own garden, and his grandfather, Professor William Vilant of St Andrews, had also demonstrated this potential. A drawing of his specimen was reproduced in the paper. Duncan was awarded a silver medal for his experiments.

From the start Duncan appreciated having the then youthful Patrick Neill as secretary and there is no doubt that the early success of the society was due largely to the joint partnership of Duncan and Neill.

Patrick Neill, first secretary to the society

Patrick Neill, a printer to trade and responsible for the printing of many of Duncan's writings, was a keen naturalist. His company printed the *Encyclopaedia Britannica,* to which he also contributed the entry on gardening. Such was his personality that his business premises in 10 Fishmarket Close was a meeting place for scientists and men of learning. Dr Andrew Duncan said of him that 'his superior knowledge in every branch of natural history is universally admitted by all who have science enough to appreciate that knowledge'. Henry Cockburn said that he was 'a useful citizen, a most intelligent florist, and one of the few defenders of our architectural relics'. Neill was secretary of the Wernerian Natural History Society throughout its existence and vice president of the Botanical Society of Edinburgh, which was founded in 1836. He kept a menagerie and an exotic garden at his home at Canonmills which overlooked the loch created there by the mill dam – a feature which has long disappeared. The loch was necessary to provide water for the daily watering of his 2000 pot plants. The ornithological illustrators, John James Audubon and Thomas Bewick, were fascinated by his 'little paradise'.[8]

Neill is also remembered as the individual responsible for the creation of the East Princes Street Gardens on the site of the Nor' Loch, lying at the foot of the Castle rock, which had been drained in 1820. In 1818 Duncan had suggested plans for this area. In a letter to the Lord Provost, Kincaid Mackenzie, he wrote that 'it has remained for nearly half a century in the state of a morass often yielding putrid and noxious effluvia'. He suggested establishing fruit and flower markets and creating a pond for rearing ducks and geese and perhaps some swans. The bleaching ground could be continued by hanging the linen from ropes instead of laying it on the ground. Neill had more realistic plans which were accepted. Between 1829 and 1831 he organised and supervised the planting of many thousands of trees and shrubs which transformed the polluted foetid marsh into one of Edinburgh's most attractive features. Such was his persuasive power that donors – no doubt members of the Caledonian Horticultural Society – contributed their plants freely and the cost to the Edinburgh Town Council of the entire planting was less than £5.

The annual dinner

No society with which Duncan was associated could exist without at least an annual dinner, and true to type he commenced a tradition of holding a dinner to follow the annual general meeting in September, the first being held in 1810 in MacEwan's large room.

On 14 September 1813, 50 members dined; fruit presented for prizes by the members provided 'a very ample and elegant dessert'. A large pot with a growing vine of Black Hamburg grapes from the Duke of Buccleuch's garden at Dalkeith was placed at the head of the table. These dinners became very popular and the home-grown desserts remained a feature. Members paid six shillings and sixpence to dine.

On 4 September 1823, the 14th anniversary dinner was celebrated in Oman's Waterloo Tavern, when more than 120 members sat down to dine. The table was tastefully ornamented with living plants and bouquets of flowers. Among the plants were several vines growing in flower pots and bearing fine bunches of grapes from Dalkeith Garden and several balsams of uncommon size and beauty from the Royal Botanic Garden. Considering the very unfavourable season, the dessert was ample and of excellent quality. It was composed of more than 200 dishes, of which about 80 were grapes, 40 of peaches, nectarines, apricots and plums, 30 of apples and pears, and 20 of gooseberries, with 22 melons and 10 pineapples.

At the dinner in 1827 in Gibbs Waterloo Tavern, 150 attended and the dessert consisted of 288 dishes of fruit 'affording most decisive proof of the excellence of the practical gardeners of Scotland'.

Duncan's discourses

Duncan reported the progress of the society in a series of annual discourses delivered at the December meeting. Some of these were published in the society's *Memoirs* and others were printed and distributed by Duncan.[9] In his discourses, Duncan reported the winner of the year's gold medal and outlined the progress of the society during the year, commenting on the deaths of notable members. He then introduced his ideas about future development, often at great length – justifying Cockburn's criticism (see page 29). Two recurring themes dominate his discourses; one, a very reasonable ambition for an Experimental Garden and the progress, or otherwise, towards its fulfilment; the other, his plan for the establishment of a Chair of Horticulture. This is ventilated in almost all of his discourses with ever increasing elaboration. Duncan wanted it to be a Regius Chair because 'the same narrow-minded monopolizing corporation spirit, which has opposed the introduction of almost every new Professorship' would be against it. This refers to Edinburgh Town Council which, as Patrons of the University, had frustrated Duncan's plans for a Chair of Medical Jurisprudence (see chapter VI).

The particular value of the Chair of Horticulture for the benefit of students of divinity was repeated in nearly every discourse with ever increasing absurdity. They 'might exhibit to their parishioners an example worthy of imitation from the glebe and garden attached to the manse, and thus spread horticulture to every corner of Scotland, and contribute to the health and happiness of the clergy'. It would 'contribute to the longevity of the sedentary Divine and furnish healthful viands to his table. The daily boiling of the Clergyman's pot for necessary culinary purpose, may, at the same time ripen his grapes and figs without any expense of fuel. It would improve the British Empire on which the sun never sets.' If he succeeded in the establishment of the chair, he would 'consider myself as having bestowed a boon upon the Church of Scotland which will be remembered with gratitude long after (to use the words of the admirable Shakespeare) *Duncan is in his grave*'. References to the Chair of Horticulture and its benefit to the clergy reached such a pitch of fatuity that the council of the society refused to allow his last discourse of 1825, which Duncan had printed at his own expense, to be distributed. Perhaps Duncan's pride in his longevity, which must have been unusual at that time, coupled with his undoubted sense of duty, persuaded him to continue with his responsibilities longer than it was wise, just as it had with his teaching.

Research encouraged by the society

In his first discourse to the society in December 1811, Duncan made a plea that the society should support experimental activity:

> *Discoveries are chiefly to be made by judicious experiment. And it is by the test of experience alone, that the suggestions of genius can be duly appreciated, can be confirmed, or refuted. It is therefore an object of great importance, not only to encourage a zeal for experiment by proper rewards, but to recommend it by example, and to put the alleged results of the experiments of others to future trials under our own inspection.*

Research was encouraged by the award of medals or premiums. The society did not seem short of money in its early days, for silver and gold medals and other silver items were awarded freely.[10] During the society's first year, 52 were awarded for fruit, flower and vegetable growing, including several 'to the ladies for their excellence in the preparation of currant wine' – an object of great importance at a time when 'the tyranny of war' had cut off supplies from France. Ladies were not then entitled to be members, but spouses and family members were allowed to submit entries on their behalf. In 1810 there were 19 entries of home-produced wine (16 currant and three gooseberry) which were judged by the committee in MacEwan's Tavern, Royal Exchange. The one marked '*vino petite curas*' was voted the best, and when the sealed letter was opened was found to belong to Mrs Duncan, Adam Square.[11] Elizabeth Duncan was successful again in 1821, when in her eightieth year. On this occasion she was awarded a silver wine label in the form of a cross.[12]

So popular was currant wine at that period that it was produced in commercial quantities. George Montgomery of Princes Street was awarded a medal by the society for the production of 866½ gallons in 1814, on which he had to pay duty.

Ladies were given a further opportunity to participate in the activities of the society by the introduction of prizes for the best paintings of botanical objects.

In 1823 Andrew Duncan was awarded a silver medal for the best summer apples from his garden on St Leonards Hill. On another occasion he wrote an undated letter to the president of the society, accompanied with a few gooseberries and apples on the branches on which they grew. The letter characteristically took the form of a poem:

> *While veteran Gardeners strive to gain the prize,*
> *By all the beauty Flora's aid supplies,*

Permit, good Sir, a raw but old recruit,
In place of Flowers, to send a gift of Fruit;
His full sized Berries, fit for present use,
May serve as tasteful sauce for any goose;
His Apples will, he trusts, no discord bring,
Midst brethren met to sing, 'God save the King'.

On 6 September 1826, Duncan sent to the meeting ten very fine specimens of apple, being the last produce of his garden at St Leonards Hill, the site now being required for public improvements. They were accompanied by a letter bearing this quotation from Virgil:[13]

Quod potui puero, sylvestri arbore lecta, aurea mala decem misi.
[Ten golden apples have I sent my boy, all that I could.]

The Royal charter and the founding of the Experimental Garden

In 1821 Duncan proposed the formation of a committee to apply for a Royal charter for the society, and this was granted in 1824. He was well practiced in this procedure, having already obtained charters for the Medical Society, the Lunatic Asylum and the Public Dispensary. In his discourse of 1824, in gratitude for the award of the Royal charter, he suggested to his audience, 'Let us then, Gentlemen, with united hearts, send up our sincere, though silent prayers to Heaven, for His blessings on our truly patriotic Sovereign'. Duncan had enormous regard for the dissolute King George IV, which was not universally held.

The effort to obtain an Experimental Garden was a recurrent preoccupation of the early minutes of the society and Duncan's discourses. Various sites were considered, including a plot adjacent to the Palace of Holyroodhouse. In 1816 gold and silver medals were offered and awarded as prizes for the best plans for an Experimental Garden, even though no site was yet available. Committees were set up to look into the matter; one, consisting of the Duke of Buccleuch, the Earl of Wemyss, Sir George Mackenzie and Andrew Duncan, to seek government aid for the purpose. This was finally successful in 1824 when the society was proud to acknowledge that the government had purchased a piece of ground and granted it to the society on a 70-year lease.

The site, consisting of eight Scotch or ten English acres on Herd's Hill, was situated immediately to the south of the recently relocated Royal Botanic Garden at Inverleith.[14] It was considered that the juxtaposition of the two gardens would be of mutual value in sharing knowledge and facilities. The funds of the society were sufficient to pay for the rent, but for the development of the site more money was required. It was decided that members should be invited to buy shares at 20 guineas. The response was gratifying; many members, including all the Duncan family members, bought one or more shares. Those who did not would pay one guinea annually, in addition to their society subscription, to support the garden, and visitors would be charged an admission fee. Thus money was obtained which enabled the levelling of the site, the building of surrounding walls and a house for the head gardener, designed by the leading architect William Playfair (who was a member). The construction of glasshouses had to be delayed because of the heavy taxation on glass. Trees, shrubs and seeds were contributed by numerous individuals, nurseries and organisations from near and far, including donations from the Marquis of Hastings, the Governor General of Bengal and Duncan's son, Lt Col. Alexander Duncan in India. The first donation, in February 1825, was made by Andrew Duncan of fruit trees from his own garden. The Horticultural Society of London sent uncommon fruit trees and more than 50 different types of strawberries.

In his discourse of 1820, Duncan had said:

> *My zeal for the immediate commencement of our Experimental Garden is not altogether disinterested. I may venture … to affirm that now, far advanced in life, I cannot expect to obtain from it any addition to wealth, to fame, or honour, but I have no doubt that it would materially promote both my health and happiness. Even now, anticipating what may happen, and in the hopes of being able to walk in a Royal Garden at Edinburgh, where I may witness experiments conducted by the Caledonian Horticultural Society, I enjoy in imagination, pleasures perhaps superior to those of sense. Shall I ask, gentlemen, in the words of Horace;*[15]
>
> > *An me ludit amabilis insania?*
> > *Videor pios errare per lucos.*
> > [Or is some delightful madness sporting with me?
> > I fancy myself wandering through sacred groves.]

The Garden would give professional gardeners the opportunity to witness the effects of different modes of culture, and of various kinds of manure on culinary vegetables. They would be able to buy, at the cheapest rate, best quality seeds of new and rare vegetables and scions of every variety of fruit for grafting. 'Thus the Experimental Garden might confer a lasting blessing on the British Empire.'

When Duncan chaired the first meeting in the newly built council and committee room within the Experimental Garden on 15 June 1826, he must have been very proud to see the fulfilment of his dream.

Celebration

On July 1830 the society held a 'promenade with music and dessert' to celebrate its 20th anniversary and the establishment of the Experimental Garden. It had been due to take place on 3 July, but had to be delayed until the 15th because of the death of the society's Royal patron, King George IV. It was eventually held on the green in front of the vinery in the Experimental Garden. A large tent measuring 130 feet by 29 feet was erected, with staging to hold the exotic plants. Opposite, a smaller tent was provided for a military band, but as the Royal funeral had not yet taken place, etiquette prevented procuring such a band and the committee were obliged to hire performers from the orchestra of the Caledonian Theatre. Sufficient flooring was laid down for two quadrilles. A dozen policemen under a sergeant were stationed at the gates and around the fences to prevent intrusion.

From 1-3pm the company arrived chiefly in carriages. Among the lady patronesses were the Dowager Lady of Torphichen, the Countess of Hope, Lady Gray, Lady Charlotte Hope, Lady Keith and Lady Jardine. The patrons included Lord Gray, the Lord President, the Lord Justice Clerk, Lord Pitmilly, Lord Cringeltie, Lord Gillies, and some lesser dignitaries. Tickets had been sold to 228 ladies and 189 gentlemen, and about 14 tickets were sold at the gate to persons of known respectability. The display of fine flowering plants, many supplied by Patrick Neill and the Royal Botanic Garden, 'was probably never surpassed in Britain'. Three hundred people were seated in the great tent for the dessert, 'without the slightest crowding or confusion owing doubtless to the polite and well bred conduct of the whole company'. Soon after 4pm it began to rain and the festivity was cut short, but it had been a splendid event which demonstrated the extraordinary flowering of the society in only 20 years. Andrew Duncan would have been thrilled had he survived.

Duncan chaired his last general meeting of the society on 2 March 1828. He was absent from the next meeting on 5 June 1828 when

> ... it was unanimously agreed that there be entered in the minutes of this day, an expression of the Society's deep regret at the absence, owing to indisposition, of Dr Andrew Duncan Sr, Father of the Society, and Permanent First Vice President; and the secretary be directed to convey to Dr Duncan the expression of the Society's condolence, and their lively gratitude for his unwearied past service to the institution.

Duncan died a month later. A large deputation from the Royal Caledonian Horticultural Society led the funeral procession, the Right Honourable Sir Robert Liston GCB as vice president in the rear.

Recognition of the contributions of Andrew Duncan and Patrick Neill

The outstanding contributions to the society made by Duncan and Neill were recognised in several ways. Neill was presented with the society's gold medal in 1817 for his report on the Horticultural Survey of the Netherlands. This survey had been undertaken on the society's behalf by Neill, together with John Hay and James McDonald.[16] In their travels they had seen the results of the depredations of Napoleon's army: 'These barbarous Goths of modern Europe ... the ruffian French soldiers, under such a leader of banditti as Buonaporte [sic], treated the Netherlands even worse than they had either Rome, Venice, or Naples.' Villas had been destroyed which were quickly rebuilt, but fruit trees, which had been protected and nourished for years, were wantonly cut down for fuel and were less easily replaced. Clearly feelings still ran high so soon after Waterloo.

In 1821 Patrick Neill was again awarded the society's highest award, but because he already had a gold medal and his contributions to the society were so outstanding, he was presented instead with a more valuable piece of silver plate. In 1848 he was given a splendid silver cup, funded by 600 'practical' gardeners.[17] The cup was inscribed 'In testimony of their high esteem for his personal character, and gratitude for the zealous and long continued devotion of his time and talents to the cause of horticulture and the interest of its cultication.' Busts of both Duncan and Neill were placed in the new Exhibition Hall in the Experimental Garden (now the Caledonian Hall) at its opening in 1843, and both men were featured in profile in a Certificate of Merit (*fig.* 42) commissioned in 1851.[18] Patrick Neill received the first of 525 prints of this certificate shortly before his death at the age of 75. The certificate was designed by Louis Ghémar and the profiles were drawn from busts of Duncan and Neill. Neill's bust by John Steell remains in the society's possession. Duncan's bust was a cast of the missing original by Lawrence Macdonald (*fig.* 32).

Patrick Neill bequeathed £500 to the Royal Caledonian Society to provide a medal, every two to three years, to a deserving horticulturist, and a similar amount to the Royal Society of Edinburgh for a medal to be awarded to a distinguished Scottish naturalist.

It is outside the scope of this book to give a full history of the 'Caley', as the society is now commonly referred to. By 1843, when the Exhibition Hall was opened, the Experimental Garden had a camellia house, two conservatories, a propagation house, and a grand three-bayed Winter Garden. The garden contained a splendid collection of fruits, including oranges as well as camellias, azaleas, rhododendrons, and plants from China, the Himalayas, Australia and South America.

In 1839 the excellent supervisor James MacNab, under whose guidance the garden had prospered, succeeded his father as manager of the Royal Botanic Garden which flourished while the Caledonian Garden went into a period of decline. Funding became difficult due to a reduced membership and non-payment of subscriptions and the society ran into debt. In 1859 the council decided that the only solution was to abandon its lease and allow the government to merge its garden with the Royal Botanic Garden. In 1864 the handover was completed, the government contributing £1000 for the surrender of the lease in order to allow debts to be cleared. The Exhibition Hall became a store for the Botanic Garden's rapidly expanding herbarium and library, and remained thus until 1964 when new accommodation was built allowing the building, now named the Caledonian Hall, to return to its original function. In 2008 it became a tea room. The Winter Garden was demolished to allow the development of the rock garden. The only remnants of the Caledonian Garden, apart from the hall, are the gardener's house which is now the lodge at the East Gate and a fragment of the original brick wall, which separated the two gardens, adjacent to it.

Relieved of its financial burden, the Royal Caledonian Horticultural Society recovered slowly. Donald Mackenzie[19] gives a good account of the lengthy period of financial difficulty, with its eventual solution after the First World War, when the Caley amalgamated with its rival the Scottish Horticultural Association which was in similar difficulties.

The society is once more thriving. Membership is now nearly 1000 and women members have been admitted for many years. Royal patronage continues in the person of the Princess Royal. Meetings are now held in the premises of the Royal Botanic Garden, with which the society has had a close association since their gardens merged. The Regius Keeper of the Royal Botanic Garden and the President of the Royal College of Physicians of Edinburgh are honorary vice-presidents in recognition of the past links with these institutions. Talks are given fortnightly during the winter months, and flower shows remain a major feature with the award of trophies for prize-winning presentations. The Patrick Neill and Andrew Duncan Medals are awarded to gardeners and horticulturists who have made significant contributions.

Alas the splendid dinners of Duncan's day are no longer held. The bicentenary, in 2009, of the society was celebrated with an exhibition held in the Royal Botanic Garden.

Notes

1 A history of the founding of the Caledonian Horticultural Society is given in Byrom (1999), pp. 5-14.
2 The early minute books of the Caledonian Horticultural Society are held in the library of the Royal Botanic Garden.
3 Sir James Hall (1761-1832) was a geologist and friend of and collaborator with James Hutton, whose theories of formation of the Earth he endorsed and confirmed by laboratory experimentation. He became President of the Royal Society of Edinburgh and from this position of influence was instrumental in getting acceptance of Hutton's theories in the face of much opposition by the religious establishment.
4 Cited in Abraham (1933), pp. 425-26. Lettsom was subjected to some ridicule for his enthusiastic promotion of mangelwurzel as a cattle food.
5 Pettigrew (1817), vol. 2, p. 100.
6 *Memoirs of the Caledonian Horticultural Society* (1814), vol. I: pp. 160-68.
7 *Ibid*, pp. 237-45.
8 Chalmers (2003), pp. 36-37.
9 Discourses for the years 1811, 1814, 1815 and 1816, appear in the Society's Memoirs. Printed copies for the years 1814 and 1818-25 are held in the CRC, EUL.
10 The Society encountered temporary financial difficulties during the mid-19th century due to declining membership and competing societies. See Byrom and Dalgleish (2003), pp. 47-61.
11 Mrs Duncan's recipe for white currant wine was recorded in the minutes of the Society (1810): 'To every pint of the juice of fully ripe white currants, are added two pints of water and one pound of raw sugar, the fermentation is promoted by gentle agitation every day for eight or ten days. When it appears from the taste that the liquor has obtained the pure vinous state without either great sweetness on the one hand, or any obvious acidity on the other – which state it has in general acquired in a month or six weeks, the progress of the fermentation is stopped, by the addition of a small quantity of pure ardent spirit. One or two bottles of good whisky … are in general sufficient for a hogs head. After the obvious fermentation is terminated, the cask is bunged up and allowed to remain at rest for six months. The pure liquor is then racked off into another cask, in which it is allowed to remain for twelve months longer before it be bottled. …' The wine presented was of vintage 1805.
12 Byrom and Dalgleish (2001), pp. 20-36.
13 Vergil, *Eclogues* 3, pp. 70-71.
14 The Royal Botanic Garden moved to its new 14-acre site at Inverleith during 1820-23; its third move. John Hope (1725-86), Professor of Botany and King's Botanist, had supervised its second move in 1763 to a site off Leith Walk. In his Harveian Oration on the life of John Hope (1788), Duncan described the successful garden which Hope had created in its new location and commented that a suitable monument should be established in grateful remembrance of his distinguished service. Interestingly, at the present time (2009), the Royal Botanic Garden is building a splendid new educational and research facility which is to be called the John Hope Gateway.
15 Horace, *Odes* 3.4.6.
16 Reported in Neill (1823).
17 The history of this cup is given in Byrom and Dalgleish (1991), pp. 32-42. After Neill's death, the cup was given to the National Museum of Scotland where it is currently on display. It is regarded as the most elaborate piece of plate ever manufactured in Edinburgh.
18 The account of the discovery of the certificate and its history is given by Byrom, 1998, pp. 9-15.
19 Mackenzie, 1935, pp. 64-83.

CHAPTER X

Duncan's Non-Medical Clubs and Societies

JOHN CHALMERS

The many non-medical clubs of which Duncan was a member are listed below, and short accounts of those in which he appears to have greatest interest are given.

> Royal Company of Archers*
> Honourable Company of Edinburgh Golfers*
> Beggar's Benison
> Dissipation Club
> Old Revolution Club
> Six Foot Club
> Speculative Society*
> Philosophical Society
> American Philosophical Society*
> Royal Society of Edinburgh*ƒ
> Canongate Kilwinning Freemason Lodge*
> Society of Antiquaries of Scotland *

> * = still surviving
> ƒ = founder member

Speculative Society

The Speculative Society was founded in 1764 by William Creech and five others, while students at the University of Edinburgh, for the improvement of literary composition and public speaking. It was closely linked to the University in which it held its meetings. They were held weekly during the winter months and took the form of a discourse, by one of the members in rotation, on a subject of his choice. This was followed by a debate on a prearranged topic introduced by an assigned member. Ordinary membership was limited to 25 and highly prized. Among its members were many of the Enlightenment luminaries, including Lord John Russel, Walter Scott, Charles Hope, David Hume, Francis Jeffrey, Henry Brougham, Francis Horner and John Murray. Henry Cockburn became a member in 1799 and described the society as 'an institution which has trained more young men to public speaking, talent and liberal thought, than all the other private institutions in Scotland. ... No better arena could possibly have been provided for the exercise of the remarkable young men it excited.'[1] Brougham in particular impressed him as an outstanding speaker.

Duncan was admitted in 1770 and at first his attendance was very regular. Failure to attend a meeting without cause incurred a penalty of half a crown (2/6), and absence on three consecutive occasions led to the possibility of expulsion. On 8 January 1771 Duncan requested permission to be absent because of his particular situation which prevented regular attendance. He was granted leave for six weeks without being subject to fines, but his was not to be regarded as a precedent. The nature of his 'particular situation' was not recorded, but it coincides with the time of his marriage.

The subject of one of Duncan's discourses was 'Youth'. On 18 December 1770 he opened the debate on the question, 'Ought the Crown of Britain to be Elective or Hereditary?' Alas the outcome of the debate is not recorded in the minutes.

Members who had attended for three sessions and had delivered three discourses became eligible for extraordinary membership. Duncan was elected to this category on 1 December 1772, although it is doubtful if he had fulfilled the necessary requirements. Extraordinary members were not subject to the discipline of regular attendance and Duncan's attendances after his election became infrequent. His contribution to the society, nevertheless, must have been appreciated, for he was elected an honorary member in 1799 'as a testimony of the high esteem of his talents and his able and effectual support'.

The Speculative Society survives to this day.

The Philosophical Society

In 1731 Dr Alexander Monro *primus*, the first Professor of Anatomy in Edinburgh and founder of the Edinburgh Medical School, established a society for the improvement of medical knowledge which published five volumes of *Medical Essays and Observations* between 1733 and 1744. (These were translated into several languages.) Later it was proposed that literature and philosophy should be included and a conjoint society was established with the cumbersome title of the Edinburgh Society for improving Arts and Sciences and particularly Natural Knowledge – or more shortly the Philosophical Society – with David Hume and Alexander Monro *secundus* as secretaries. This society published three volumes of essays, under the title of *Essays and Observations, Physical and Literary* in 1754, 1756 and 1771, precursors of Duncan's *Medical Commentaries*. Joseph

Black's 'Experiments on Magnesia Alba', which had been the subject of his essay for the degree of Doctor of Medicine, was published in *Essays and Observations* (vol. ii, p. 157).

The Philosophical Society, of which Duncan was a member, evolved into the Royal Society of Edinburgh.

The Royal Society of Edinburgh and the Society of Antiquaries

In 1782, at a meeting of professors of the University of Edinburgh, The Reverend Dr Robertson, Principal of the University, proposed that a more all-embracing society be created to include medical and physical science and 'every branch of science, erudition and taste'.[2] Dr Robertson's motivation was not entirely altruistic as politics played a part. The Society of Antiquaries, founded in 1780 by Duncan's Whig friend, the 11th Earl of Buchan (elder brother of Duncan's friends, Thomas and Henry Erskine), was threatening to encroach upon matters which were regarded as being within the province of the University. The principle aggravation rested with William Smellie, founder of the *Encylopaedia Britannica* and printer of Duncan's *Commentaries,* who himself was also a natural historian of distinction. Smellie, who had been an unsuccessful applicant for the University Chair of Natural History which was awarded to the Rev. Dr John Walker, proposed in his capacity as Superintendent of Natural History of the Society of Antiquaries to deliver a series of public lectures on natural history. This was regarded by the University as an unwelcome challenge. The professors, backed by the Faculty of Advocates, hoped by inviting the Society of Antiquaries to join in the formation of the new society that their threat might be contained. In the event the Antiquarians resolutely refused to become involved. Nevertheless the University, supported by the Philosophical Society, decided to go ahead, and in 1783, having been granted a Royal charter, the Royal Society of Edinburgh (RSE) for the Advancement of Learning and useful Knowledge was founded. The Duke of Buccleuch was elected president and 58 of the 60 members of the Philosophical Society, Duncan among them, became founding Fellows of the RSE.[3]

The RSE flourished while the Antiquarians went into a period of decline. It met first in the University library and later in the Physicians' Hall in George Street until they obtained their own premises in 42 George Street in 1810. In 1826 they moved once more to the newly opened Royal Institution at the foot of the Mound. Duncan, surprisingly, makes little mention in his writings of either the Philosophical or the Royal Society, although he was an active member of both. Initially the Royal Society was divided into literary and physical sections which met on separate evenings. Duncan, whose profession would have placed him in the physical section, is on record as having chaired literary sessions, no doubt a tribute to his classical education.

The early *Transactions* of the society indicate the very high standard of communications which have characterised its meetings ever since. James Hutton, for example, published his *Theory of the Earth* in the first volume. Sir Robert Christison, in his presidential address in 1868, commented that 'medicine makes only a rare, and for the most part insignificant appearance in the business of the society', and attributes this to the competing medical societies and publications such as the *Edinburgh Medical and Surgical Journal*. One of the insignificant papers that he mentions was Duncan's report of a case of inveterate hiccup cured with a dose of dilute sulphuric acid. He advised against a further trial.[4]

A more substantial paper by Duncan was his 'Account of Sir Alexander Dick, Bart. of Prestonfield, late President of the Royal College of Physicians of Edinburgh and FRS Edin'.[5]

Alexander Dick (1703-85) studied medicine in Edinburgh and obtained a MD from the University of St Andrews. He was elected President of the Royal College of Physicians for seven years – a uniquely long term of office. He is now chiefly remembered for his part in the introduction of rhubarb into Britain. Rhubarb, an essential ingredient of James Gregory's famous powder,[6] was grown in profusion in Dick's garden at Prestonfield. He was awarded a gold medal by a society in London for growing and preparing rhubarb for the market.

Dick gave hospitality to Benjamin Franklin during his two visits to Edinburgh. Franklin loved Edinburgh which honoured him with the Freedom of the City. He wrote that, in Edinburgh, 'I think the time we spent there, was Six Weeks of the *densest* Happiness I have met with in any Part of my Life. And the agreeable and instructive society we found there in such Plenty, has left so pleasing an Impression on my Memory, that did not strong Connections draw me elsewhere, I believe Scotland would be the Country I should chuse to spend the Remainder of my Days in'. The hospitality received from Dick must have contributed to his favourable impression. He sent a thank you letter in verse, which included the following:

> *Cheerful meals and balmy rest,*
> *Beds that never buggs mollest,*
> *Neatness & sweetness all around*
> *These at Prestonfield we found.*

In the conclusion to his paper on Alexander Dick, Duncan makes a statement which was to have a curious parallel with his own experience:

Although he [Dick] had already passed the 82nd year of his age, a period at which the faculties both of mind and body have in general so far failed, that death is rather to be wished for than otherwise, yet not only his judgement, but his spirit for exertion, still remained unimpaired. His death, therefore, even at that advanced age, was a great loss to society.

The Royal Company of Archers

The Royal Company of Archers, the oldest sporting club in Britain, was founded in 1676 by 'an influential body of Noblemen and Gentlemen, who met for the purpose of encouraging the Noble and Useful Recreation of Archery, for many years much neglected'. There was a realisation that Scotland was falling behind England in this regard. In 1704 Queen Anne granted the company a Royal Charter in return for which she was entitled to a yearly gift of one pair of barbed arrows if requested. In its early days the Royal Company had no official duties and took the form of the many other clubs and societies which flourished in Edinburgh at that time, of being a vehicle for social intercourse and good fellowship as well as an opportunity to develop toxopholite skills. The Royal Company consisted of an undefined number of archers under the command of a captain general, president, seven council members, various junior officers, a chaplain general, a surgeon, and most importantly an agitant [*sic*] who acted as secretary. In 1776 the Royal Company, which had hitherto met in a variety of taverns, built their own Archer's Hall adjacent to their archery range in the East Meadows. For the first 100 years members were elected by an open vote, but from 1778 a secret ballot was introduced, one black ball excluding the candidate.

The Royal Company had no official military duties until the 'joyful occasion' of the visit to Scotland of King George IV in 1822 – an event which aroused great enthusiasm among the populace, as indicated in a poem quoted by Duncan which included the following verse:

Rejoice, Edina, now rejoice,
Let acclamations fill the gale;
Shout all, with loud and joyful voice,
Hail, to our Monarch! Hail, all hail!

Sir Walter Scott, chief organiser of the Royal reception and himself an Archer, was largely responsible for having the Royal Company appointed the official King's Bodyguard in Scotland – a responsibility and honour which continues to this day. Hitherto, although the Royal Company had paraded in all their finery through the streets of Edinburgh to their shooting fixtures, their military skills and discipline was not of a high order. In order to prepare for their new status, drills and routines were developed and practiced. New, even more splendid uniforms were ordered, featuring a large ruff around the neck and long leather gauntlets. The event was a great success despite torrential rain. A division of 50 formed a guard of honour at the Royal landing at Leith and a further 40 attended His Majesty at Holyrood Palace and presented him with silver barbed arrows in accordance with their charter. History doesn't record whether Duncan was one of the Royal Company involved in the ceremonial greeting of George IV, but he did attend the Royal levee at the Palace of Holyroodhouse as a representative of the professors of the University[7] and no doubt in his capacity as the King's Physician in Scotland

At another wet reception at Hopetoun House, home of the Royal Company's Captain General, the Archers were on parade having sailed from Newhaven to Port Edgar and marched the two miles to the House. Henry Raeburn, one of their number, was knighted by the King who borrowed the Earl of Hopetoun's sword for the purpose. Rain seemed to have been a feature of Royal levees. During the 'Wet Review' of 1881 in Queen's Park, Queen Victoria, who herself sat in an open carriage protected only with an umbrella held by John Brown, was so distressed to see the officer in command of the Royal Company – the Duke of Abercorn – getting soaked that she took off her Shetland shawl and insisted that he wrapped it round his shoulders.

Andrew Duncan was proud to be elected a member of the Royal Company of Archers, having been proposed by his friend Henry Erskine. In his writings about the Royal Company he lists all the members from its foundation until 1819, a list which includes nearly all the notable figures of Edinburgh and its environs, many of them doctors. Nathanial Spens, who was elected President of the Royal College of Physicians in 1794, wearing his uniform of Adjutant General, was the subject of one of Raeburn's finest paintings. Duncan dates his intimate friendships with Spens and Alexander (Sandy) Wood from their meetings in this Company. During his long membership, Duncan won many trophies including the Musselburgh Arrow in 1778, the Silver Bowl and Kings Prize in 1799, and the Bugle Horn in 1808. Andrew Jr won the Goose Prize in 1800.

On 29 October 1821, at the age of 78, Duncan completed 50 years as a member. At this meeting he won the Pagoda Medal, the Prize at the Butts – the short range contest. (All the other members refrained from competing with the venerable archer!) At the dinner given in his honour, Duncan wore the same uniform he had when he first joined. His health was drunk and in his reply he noted that in 1771 three memorable events had happened to him. First he had been elected to the Royal Company of Archers and second he had married Elizabeth Knox. He said that among the fruits of his marriage he had two recruits to the Corp. He had a dozen grandchildren in Europe, and three in Asia. The majority were female, but he hoped that they too might become toxopholites (archers). The third memorable event was his creation as a Knight of that most ancient Order of Merit, the Beggar's Benison – a most curious conjunction to be bracketed with the other most respectable activities. He concluded with a respectable version of the beggar's benediction (see below) to the King:

> Long may you live in harmony and ease
> And never want, or purse, or power to please.

The Beggar's Benison

Duncan's proud declaration of his membership of the Beggar's Benison reveals a totally unexpected and surprising side to his character. David Stevenson[8] gives a scholarly account of the Beggar's Benison, a club dedicated to good fellowship and sexual licence, with an emphasis on masturbation. The Beggar's Benison came into being, surprisingly, in the Fife fishing and smuggling village of Anstruther, not far from Duncan's birthplace of Crail in 1732. The name derives from a legend that the promiscuous King James V, who was wont to wander about disguised as a commoner, came to the Dreel Burn which separates East and West Anstruther. In order to avoid getting wet he persuaded a beggar lass to carry him over, for which (and perhaps other services) he gave her a gold coin. In return she is said to have given thanks in the form of a benison:

> May your purse naer be toom   [toom = empty]
> And your horn aye in bloom

The club adopted this benison as its motto in the shorter version: 'May Prick nor Purse never fail you.' Its seal has the inscription 'The Beggars Bennison' [sic] and, under an anchor, an erect penis with a purse dangling from it.

In 1739 the club had 32 members, all local burgesses including local gentry, teachers (including one of Duncan's school teachers Sandy Don), Church of Scotland elders and commissioners, custom officers and smugglers, and a town clerk, Thomas Dishington of Crail, whom Duncan describes 'as being one of those choice spirits to whom the world is indebted for the revival of the most ancient order of Knighthood, *The Beggar's Benison*: an order of which I am proud to say I have had the honour of being one of the Knights Companions for many years'. Elsewhere in a Monro *secundus* oration, Duncan credits Sir John Macnaughton as being the founder and long serving sovereign of the Beggar's Benison.

Several clergymen were among the members, including David Low, an episcopalian minister in Pittenween who later became Bishop of Ross, Moray, Argyll and the Isles. He later requested that his name be removed from the club records and this request was duly recorded in the minutes. Perhaps not surprisingly most of the records of the club have been destroyed, but it clearly had much support and satellite branches were created in Edinburgh and Glasgow and even St Petersburg.

Membership became increasingly aristocratic and included Thomas Erskine, 6th Earl of Kellie, Sir Thomas Wentworth, David Steuart Erskine (Lord Cardross), who later became the second Earl of Buchan and the founder of the Antiquarian Society of Scotland, Sir Thomas Dundas, and Nathanial Curzon, 2nd Lord Scarsdale. The Edinburgh branch, established in 1752, was regarded as being particularly upper class. The Prince of Wales was created a member in 1783, but it is not known if he ever attended a meeting (although his proclivities would have fitted well with the tenor of the club). Duncan, the Prince's Physician in Scotland at that time, probably proposed him for membership.

Perhaps the most surprising member was the Italian Vincenzo Lunardi, who flew a hydrogen balloon across the Firth of Forth from Heriot's Hospital in Edinburgh to Ceres in Fife in 1785. This feat was rewarded with several honours, including membership of the St Andrews Golf Club and a diploma of membership of the *Beggar's Benison* adorned, as were all the club's memorabilia, with phallic images.

Lunardi wrote:

I am just now favoured with a Letter and Diploma from Sir James Lumsdaine, constituting me a member of a very respectable Society called Knights Companion of the Beggar's Benison: and I am the more elated with this new honour as I understand that my Patron the Prince of Wales had the same conferred on him a few months ago. I cannot now explain to you the enigmatical meaning of the Beggar's Benison but shall endeavour to do it ad aures. ...

No shame was attached to membership and notices of meetings were advertised in the local press. The *Edinburgh Advertiser* (29 January 1765) reported:

... that there was a very numerous meeting of the Knights Companions of the ancient Order of the Beggars' Benison, with their sovereign on Friday last, at Mr Walker's tavern, when the band of music belonging to the Edinburgh Regiment (25th Foot) attended. Everything was conducted with the greatest harmony and cheerfulness, and all the knights appeared with the medal of the order.

33

34

Figure 33. Henry Raeburn's portrait of Andrew Duncan.
(BY COURTESY OF THE ROYAL COLLEGE OF PHYSICIANS OF EDINBURGH)

Figure 34. Andrew Duncan's armorial bearings as it appears above the fireplace in the Dining Hall of New Craighouse.
(COURTESY OF NAPIER UNIVERSITY/ PHOTOGRAPH BY J. CHALMERS)

Figure 35. Portrait of Elizabeth Duncan by David Martin, currently displayed in Duff House.

(SCOTTISH NATIONAL PORTRAIT GALLERY)

Figure 36. Portrait of Andrew Duncan Sr by Sir John Watson Gordon, currently displayed in the Chancellor Building of the Edinburgh Medical School.

(WITH PERMISSION OF THE UNIVERSITY OF EDINBURGH FINE ART COLLECTION)

Figures 37 and **38.**
Duncan's memorial plaque on the wall of McKinnon House together with other pioneers of mental health. The bust at the top is of Philippe Pinel (1745-1826), Duncan's contemporary, who is credited in France as being the initiator of humane mental care. The others are William Tuke (1732-1822), Florence Nightingale (1820-1910), Robert Gardiner Hill (1811-78), Dorothea Lynde Dix (1802-87) and Campbell Clark (1852-1901).

(PHOTOGRAPH BY J. CHALMERS)

Figure 39. Frontispiece from the Harveian minute book.

(THE HARVEIAN SOCIETY)

Figures 40a and **40b.** The Gymnastic swimming cup. The medal on the right reads 'A. Duncan Sr M.D. & P. *Victor Quartum* [victor for the fourth time]'. The two adjoining medals show the Duncan armourial bearings.

(PHOTOGRAPH BY IAIN MILNE)

Figure 41. The Bur-knot tree. This drawing by Patrick Syme (official artist to the Society) is of a tree from Dr Duncan's garden. It was about three feet in height and was cut from a much larger tree early in the spring of the preceding year.

(COPYRIGHT ROYAL BOTANIC GARDEN EDINBURGH/ PHOTOGRAPHER LYNSEY WILSON)

Figure 42. The Certificate of Merit. Andrew Duncan is on the left and Patrick Neill on the right. The buildings are the Caledonian Hall on the right and the Winter Garden on the left.

(COPYRIGHT OF THE ROYAL CALEDONIAN HORTICULTURAL SOCIETY)

Figure 43. Patrick Neill. A portrait by
John Syme

Figure 44. James Gregory. A copy of a painting
by Henry Raeburn by an unknown artist.

Figure 45. Andrew Duncan's family vault in
the Buccleuch Churchyard.

The club was not entirely self indulgent. The *Advertiser* of 4 March 1778 carried the following notice:

For the encouragement of all young fellows of spirit who wish to maintain the dignity of Great Britain, by serving the best of kings, the Knights Companions of the most ancient and Puissant order of Beggar's Benison and Merryland of Glasgow, hereby offer a reward of Five Guineas to every able man who will enlist with their Knight Companion Sir Henry Wilsone, Lieutenant of the Glasgow Volunteers, until his number of men is completed.

It is difficult for us at the present time to understand this tolerance, for even in the present acceptance of liberal sexual freedom we might look askance at someone who openly declared his membership of such a society. Many public figures and Members of Parliament have been disgraced for less. In Duncan's day attitudes were clearly more tolerant. His standing as a pillar of society and the church, and a family man, does not seem to have suffered as a consequence of his participation, of which he was proud.

Relaxation of sexual morals was however a feature of the Enlightenment. Perhaps the example set by some members of Royalty contributed to this attitude. Sex was regarded by many as a God-given gift to be enjoyed and not taken too seriously. Indeed, notable figures such as James Boswell, Erasmus Darwin and David Hume wrote freely about the pleasures and benefits of sex and encouraged following one's sexual urges in the belief that this was good for one's health. Erasmus Darwin, father of twelve legitimate children and several others, felt that it prevented mental dysfunction.

Another even more select Edinburgh society dedicated to the same end – the Wig Club[9] – founded in 1775, had as its emblem a wig allegedly made of the 'privy hairs of Royal courtezans'. Membership was limited initially to 25, but later increased to 50. Among its members were three dukes, one marquis, six earls, nine lords, and other notables including Henry Dundas, Viscount Melville, the senior government official in Scotland. Initiates were required to drink a quart of claret without pausing from a glass vessel of 'curious design'. Their more usual fare was twopenny ale and a coarse bread known as Soutar's clod.

Many of the more serious and learned societies which flourished during this period allowed some bawdiness to enter into their proceedings. The poets Burns and Fergusson are known to have entertained members of the Crochallan Society and Cape Club with their double entendres, and even Duncan, although by no means in their class, composed a bawdy poem for the *Ludo Apollinares*. Golfers had been called 'a set of idle loungers' by Judge Middleman in an action involving the threat of developments encroaching on Leith Links. Duncan wrote a poem in response,[10] ending:

But, with all his grave knowledge, Middleman may go wrong,
And his deep Metaphysics sell for an old song;
For he ne'er made a speech more absurd in his life,
He says 'Golf is lounging.' – We appeal to his Wife.

His wife is a mother, and surely will say,
That at the short strokes, the stiff shaft is the play;
A friend to good golfing, she'll wish, honest soul,
Success to the Putter, the Baas, and the Hole.

The surviving artefacts of the Beggar's Benison which exist in several museums and libraries recall the artefacts and wall paintings which commonly decorated domestic dwellings discovered during the excavations of Pompeii and Herculaneum. The Roman Empire at that time appears to have accepted sex as something to be regarded openly as a normal activity without any prurience. Again the example of their leaders, such as the notorious Emperor Nero, may have contributed to this liberality. However, attitudes towards sex have fluctuated over the years. The Beggar's Benison was disbanded in 1836, presumably reflecting changing public opinion, and its residual funds amounting to £70 were donated to the school of East Anstruther to fund prizes for 'two co-equal girls'. During the Victorian age which followed, attitudes to sex were to change dramatically. Any sexual activity, other than that directed to procreation within marriage, came to be regarded as sinful. No doubt things continued much as before, but in a more secretive and perhaps less wholesome and certainly less enjoyable atmosphere. Perhaps Duncan's acceptance of free and guiltless sex might be regarded as one of his contributions to the well-being of mankind.

Freemasonry

The one society of which both James Gregory and Duncan were members was the Canongate Kilwinning Freemason Lodge. Freemasonry was very popular in Duncan's day, there being twelve lodges in Edinburgh. The Canongate Lodge to which Duncan was initiated in 1774 still exists in St John's Street. Its members included a number of the aristocracy and many of Edinburgh's most distinguished citizens. Among the legal members were Duncan's lifelong friend Henry Erskine, Dean of the Faculty of Advocates, and James Burnet (Lord Monboddo). The world of literature was represented by the writer Henry Mackenzie, to whom Scott dedicated his Waverley novels, William Creech, the prominent publisher, bookseller and Lord Provost of Edinburgh, and William Smellie, printer. Medical members included James Lind, discoverer of the cure for scurvy, and Duncan's great friends Sandy Wood and James Hamilton Sr. It is an interesting insight into the ways of masonry that the Lodge could accommodate two of Duncan's greatest antagonists, James Gregory and James Hamilton Jr, each of whom became involved in a series of bitter legal actions against the others, explored in chapters XII and XIII respectively.

The poet Robert Burns, a keen mason, was introduced by Henry Erskine to the Canongate Lodge during his time in Edinburgh and was, according to a disputed legend, appointed Poet Laureate of the Lodge in 1787. The artist Stewart Watson (1800-70) created a well known painting of the ceremony 60 years later. If the event took place as depicted, one can be sure that Duncan was present, for he was a great admirer of Burns and was one of the subscribers to the Kilmarnock edition of Burn's poems. Other events link Burns with medical members of the Lodge. Sandy Wood treated Burns for an injury to his leg, sustained when he fell from a coach. Burns greatly respected James Gregory and sent him poems for his criticism. Both men shared an admiration for Lord Monboddo's beautiful daughter Eliza Burnet, who lived across the road from the Lodge in St John's Street. Gregory proposed marriage to her and Burns wrote an elegy on her early death at 24, which included the following lines:

> Life ne'er exulted in so rich a prize,
> As Burnet lovely from her nature skies;
> No envious Death so triumph'd in a blow,
> As that which laid th'accomplished Burnet low.
>
> The form and mind, sweet Maid! Can I forget?
> In richest ore, the brightest jewel set!

There is no record that Duncan held office or took an active part in the affairs of the society.

The Old Revolution Club

Duncan joined this club on 11 November 1788. His membership certificate, which exists in the Duncan Archive in Edinburgh University Library, states that a member was required

> ... to declare the grateful sense he has of the Deliverance of the Kingdom of Great Britain and Ireland from Popery and Slavery by King William and Queen Mary of Glorious and Immortal Memory and of the further security of our Religion and Liberty by the Settlement of the Crown upon the Illustrious House of Hanover, and his zealous attachment to his Majesty

King George the third and our present happy Constitution in Church and State.

Duncan makes no reference to the club or its activities, but the very fact of his membership of this club, with its staunch Tory declaration, gives an interesting insight into his political leanings. Despite his close friendship with the Whig brothers, Thomas and Henry Erskine, and his reliance on them in his approaches to Parliament, Duncan clearly liked to keep a foot in both political camps.

A brief account of the Honourable Company of Golfers is given in chapter VII where the Dissipation Club is also mentioned, although nothing can be found otherwise about its purpose.

THE MUSSELBURGH ARROW

The archery prize won by Duncan in 1778.

(NATIONAL MUSEUMS SCOTLAND)

Notes

1   Sir Robert Christison did not share this opinion of debating societies: '… the good done by these societies is, if I mistake not, attended with an irreparable evil. They make some men pragmatical and offensively disputative. I, at least, have known several … whose acquired glibness of tongue misled them afterwards, and made them … contentious, noisy, troublesome obstructives in the real business of life …', in Christison (1885), vol. I, pp. 52-53.
2   Cullen (1783), p. 676.
3   A full account of the dispute with the Antiquarians is given in Shapin (1974), pp. 1-41.
4   Duncan (1784), p. 27.
5   Duncan (1789), pp. 58-62.
6   Gregory's powder, a mixture of rhubarb, magnesia and ginger, remained a popular remedy for intestinal upsets well into the twentieth century.
7   Craig (1976), p. 981.
8   Stevenson (2001).
9   Cockburn (1910), pp. 135-41.
10   Duncan's Miscellanies, (RCPE Library, LC 1021 (19)).

CHAPTER XI

Duncan and
the Brunonian Society

JOHN CHALMERS

They are now printing at Milan the works of Mr Brown ... and it seems that our young people, as everywhere are carried away by theoretical dreaming and give this author more value than ... he seems to merit.[1]

In 1781 Duncan became involved in a bitter dispute with an eccentric doctor, John Brown (1735-88), who was born and brought up in a Scottish Border village where his father was a weaver. Brown was educated in Duns where he acquired an excellent grounding in Latin which was to serve him well in his career. At the age of ten he was apprenticed to a weaver, but abandoned this after three years to become a pupil teacher and tutor. Aged 18 he went to Edinburgh to study divinity, later changing course to the study of medicine. His skill with Latin enabled him to earn a living as a tutor to William Cullen's children, and by acting as a 'grinder' he helped other students to prepare for their MD exam. So highly did Brown regard Cullen at that early stage of his career that he named his first son William Cullen. Later he was to become Cullen's critic and bitter opponent. He acquired an MD at University of St Andrews in 1779.

Although Brown's clinical experience had been very limited, in 1778 he began to give an extramural course of lectures on the practice of physic just two years after Andrew Duncan had commenced his extramural teaching. Brown had developed a novel theory of disease and its treatment which, by virtue of its simplicity, had great popular appeal among the medical students of his day, and was hotly debated by the members of the Royal Medical Society of which Brown was twice president (see chapter VIII).[2]

The controversial Brunonian theory, published in *Elementa Medicinae* (1780) in Edinburgh by Charles Elliot, stated that all diseases were due to an imbalance between too great or too little excitability of the tissues and should be treated either by sedatives or stimulants. This challenged the conventional teaching of the Edinburgh medical establishment. William Cullen, who had published his own classification of diseases, *Synopsis Nosologiae Methodica* in 1769, was particularly incensed and blackballed Brown's application to join the Philosophical Society. The Brunonian theory, however, acquired transient popularity elsewhere in Britain, on the Continent, and even in Philadelphia. Andrew Duncan Jr wrote to his father from Florence on 16 October 1797: 'The Italian physicians in the northern parts are divided into two opposite sects. The old school bleeds and purges every patient and the young men are all mad Brunonians.' In another letter from Leghorn on 1 January 1798: 'The whole medical world here are taken up with disputes about Brown's doctrines and in conformity with the national character, the young are its enthusiastic supporters on account of its apparent simplicity while the old practitioners decry it as furiously without knowing it.'

Guthrie states, with possibly some hyperbole, 'that it has been remarked that the Brunonian methods killed more persons than the French Revolution and the Napoleonic wars taken together'.[3] In fact, Brown's conservative approach to the prevalent depleting measures of blood letting, purging and emetics probably did more good than harm.[4]

Andrew Duncan became involved with the Brunonians in connection with his management of a sick medical student who, according to their theory, was suffering from too little excitability (asthenia) which, therefore, required correction by liberal ingestion of opium and alcohol. In a book published by one of Brown's followers, Robert Jones,[5] Andrew Duncan and Alexander Monro *secundus* were criticised over their management of the case. Monro was prepared to let the matter rest on the grounds that he did not want to damage the career of Brown who had a large family and who had already been imprisoned for bankruptcy. Duncan, however, could not tolerate criticism and published a lengthy account of the case.[6]

According to Duncan, in October 1780 he was asked by medical student Edward L. Fox to visit his friend and fellow student John Braham Isaacson who was very ill. Duncan found Isaacson to be suffering from 'a distinctly marked fever with a disposition to the putrid state'. The patient's condition gave him grounds for concern and he asked his friend and colleague Dr Alexander Monro *secundus* for a second opinion. The two physicians agreed on a course of treatment which consisted of Peruvian bark, acid elixir of vitriol, fresh air and port wine, liberally employed together with considerable quantities of strong cider. The patient was left in his lodgings under the care of a nurse and a fellow lodger, Mr Goodwin, also a medical student.

Duncan visited at least twice a day. Isaacson became delirious and a sore under his arm discharged a large quantity of an 'ichorous' and bloody matter with 'foetor'. Eventually he made a slow and complete recovery.

Duncan went on to relate:

No sooner was Mr Isaacson in this state, than it began to be reported that he was cured by Dr Brown, and [that] Dr Monro and Dr Duncan had given him over. This story was particularly told in a pretty large company by a pupil of Dr Brown ... who went so far as to say ... that if he had not boldly interfered, Dr Monro and I would have killed our patient in one day longer.[7]

The following version was given by Robert Jones.

A friend of mine lay in a fever. He was treated in the ordinary way, excepting that he had a scanty allowance of wine; which is a practice beginning to take place among the most violent and powerful opposers of Dr Brown, in consequence of these practitioners perceiving, from its successful use in his own hands ... that it will obtrude itself upon them at last. But their prejudices ... oppose ... that liberal and copious manner in which only it can be of use. ... The weakness went on ... till it was plain, that death must be the consequence of the plan of cure. ...[8]

Jones goes on to state that the physicians in charge of the case suspected that there was a Brunonian among the friends who visited the patient and instructed the nurse to allow no other treatment than that which they had prescribed. He stated that the nurse was, however, persuaded to give additional treatment, although she acknowledged, 'I am ruined if what I am about to do be divulged. And if ever it comes out ... I will deny the whole matter.'[9] Opium in large quantity, and the strongest cinnamon spirit and rum, were said to have been administered, leading to the patient's recovery.

This attempt to interfere in the treatment of a patient without the knowledge and consent of his appointed physicians was highly irregular. Duncan took legal advice, which was unanimous, and he informed Jones that if the circumstances were proved, 'imprisonment, pillory or banishment, would have been the punishment inflicted upon you. And they were farther of the opinion, that if your rum and laudanum had really been exhibited, and if Mr Isaacson had died ... you could not have escaped the gallows ...'.

Duncan averred that the circumstances were as follows:

The nurse informed me, that, during the course of Mr Isaacson's illness, you [Jones] had made repeated applications to her to exhibit to Mr Isaacson, without the knowledge of his physicians, medicine which you would bring her: that you had offered her money to comply with this request ... that ... you prevailed upon her to go to Dr Brown's house where ... Dr Brown had urged the same request and had given her particular directions about exhibiting to Mr Isaacson rum and laudanum in large quantities.[10]

The nurse, according to Duncan, refused and continued to follow Monro and Duncan's routine. One night Jones personally attempted to get the patient, who was delirious, to swallow a cup of medicine which he spat out.

In the rumours which circulated after these events, each party accused the other. Jones wrote:

> *Without giving Dr Brown the least opportunity to vindicate himself from their accusations, by spreading these through all the numerous circles of their friends and his enemies, they* [Duncan and Monro] *had very near ruined his character as a physician, and as a man.*

Duncan replied that, with regard to the accusations against him, 'if this be criminal, I pretend not to innocence. ... If a fair relation of facts was any prejudice to his [Brown's] character, he had himself only to blame.'[11]

To Jones, Duncan wrote, 'I hope, Sir, that notwithstanding the thorough conviction which you possess in the truth of the New Doctrine, you will allow yourself to reflect, that you, as well as others are liable to error'. Of Brown, he suggested, 'It would have been much for ... his interest, if, in place of coming to Edinburgh as a teacher of Latin or of medicine, he had still continued to exercise his original occupation of an operative weaver in a country village'.[12] Duncan added to his published letter several supporting statements. As soon as Isaacson was able to get about, he

> *in language expressive of the most sincere regard, returned me his best thanks. ... He pressed me to accept a proper pecuniary compensation for my trouble. This however, I declined; as it is a general rule with me, as well as with almost all the other medical practitioners in Edinburgh, never to accept a fee from any student of medicine. But he afterward sent me a book inscribed 'To Dr Duncan as a tribute of gratitude from his humble servant'.*[13]

Isaacson confirmed that he had never requested Jones' help, nor had he accepted his treatment. Monro and Mr Goodwin confirmed Duncan's account of events, as did Isaacson's landlady and two nurses who all made depositions on oath. The landlady said that she had tried to stop Jones' visits which were disagreeable to the patient, and one of the nurses said that Jones had offered her two guineas to carry out his treatment. Jones, who stated that he attended the patient four or five times a day and witnessed the nurse administer his treatment, maintained that the nurse had been intimidated:

> *She was said to have confessed that she had deceived me, to get rid of my importunities; and they even circulated a story that I had offered her a*

bribe. All this was weakness and impotence. It was devoid of truth ... and the whole fact hung upon the testimony of a poor woman who, if she acted the part that was alleged, was impelled to it by her situation in life, indigent and at their mercy.[14]

The truth of the matter will never be known. In the light of modern knowledge, one thing is certain: that whichever therapeutic routine was followed, it played no part in Isaacson's recovery.

The case highlights Duncan's intolerance of criticism which was to plague him throughout his life. If he had followed Monro's wise judgement, the comments of two inexperienced doctors would soon have been forgotten. The case also draws attention to the intensity of feeling generated by the Brunonian theory. Jones quotes Brown as saying 'that his doctrine and practice had touched them [the Edinburgh establishment] so much in their tenderest and most exposed parts, that their passion and hatred to him had got the ascendant over their reason, so that there was not the most distant hope that a meeting betwixt him and any of them, would be productive of either harmony or common decency'.[15] Jones goes on to compare Brown with Martin Luther whose 'spirited boldness ... called in question the infallibility of the Pope'. Even after his death his influence lingered among the students of Edinburgh, one of whom wrote:

> *... the students ... would do well to study the principles of medicine which the immortal Brown has left as an invaluable legacy to mankind. While he lived, his indiscretions were such, and his personal conduct so offensive to the professors at Edinburgh, that I do not wonder at their obstinately rejecting his doctrine. But, now that he is dead, and his ashes are cold, it would be more manly and more just to open their eyes to the light of his precepts, than wilfully to remain in the thick mist and darkness of their incomprehensible jargon.*[16]

Brown, having failed to gain acceptance or make a living in Edinburgh, moved to London with his family in 1786 to seek his fortune. There he eventually established a modest practice and made some money from his book *Elementa Medicinae*, republished in London in English translation, which Erasmus Darwin described in *Zoonomia* as 'a work (with some exceptions) of great genius'. Beddoes thought it 'disgustingly uncouth throughout, and in many passages almost impenetrably obscure'.[17] Brown's addiction to his favourite remedies – alcohol and laudanum – contributed to his lack of success and he was again imprisoned for debt. He died of apoplexy in 1788. His son, William Cullen Brown, followed him in medicine, and the artist Ford Madox Brown was a grandson.

Notes

1. From a letter by Johann Peter Frank, cited by Baumgartner and Ramsey (1933), p. 531. Frank adds in this letter that his son Joseph had accepted the Brunonian teaching, but in a later letter Joseph said that he had abandoned the Brunonian system: 'I am convinced his principles cannot be adopted as foundation of the science of medicine' (1806), in *Edinburgh Medical Surgical Journal* II, p. 499.

2. A full account of the significance of Brunonianism is outside the scope of this book. Details of its impact is given by Mike Barfoot in *Brunonianism under the bed: an alternative to university medicine in Edinburgh in the 1780s*, in Bynum and Porter (1988).

3. Guthrie (1945), p. 219.
4. Risse (2005), p. 108.
5. Jones (1781).
6. Duncan (1782).
7. *Ibid.*
8. Jones (1781).
9. *Ibid.*
10. Duncan (1782).
11. Jones (1781).
12. Duncan (1782).
13. *Ibid.*
14. Jones (1781).
15. *Ibid.*
16. Bristed (1803), p. 620.
17. Thomas Beddoes writing in the preface of Brown (1795).

CHAPTER XII

James Gregory's attack on the Royal College of Physicians and on Andrew Duncan

JOHN CHALMERS

But ye are forgers of lies, ye are all physicians of no value,
Oh that ye would altogether hold your peace! and it should be your
wisdom.   Job 13: 4-5, quoted by James Gregory

When malignant lies are invented and seriously told in presence of
respectable people, a man must have lost all respect for reputation, if he
takes not the proper steps to contradict them.
                  From *Memoirs of William Smellie*, quoted by Andrew Duncan

James Gregory's dual personality

In 1804 Duncan became involved in a protracted dispute that James Gregory
launched against him and the Royal College of Physicians. Gregory was a
curious individual with characteristics not unlike those of Stevenson's Jekyll
and Hyde. He was a brilliant lecturer, popular with his students, but a thorn
in the flesh of his colleagues. Robert Christison, who had been one of his
students, said of him:

> [His] *expression, voice and manner, – all betokened the vivacity, self-reliance,*
> *boldness, and determination of a powerful intellect. Equally in fluency as in*
> *choice of language, he surpassed all lecturers I had ever heard before. His*
> *doctrines were set forth with great clearness and simplicity. … His measures*
> *for the cure of disease were sharp and incisive. …With such a union of*
> *attributes, precept and preceptor could scarcely fail to captivate a youthful*
> *audience. … England and Ireland, as well as Scotland, together with our*
> *colonial dependencies, were overrun by his disciples and his doctrines.*[1]

However, another of Gregory's students, John Bristed, was less enthusiastic. While acknowledging that James Gregory was a 'man of sense, and of
extensive acquirements', he criticised him for wasting time with opportun-

ities for displaying his wit by 'the numberless tales and little stories which he continually recites, for the purpose of making his hearers laugh, and of showing that he considers all medicine, as a farce and a cheat put upon the public'.[2]

Henry Cockburn described him as:

... a curious and excellent man, a great physician, a great lecturer, a great Latin scholar, and a great talker; vigorous and generous: large of stature and with a strikingly powerful countenance. The popularity due to these qualities was increased by his professional controversies, and the diverting publications by which he used to maintain and enliven them. The controversies were rather too numerous; but they never were for any selfish end, and he was never entirely wrong. Still, a disposition towards personal attack was his besetting sin.[3]

James Gregory seems to have positively enjoyed baiting his colleagues and it is probable that the dispute recorded in this chapter was primarily due to Gregory indulging this unpleasant trait. He stated that his 'veneration for my own profession, and for those who practise it, is not excessive and many things in theory and the practice of it I consider as fair objects of ridicule, contempt and reproach'.[4] Unfortunately his colleagues tended to take him seriously, which led to a number of squabbles. (In chapter XIII reference is made to his contretemps with James Hamilton and John Hope, and there were several others which are outside the scope of this book.) Gregory's behaviour must have seemed so strange that some must have doubted his sanity. Andrew Duncan Jr, in a letter to his father from Leghorn dated 18 April 1796, wrote: 'I had a strange piece of news from Göttingen that Dr Gregory is deranged in his mind. I think you would not have omitted mentioning so important an event and I most sincerely hope it may not be true.'

The cause of the dispute

In modern times the issue which caused great turmoil in the Royal College of Physicians 200 years ago seems rather trivial. It concerned whether or not physicians should be allowed to dispense medicines. There was of course a hidden agenda. The surgeon apothecaries, who were manual workers and trades people, were allowed the privilege of dispensing drugs and this was one of the defining factors which distinguished the university educated physicians from their more lowly brethren.[5] The matter would probably have been resolved pragmatically and long forgotten had it not been for the intervention of the argumentative Professor James Gregory.

The College of Physicians in 1750 passed a bye-law prohibiting Fellows from practising surgery or pharmacy. This was reinforced by another bye-law of 1754 which extended the prohibition from practising pharmacy to licentiates, as well as Fellows, and their co-partners and servants residing in Edinburgh.[6] No licentiate or Fellow of the Corporation of Surgeons was allowed to become a member of the College of Physicians.

In 1765 a third bye-law added midwifery to the list of prohibitions, although this was repealed in 1787. These restrictions were the subject of recurring debate and disagreement among members of the College. A number of eminent physicians, including William Cullen, John Gregory and Joseph Black, objected to the restriction being applied to licentiates on the grounds that they would be deprived of income and training opportunities.

Professor John Gregory, the father of the contentious James, had published his influential *Lectures on the Duties and Qualifications of a Physician* in 1772, containing the following passages which were to be much quoted in the future:

> *There have arisen at different periods ... great disputes about the boundary of physic and surgery and the proper subordination of surgery to medicine. A dispute hurtful to mankind. ...*
>
> *In regard to pharmacy, it were much to be wished, that those who make it their business should have no connection with the practice of physic, or that physicians should dispense their own medicines, and either not charge the expense of them to their patients at all, or charge it at the prime cost.* [In this way we] *can expect to see physicians placed in the honourable independence, which subjects them to no attentions but such as tend to the advancement of their art.*

The passage with regard to pharmacy is rather ambiguous and was interpreted by Duncan as being in favour of, and by James Gregory as against, the dispensing of drugs by physicians in the subsequent discussions.

In 1796 Dr Thomas Spens moved to have the bye-law of 1754 repealed so as to allow all Fellows and licentiates to dispense drugs. There was much opposition to this proposal, by Andrew Duncan among others, and no vote was taken. (Duncan was later to change his mind and this was to become one of the contentious issues.) When Spens became president in 1803, one of his first actions was to set up a committee to review the laws of the College and suggest amendments. The committee which he appointed consisted of five members – himself as president, Andrew Duncan Sr, Andrew Duncan Jr, Thomas Hope and James Buchan, all past or future presidents of the College, and all, except Duncan Sr, at that time holding office in the College. Duncan Jr was librarian, Hope the secretary and Buchan the treasurer.

The committee suggested a number of amendments, among which was the proposal that the bye-law of 1754 could be interpreted as permitting members, when they thought fit, to prepare and dispense medicines to their own patients, provided that they did not charge for them or set up apothecaries' shops for the purpose of selling medicines. This interpretation of the ruling provoked such an intense reaction from some members of the College that the committee decided to withdraw this recommendation and there the matter should have rested for the time being.

James Gregory's attack

Despite the fact that the proposed amendment had been withdrawn, James Gregory, who had been president of the College from 1798-1801, commenced a violent public attack on the College and its committee which he sustained for six years. Within six weeks of the committee's retraction, Gregory published two lengthy pamphlets, the first a 'Review of the Proceedings of the Royal College of Physicians of Edinburgh from 1752-1804, both inclusive, with respect to separating the practice of medicine from the practice of pharmacy, and preventing any of their own Fellows or licentiates residing in Edinburgh from keeping an apothecary's shop, or practicing pharmacy, by himself, his copartners, or his servants'.

The pamphlet was published for public distribution and not officially given to Fellows of the College, although Andrew Duncan, against whom much of the invective was directed, received a personal copy inscribed from the author. In his copy, Duncan has inserted handwritten notes criticising James Gregory for ignoring the advice of his father, John Gregory, whose

> ... lectures on the duties and qualifications of a Physician contain many excellent admonitions to medical practitioners and it is truly wonderful that they have had so little influence on his son. For it is an undeniable fact, that no member of the College of Physicians has so frequently and shamefully acted in contradiction to the injunction of Dr John Gregory, as his son. ... How little regard has he paid to the following sentence 'The quarrels of the Physicians when they end in appeals to the publick generally hurt the contending parties but what is of more consequence they discredit the profession and expose the faculty itself to ridicule and contempt'.

Gregory's pamphlet reviewed the College history, particularly with regard to dispensing, and made a powerful case against changing the bye-law of 1754. The committee had by then agreed that there should be no change, so Gregory's fulminations were quite inappropriate. He made a number of attacks on the committee, which he accused of 'base and sordid motives' and endeavouring by 'falsehood, chicane, and breach of faith' to accomplish a 'most dishonourable and illegal object'. He was particularly critical of Spens, whom he accused of holding discussions from which Gregory had been excluded and of selecting committee members who were inclined to his views. In fact, with regard to the matter of dispensing medicines, the committee had been initially divided three to two against change. However, according to Duncan Sr, Buchan had studied the College's historical records in such detail that he persuaded the members of the committee to alter their opinions in favour of the amendment.

Spens and Hope responded to Gregory on 29 January 1805:

> We have just now heard, that you have printed ... some observations upon the alterations of the byelaws of the College of Physicians, which were some time ago submitted to the consideration of the College. ... It has been long known to you, that most of us, who saw little objection to the proposed alterations, except that they did not meet with the approbation of some of our friends in the College, considered it to be of more importance to maintain the unanimity of the College, than to carry through those changes, and that ... the Committee, and some other members, had agreed that the measure should be dropped.
>
> Now, it would be extremely unpleasant to us, both as individuals and members of the College, to have such matters made the subject of public talk and discussion, when no public good can attend that discussion, and certainly no benefit to the College as a body. It would be very unpleasant to us that our private or confidential opinions should be published ... particularly by a person with whom we have been so long in such habits of friendship, and the more especially as with a view to prevent a division in the College, the prevailing opinion was, that the changes proposed were not to be persisted in.
>
> This unanimity would be completely destroyed by any publication on the subject; and, if we recollect distinctly, it is contrary to our solemn obligation as Fellows, that such transactions should be disclosed.
>
> But, independent of all reasoning on the subject, any publication would be so very disagreeable to us, that, we think, our long friendship warrants us earnestly to request, and entitles us confidently to expect, that, if such ever were intended, it may be suppressed.

Gregory responded that he could not comply, for his next pamphlet had already been distributed to the public. This 'Censorian Letter to the President and Fellows of the Royal College of Physicians of Edinburgh', dated 25 January 1805, consisted of 142 pages of rambling invective covering much the same ground. He criticises each member of the committee and describes his attempt to outsmart Duncan Sr. This is quoted as a sample of his prolixity and bias:

> *I made one feeble attempt to converse with Dr Duncan senior ... to enquire at what time he had changed that opinion on the subject, which, but about eight years before, he had expressed so strongly. ... I explained to him, that I wished to know whether it was before that Committee was appointed, ... or after the subject had been discussed. ... He told me, that it was just at the time when the President first proposed the subject to the Committee; and added, that he had now a very different view of the subject from what he had formerly. ... In that manner he escaped from the dilemma that I had prepared for him, which in general is no easy matter. If he had told me he had changed his opinion before that Committee was appointed, I meant to have asked him whether the President knew of the change of his opinion before he appointed the Committee; ... If he had told me, that he changed his opinion only after hearing the subject discussed in the Committee, I meant to have asked him, what new arguments had been suggested to him on the subject, ... had now induced him totally to change his opinion. From the very peculiar tenor of his answer, which disarmed me at once of both those weapons, I presume he had a shrewd suspicion of what I intended by my dilemma, and what my next question would be.*

According to Duncan, this conversation took place in Gregory's carriage as they were going to visit a patient. Gregory had asked him:

> *'Oh Doctor! ... I do not ask you how you got the New Light; but will you tell me when you got it?' To this I ... replied, that I really could not precisely tell when I changed my sentiments, but that it was chiefly in consequence of the discussions which took place in the Committee, and particularly from what Dr Buchan had discovered in the old minutes. ... I read with astonishment the erroneous and unfair conclusion which you have drawn from this conversation in your Review and Censorian Letter.*[7]

Having slated the members of the committee at length, collectively and individually, Gregory, towards the end of his 'Censorian Letter', makes the hypocritical statement that, '... no five men could be found in the world, towards whom I was more perfectly free from every kind of ill-will; nay, there is not one of them to whom I did not bear very hearty goodwill. I am sure none of them ever had the smallest reason to suspect me of any ill-will towards them; and all but one of them have had actual experience of my goodwill, and my zeal to serve and oblige them.' [All except Duncan Sr had been his students.]

Gregory's protests were to preoccupy the quarterly and council meetings of the College for several years and have been well documented by Craig.[8] At the first quarterly meeting (5 February 1805) after Gregory's 'Censorian Letter' was issued, the members declared that the president and committee 'had acted from purest motives, and in the most honourable manner, and that they well deserved the thanks of the College'.

In 1806 the College council reminded its members not to mention, out of doors, what passed in any of the meetings of the College, and recommended a strict observance of secrecy with regard to all such proceedings. Gregory took this injunction as a personal attack on himself, although it was not intended as such. He attended the next College meeting and delivered an address which was so offensive to the members that they voted that his indecorous and improper conduct merited a 'very severe Censure from the College'.[9] Gregory responded with a lengthy paper entitled 'Reasons of Protest against the Admonition to Secrecy and the vote of Censure' which was read to a quarterly meeting of the College in May 1807. The council considered it so insulting and disrespectful that it was not entered into the minutes.

At a College meeting on 24 November 1807, Gregory's latest outburst was discussed and he was found guilty of a deliberate violation of the truth in respect of some of his statements. He was invited to present his defence. After much procrastination, Gregory delivered in August 1808 his third pamphlet, 'Defence before the Royal College of Physicians of Edinburgh'. This lengthy pamphlet of 510 pages of confused and rambling nonsense is liberally decorated with Latin and Greek quotations, the only possible purpose of which was to display his (undisputed) wide classical education. In it he singled out seven members of the College, Andrew Duncan Sr among them, as being responsible for the 'most foul injustice' against him and raised the possibility of taking legal action against the College and the seven members who had voted for his 'severe censure'.

In the copy of Gregory's 'Defence' which Duncan had received from the author, Duncan wrote in the title page:

Character of the Author from S. Butler

He was in logic a great Critic
Profoundly skilled in analytic,
He could distinguish and divide
A hair, twixt south and southwest side
On either which he would dispute,
Confute, change sides, and still confute.

Duncan delivered to the College council an 'Opinion in the College of

Physicians of Edinburgh upon a charge against Dr Gregory for wilful and deliberate violation of the truth'. In the preface he wrote:

> *I have long had reason to believe, that it was Dr Gregory's earnest wish to force me, either into a paper war, or into a lawsuit. ... I have, however, a strong aversion, both to courts of justice and to literary warfare. ... Dr Gregory, indeed, I am told, treats the whole of this matter as a subject of merriment ... he has told some respectable citizens, that he would send them a book which would give them a good laugh. On my mind this controversy has had a very opposite effect, and I may affirm that, in the short space of three years, it has done more to interrupt my happiness, than all the other occurrences of my life for thirty years before.*

Duncan, privately, sought legal opinion from his friends, the Lord Advocate Henry Erskine and John Clerk KC, the Solicitor General, with respect to several queries. Erskine, in a friendly aside, wrote, 'I most earnestly beg leave to recommend to the parties, concerned, not to make them the subject of judicial discussion'. One of Duncan's questions was whether a member of the College would be transgressing the Act of the College if he were to supply his patients with medicines, although he made no charge, but was paid only for his advice and attendance. Erskine opined that he would not be guilty of transgression of the Act. Clerk, on the other hand, pointed out that the physician's fee is an honorary and 'the whole being paid for his services without distinction, some part of it is for the medicines. ... I am not aware of any case in which they could be said to have been given for nothing, unless it were where the Physician takes no fees at all, even for attendance.' What a pity that this legal opinion had not been available when the committee first considered the matter – it might have prevented the subsequent furore.

By September 1808 the patience of the College was exhausted. It was regretted 'that any one of their body should have acted so as to call forth an animadversion and censure of this nature', and declared by a majority vote that Dr Gregory 'had been guilty of a wilful and deliberate Violation of the Truth'. The council was instructed to draw up its own account of the transactions relating to Dr Gregory. This 'Narrative of the conduct of Dr Gregory' was published in 1809. Its style suggests that Andrew Duncan was much involved in its composition. It was released for public distribution as a counter to Gregory's published pamphlets. The 'Narrative' gives a history of the events leading up to the dispute of 1804 and Gregory's subsequent behaviour. It points out that he had broken the promise which each Fellow made when taking his seat, 'that [they] shall never divulge anything that is acted or spoken in any meeting of the College'. It stated that in his publications, Gregory had laboured to persuade his readers with gross misrepresentations and goes on to refute each of his allegations in detail.

Gregory responded to the 'Narrative' with an angry protest letter dated 7 February 1809, in which he named eight individuals who had displayed gross falsehood and malevolence towards him. Those named included Spens and five of his fellow professors: Duncans Sr and Jr, James Home, Thomas Hope and James Hamilton Sr.

This paper was remitted to a committee who considered it 'both in its matter and style to be equally inconsistent with truth and decency, and recommended Gregory's suspension from the rights and privileges he enjoyed as a Fellow of the College', until he made satisfactory acknowledgement of his wrongs.

This marks the end of Gregory's tirade against the College, but not of his war with Duncan.

The 'Viper and File'

In 1811 James Gregory circulated among his acquaintances in Edinburgh a number of poems in English and Latin and a short tale. All of them seem puerile and pointless, until their mystery is revealed. They are addressed 'To a Fellow Professor' and signed with the pseudonym Nestor Ironsides,[10] but Gregory made no attempt to deny that they were his.

One of the poems was the 'Viper and File' derived from the fable of Phædrus, *Vipera et Lima*. Gregory's poetic ability was even worse than Duncan's and this lengthy epic does not merit reproduction. In brief it is an account of a viper attacking a file and coming off worse against the teeth of the file. Accompanying this poem was a 'An old Story':

A Gentleman, one day, writing a Letter in a Coffee-House, observed that a person looked over his shoulder, and read what he wrote. Without saying a word, he wrote, – 'But I must write no more at present; for an impertinent scoundrel is looking over my shoulder, and reading every word that I write.' 'You lie, you damned rascal!' said the looker on, 'I am not reading what you write!' The moral of this Story, if any person shall have sense enough to find it out, will be most acceptable to all the parties concerned.

The clue to these apparently obscure writings was given in a footnote.

Written on perusing a smart Review of two Works never published, never distributed, never printed, never written, NEVER COMPOSED!!! and not likely soon to be so: of which works only A FEW SHEETS HAD BEEN PRINTED!!! See Articles xxv, xxvii, pages 155-169 of 'The Annual

Medical Review and Register for the year 1809'. By a Society of Physicians Vol II. Printed for John Murray, 32 Fleet Street, London.[11]

The two articles referred to in the *Annual Medical Review and Register* were included in a paper entitled 'Review of Publications on the Disputes in the Edinburgh College of Physicians'. The fact that a London medical journal should devote space to Edinburgh's medical dispute is an indication of the wide interest in the matter. Three publications were reviewed – the 'Narrative of the conduct of Dr James Gregory', the 'Opinion delivered by Dr Duncan Sr' and 'Historical Memoir of the Medical War in Edinburgh in the Years 1805, 1806 and 1807' by Dr Gregory. The anonymous reviewer gives a good analysis of these papers, even commending Gregory for his stand against altering the interpretation of the Act of 1754, by which he anticipated the opinion of Counsel John Clerk KC referred to above. He is otherwise highly critical of Gregory and sympathetic to Duncan. The point at issue, however, is that he refers to Gregory's 'Historical Memoir', which, although printed, had been withdrawn from publication and was never issued. Gregory's conclusion was that it must have been stolen by someone from the printer (Messrs Ballantyne) and made available to the reviewer. Duncan became aware that his colleagues regarded Gregory's innuendos as being directed at him. Duncan was the viper and the 'looker-on' in the 'Story', and Gregory was the file. The innuendo was the Duncan was both the thief and the reviewer.

In a 'Letter to Dr Gregory', Duncan wrote:

Although these Poems, in the opinion of many ... shew no great marks either of genius or of judgement, and afford no proof either of a good head or a good heart; yet at a distance from Edinburgh, they may do me much mischief. With strangers, they may not only hurt my present character, but my posthumous reputation; and I own I am ambitious to hold some share in the esteem of posterity, to be holden and reputed an honest man.

Gregory approached John Murray II, publisher of the *Annual Medical Review,* to find out how he obtained the 'stolen' sheets. Murray replied in a letter dated 2 June 1810:

When Mr John Ballantyne was in London last year, he told me that he was printing a new work of yours, on the subject of the medical controversy at Edinburgh: his account of it interested me; and having so very much enjoyed the wit and talent displayed in your two former publications upon the same subject, I asked him if he might give me a copy to which he immediately assented.

Ballantyne sent Murray the relevant copy which Murray lent to 'two gentle-men' in London, not having time to read it himself. He professed not to know who were the authors of the *Review*.

The editors of the *Annual Medical Review* also sent a lengthy statement confirming Murray's letter. Murray, the son and successor of Duncan's first publisher, wrote a separate letter to Duncan dated 23 June 1810:

> *It will afford me pleasure to assist, by every means in my power, in exposing the complete fallacy of the report, which you tell me has been circulated, of your having written an article upon the subject of Dr Gregory's work. ... I shall immediately inclose [sic] your letter to the Editor of the work, and I have no doubt but that he will easily induce the actual writer of the article in question to declare himself. ...*

The editors of the *Review* issued a DECLARATION dated 2 July 1810:

> *A letter from Dr Duncan senior of Edinburgh, in which he states, that he has been charged with having written the articles ... relative to the disputes in the Edinburgh College of Physicians, having been communicated by Mr Murray to the Editors ... [they] authorise him to declare, that Dr Duncan did not write the articles in question, and that they have not had any communication with or from him upon that or any other subject.*

Despite these letters which cleared Duncan of any involvement, Gregory refused to back down or make any apology. Thus an unsatisfactory conclusion was drawn to the dispute which had lasted six years, wasted an inordinate amount of College time, and caused the vulnerable Andrew Duncan great distress. The aggressive James Gregory does not emerge with any great credit either.

Notes

1   Christison (1885), vol. I, pp. 78-79.
2   Bristed (1803), p. 559. Bristed was a medical student in Edinburgh for two years and in his book gives an objective account of the University and its professors which is not entirely favourable. He appreciated Andrew Duncan, however, and notwithstanding his criticisms, states: 'I have spent two years of the most pure and unalloyed felicity, which can perhaps fall to the lot of human nature, under the fostering influence, and in the calm, the hallowed retreats of this justly distinguished and deservedly honoured university', p. 632.
3   Cockburn (1909), p. 97.
4   Gregory (1800), p.195, from which this quotation is taken, is one of James Gregory's extraordinary fulminations extending to 260 pages. It purported to be a criticism of the organisation of the surgical staffing of the Royal Infirmary –

which badly needed reorganisation – but was in fact a thinly veiled attack on surgery in general. 'It was the spark which ignited a conflagration that persisted when its original and admirable purpose was achieved, for it led to bitter personal controversies between members of the medical profession ...'. See Turner (1937), p. 126.

5   James Gregory, in *Gregory* (1803), p. 344, wrote: '... it can be no secret, that in Edinburgh a great part of the business of those called Surgeons, is physic rather than Surgery ... I have no doubt that in Edinburgh three fourths at least ... of the proper medical practice is done by members of the College of Surgeons; who in fact, though not in name, are the ordinary physicians in every family.'

6   This restriction applied only to licentiates and Fellows working within the City of Edinburgh and its suburbs.

7   Duncan (1811), pp. 23-25, Letter to Dr James Gregory.

8   Craig (1976), pp. 419-36.

9   RCPE minutes, 26 November 1806.

10 It was customary, at that time, for individuals to use pseudonyms when writing scurrilous pamphlets. Gregory was thought to have been 'Jonathan Dawplucker', the author of a pamphlet attacking the surgeon John Bell published in 1799. See Kaufman (2005), pp. 356-64.

11 *Annual Medical Review and Register,* (1809), vol. II, pp. 155-69.

Documents and pamphlets quoted in this chapter are all accessible in the library of the Royal College of Physicians of Edinburgh and listed alphabetically in the Bibliography (see p. 236).

CHAPTER XIII

Duncan's dispute
with James Hamilton

JOHN CHALMERS

Persons of good sense ... seldom fall into it, except lawyers, university men, and men of all sorts that have been bred at Edinborough.

Benjamin Franklin on disputations[1]

He who robs me of my good name, takes from me that which not enriches him, but makes me poor indeed.

Duncan in a speech to the University Senate, 15 January 1825

The Chair of Midwifery

When the Edinburgh Medical School was founded in 1726, the Chair of Midwifery was given a lower status than that of the other chairs of medicine. Midwifery was not included as a required subject for the degree of Doctor of Medicine, and the professor was not a member of the medical faculty. The early holders of this chair taught only midwives and not medical students until the appointment of Thomas Young in 1756 and his successor Alexander Hamilton in 1780 who conducted courses of lectures which were popular with the medical students, although not a compulsory subject for graduation in medicine. Alexander Hamilton (1739-1802) was an energetic and influential man who became Deacon of the Edinburgh Incorporation of Surgeons, equivalent to the President of the Royal College of Surgeons after the Incorporation was awarded its Royal charter in 1778. Alexander Hamilton was a good friend of Andrew Duncan and one of the early members of the Aesculapian Club. He also published *Elements of Midwifery* in 1775, which went through several editions. He included in his practice the treatment of women and children whom he considered were neglected by the other professors and published a 'Treatise on the Management of Female Complaints' in 1789. The founding of a Lying-in Hospital in 1793 for the wives of indigent tradesmen and unmarried women, with the professor as Physician-in-charge, further established his position.[2] Alexander Hamilton went about his practice in a sedan chair and was one of the last private owners of this method of conveyance. The sedan chair is now in the National Museum of Scotland, having been donated by Professor James Young Simpson.

His son James joined him as an assistant and shared the teaching duties with his father from 1790 until he succeeded him in 1800. The practice of sharing a chair towards the end of the primary holder's career was frequently adopted at that time. As there was no other pension arrangement, the assistant undertook to contribute part of his income to the senior partner. In the Hamiltons' case, James guaranteed to provide half of his income from class fees to his father.

[There were two unrelated James Hamiltons practicing medicine in Edinburgh at the same time, both living in adjacent houses in St Andrew's Square. The Professor of Midwifery was referred to as 'Junior' to distinguish him from the much respected physician James Hamilton (1749-1835) who became 'Senior'. James Hamilton Sr was a great friend and ally of Andrew Duncan.]

James Hamilton Jr (1767-1839) was described as having great ability marred by his aggressive and uncompromising disposition. Robert Christison described him as

> ... *a little man, frail looking, but strong, ... not at all comely, and undeniably wigged. He had a quick, short, nervous step, and a slight stoop and downward look as if his eyes took account always of what his feet were doing. His voice was harsh and his intonation Scotch, pure and unsophisticated. Nevertheless he was a man of great energy and alertness, and a powerful lecturer ... his information was inexhaustible, drawn as it was from the stores of vast experience. ... As a critic he seemed to be in his favourite element, and a snarling, unfair, unfeeling critic he was. For Dr Hamilton was always in the right – dissentients ever wrong. ...*[3]

His nephew Alexander Lesassier observed that Hamilton was 'never in an ill humour – and always in motion – like quicksilver never still – at the same time he is the Man of Science & the complete gentleman'.[4] Despite his disputative nature with his colleagues, he was considerate to the students and dealt kindly with his patients, attending to the needs of his town patients before those of the wealthy country gentry. He supported the Lying-in Hospital at his own expense. His lectures were popular with the students for their information and the pugnacity with which they were spiced. In 1815, 423 students attended his lectures. He published many articles and books on his specialty and was the first to name the condition eclampsia.

In 1792 Duncan referred to James Hamilton Jr as an 'ingenious young friend ... whose industries and abilities are already so well known and have been demonstrated on so many occasions even at his early period of life …'.[5] This cordial relationship was soon to change.

The inferior status of midwifery

The Hamiltons, father and son, became involved in a bitter dispute with James Gregory which arose over a pamphlet 'A guide for Gentlemen study- ing Medicine at the University of Edinburgh', which had been published in London in 1792 under the pseudonym of J. Johnson Esq. This purported to give an account of the various medical departments of the University of Edinburgh, apparently written by a recent graduate, and contained much useful information about the teaching practices at that time. It did, however, emphasise the importance of midwifery and it gave fulsome praise for the teaching of midwifery by the two Hamiltons:

> *It is, therefore, very surprising, that this should be the only medical class which candidates for degrees are not obliged to attend. Does this proceed from the jealousy of the other professors, the negligence of the professor of midwifery, or the ignorance of the patrons of the university?*

Some other departments were criticised, such as botany on the grounds that it was adequately covered in materia medica, and mathematics because Professor Playfair's lectures coincided with the midwifery lectures.

James Gregory, whose teaching was actually given warm praise in the pamphlet, was infuriated by this attempt to promote midwifery. Several years before, he had successfully blocked in the Senate an attempt by the Hamiltons to have midwifery included in the medical curriculum, and in response to the 'Guide' he published an astonishing 174-page harangue in which he accused the Hamiltons of being the authors of the pamphlet and detailed at length his low opinion of midwifery which could be performed by a 'discrete sober woman who hath borne 3 or 4 children':

> *… there are many young men to whom it is particularly disgusting; and many wise and good men, and women too, … to whom the practice of midwifery by men is an abomination which degrades the character of one sex, and sullies the purity of the other.*

James Hamilton responded to Gregory's letter with a vigorous 86-page rebuttal, in which he denied having anything to do with the Johnson pam- phlet.[6] It seems likely, however, despite his protestations, that the Hamiltons were behind the publication, although the Senate exonerated them both. Gregory was so incensed by Hamilton Jr's reply that he beat him with his cane, for which he was fined £100 with costs. He declared that he would willingly repeat the offence for twice the sum.[7]

James Hamilton continued to rankle at the inferior status of his speciality within the University, and its effect on his wife who was socially stigmatised. A lawyer's wife had objected to her attending a subscription ball on the grounds that she was an accoucheur's spouse. This incident, according to Christison, 'caused much excitement in Edinburgh circles at dinner-tables'.[8] Not surprisingly, Hamilton did not mix socially with his colleagues, preferring rather to spend his evenings playing whist for considerable stakes with a narrow circle of friends.

In 1788 the Royal College of Physicians of Edinburgh repealed a resolution of 1772 which prohibited members from practicing midwifery; nevertheless it continued to be regarded as beneath the dignity of many Fellows, including Duncan and Gregory. Yet despite these prejudices James Hamilton was elected President of the College in 1812. The Royal College of Physicians, London on the other hand, continued to ban their Fellows from undertaking midwifery. A report by Sir Henry Halford in 1834 stated that midwifery 'is considered rather a manual operation and ... we should be very sorry to throw anything like a discredit upon men who had been educated at the Universities ... by mixing it up with this manual labour'.[9]

The battle for recognition of midwifery

In 1817 Hamilton appealed again to the University Senate to have midwifery included in the medical curriculum. This was rejected on three grounds: the inconvenience of having a seventh member of the faculty, the absurdity of physicians having to learn to deliver women in labour, and the heinous offence of encroaching on the field of the Professor of the Practice of Medicine by proposing to lecture on diseases of women and children. Hamilton hinted that the 'inconvenience' referred to a dilution of the fees that the faculty members would derive from examining the candidates for the degree of Doctor of Medicine if a further examiner were added to the panel. The fact that he had antagonised some members of the faculty by his aggressive behaviour did not help his case. If his personality had allowed him to be on better terms with his colleagues, his request might possibly have been granted.

In 1824 Hamilton went over the heads of the Senate by sending a lengthy submission[10] to the Lord Provost, magistrates and the Town Council of Edinburgh, who were the patrons and effective governors of the University, a situation which had existed since the founding of the University by a charter of James VI in 1621. From time to time disagreements had arisen between the University and Town Council in the distant past, but harmony had largely existed for the preceding century. The Town Council allowed the Senate to run its affairs without interference (although the limits of its authority were undefined), while the Council looked after funding, maintenance of buildings and the appointment of professors. Indeed this arrangement had worked so smoothly that the Senate was inclined to forget that they were carrying out their business on sufferance and the Council had forgotten the extent of its powers. It is of interest, and perhaps not unrelated, that the flowering of the Scottish Enlightenment coincided with this period of non intervention by the Town Council. Christison wrote:

> During this period, and especially the last fifty years of it, the University of Edinburgh reached to a wonderful height of prosperity and renown; for which it was indebted mainly to the eminence of the Professors, the government of the Senatus, and forbearance of the town council.[11]

By his submission to the Town Council, Hamilton was to trigger a period of intense dispute between the Council and University of Edinburgh which lasted for 35 years. In this submission, Hamilton informed the Council that he had made a request to the Senate eight years earlier for midwifery to be included as a required course within the medical student curriculum, and that the request had been refused on what he regarded as inadequate grounds. He pointed out that circumstances had changed since the founding of the Medical School in 1726; specialties had developed within the profession and the existing medical faculty was incapable of teaching practical subjects. He presented a strong case for the inclusion of midwifery and the care of women and children as essential parts of the student curriculum. He observed that there had been 19,348 deaths in 1820 in London, of which nearly half were children under the age of ten, including 725 stillbirths. The children had died of diseases which were not taught in Edinburgh.

He spoiled his otherwise reasonable case by including a bitter criticism of the existing faculty professors and their courses of lectures. He drew attention to the fact that the terms of reference of the various professorships were vague and that there was considerable overlap in their teachings. With the exception of Francis Home, Professor of Materia Medica, he made them out to be to be incompetent and disorganised. Andrew Duncan Sr, Professor of Theory of Medicine, came in for particular criticism. Hamilton 'ventured to allege, that the Students can derive from that individual Professor no additional knowledge which may enable them to cure disease'.[12]

Hamilton's criticisms had a certain validity, for the boundaries of the different professorships were not clearly defined and the professors played a sort of musical chairs, changing from one to another as vacancies arose. Andrew Duncan Jr, for example, occupied successively the Chairs of Medical

Jurisprudence, Institutes of Medicine and Materia Medica. There was no retirement age and no pension, so that some, including Duncan, continued to teach into old age when they were well past their prime. The professors, with the exception of the Professor of Anatomy, had no salary. They competed with each other for fees derived from teaching (three guineas from each student per session), from examinations, and from the private practice in which each was engaged. Even the Professor of Anatomy, Monro *secundus*, was one of the most sought after (and prosperous) clinicians.

Hamilton, who had a thriving private practice, always maintained that pecuniary interest was not one of his motives, but Duncan doubted this. Hamilton's campaign no doubt reflected his pent up years of resentment and jealousy and a genuine and justified belief in the importance of his specialty, but his presentation was marred by the unwise criticism of other professors of medicine. Despite this tactical error, the Town Council looked favourably on his submission. They reported to the Senate:

> *That in their opinion it would be of advantage to the Public, to the Medical Profession, and to the University that attendance on a Course of Lectures on Midwifery, and on Diseases of Women and Children, of equal extent and duration with the courses given by the members of the Medical Faculty, should form a part of the course of education of every well educated medical man, whatever branch of the Profession he may be afterwards called upon to practice, and that it should therefore form a part of the education of everyone who aspires to the honour of being made Doctor of Medicine of the University of Edinburgh.*

The medical faculty initially appeared to accept these instructions and the Senate was able to reply to the Town Council that the medical faculty, as part of a review of the curriculum (*Statuta Solennia*), essentially unchanged since 1785, 'have come to the resolution of proposing ... that attendance on the Class of Midwifery shall, on certain conditions, be required of such Medical Students as may hereafter become Candidates for the degree of Doctor of Medicine'. Meanwhile, Hamilton was able to report that he 'had the honour of being received [by the Senate] in the ordinary way (with the exception of a verbal protest from Dr Duncan Sr,) as Professor of Medicine, Midwifery, and the Disease of Women and Children'.

Hamilton oversteps the mark

If matters had been allowed to rest at this stage the subsequent war between town and gown might have been avoided, or at least delayed. However, Hamilton inexplicably introduced another, unrelated matter which was to provoke the Senate into retaliation. Hamilton, who had no part in the examination of the medical students, wrote letters to the Senate in which he recommended alterations to the examination for the degree of Doctor of Medicine.[13]

What James Hamilton proposed to the Senate was a much more structured examination system, based on written answers to preset questions in place of the existing oral examination. He also suggested that the emphasis on the knowledge of Latin might be reduced and that the candidates be examined in English. He acknowledged that a classical education was useful and that some understanding of Latin was essential for every doctor, but suggested that answering questions in Latin was a waste of time. Finally he proposed doing away with the obligatory thesis required of the candidates.

History was to prove Hamilton right, but this was the wrong time to raise the matter. For Andrew Duncan Sr, the suggestion that the status of Latin be reduced, coupled with Hamilton's criticism of his teaching and the irritation of the Town Council's interference, was too much to take and it provoked a vigorous reaction. Little did the two protagonists foresee the consequences of their contretemps.

The high reputation of the Edinburgh Medical School at this period depended not only on the quality of its professors, but on the respect for the rigorous requirements of its MD degree which are detailed in chapter I. Duncan's response to Hamilton was a lengthy address to the Senate on 22 November 1824.[14] He strongly criticised the suggestion that the Latin content of the examination of the medical students be reduced, and he pointed out that the reputation of the Medical School had suffered when they had awarded the MD degree to a Dr Leeds who had been given a special dispensation to sit his examinations in English. Dr Leeds had subsequently applied for a post in London where, to the horror of the Royal College of Physicians, London he was found to be illiterate – that is, he could not speak Latin – and was therefore *non satis doctus*. Duncan argued at length of the importance of Latin to medical men, without saying quite why. He also asserted that 'we ought to send out no men into the world, honoured with our degree as a *vir doctior*, who is entirely ignorant of the Greek language'. If the partial removal of Latin from the examination was allowed, he warned:

> ... that illiterate men will soon obtain degrees here, which will disgrace every future Doctor of Medicine from Edinburgh ... a door would be opened for conferring the degree ... on illiterate apothecaries and impudent empyrics. ... If any one shall ever obtain the degree of Doctor of Medicine from the University of Edinburgh, who is not able to under-go his examen privatissimum wholly in the Latin language, the honour of that title from the

University of Edinburgh, over the same degree from St Andrews, Aberdeen or Glasgow will be completely terminated.[15]

Duncan's overreaction

Duncan, who had obtained his own MD, without examination, from St Andrew's University 55 years before, delivered a scathing attack on Aberdeen and St Andrews Universities which were entitled to award doctorates of medicine and law by the authority of their papal foundations, despite having no schools of medicine or law. He made the mocking comment that these universities 'got rich by degrees' (although he had been exempted from paying a fee for his). He then went on to state that

> *Dr Hamilton ... from motives best known to himself, but, in my opinion, chiefly with the view of promoting his own pecuniary interest ... lately presented a very extraordinary Memorial to the Patrons of the University* [Edinburgh Town Council] *in which he endeavours to demonstrate the great superiority of Midwifery over every branch of Medical Science ... [it] contained a false and calumnious libel not only upon me as an individual Professor... but on all lecturers on the Institutions of Medicine. ... Midwifery cannot be properly studied in an University. Beside this, it is by no means necessary that every Physician should qualify himself for being a* Sage Femme, *– a Houdy-wife in the dialect of the vulgar Scot. And indeed it is the opinion of many physicians, that to old women the ordinary business of Midwifery should be entirely confined.*[16]

Finally, Duncan railed against the Town Council for interfering in university affairs. Duncan at 81 was the senior member of the Senate, and his address persuaded that body to modify its decision regarding inclusion of midwifery. As a gesture of defiance, the Senate decided to delay the introduction of midwifery to the curriculum and Hamilton's admission to the faculty for three years.

Hamilton, who had been led to believe that all was cut and dried, received notice of this decision only three days before a course of lectures that he had carefully prepared was due to commence. Not surprisingly, he was incandescent and sent off another lengthy communication to the Town Council informing it of the Senate's *volte-face* and pointing out that the Universities of Glasgow and Dublin required their students to attend a course of midwifery, as did the Royal College of Surgeons of Edinburgh for their licentiates.[17]

The Council reacted by sending another commission to the Senate, insisting that Hamilton be accepted into the Faculty of Medicine without delay. The Senate refused to do this and the Council, no doubt in a conciliatory move, then compromised by insisting that any delay should be limited to one year. Again the Senate refused and each party sought legal opinion to try to clarify the matter. The University's counsel delivered a rather inconclusive opinion, while the Town Council's counsel reaffirmed an earlier opinion that the Council 'be absolute Master of the College in all things'.

The Royal Commission

In May 1825 the Senate suggested to the Town Council that to restore harmony both parties should make an 'united, cordial and earnest application to the Crown, praying that His Majesty might command a Royal Commission for the express purpose of defining the rights, powers, and privileges belonging to each body'. The Town Council, which had no doubts about their rights and privileges, declined and so war was declared. The Council announced that it intended to make a visitation to the University on 10 November 1825, an event which had last taken place in 1703. On the due date and with much pomp, the Council, robed and led by their mace-bearer, met the Senate, gowned in academic robes, and required them to acquiesce with its instruction regarding the teaching of midwifery. The Senate replied that it could not comply, whereupon Lord Provost Trotter read an Act of Visitation which declared that from that date midwifery was a necessary subject for a degree of Doctor of Medicine and that no degree should henceforth be conferred by the Senate, except in accordance with the terms of the Act. Knowing that it was shortly to receive General John Reid's bequest of more than £50,000 (nearly £3 million in today's values), the Senate felt emboldened to resist the Council, but in the subsequent action at the Court of Session they lost their case and the authority of the Town Council was confirmed.

Andrew Duncan Jr detailed the unsuitability of the Council for the task of running an academical body. The members were appointed for only one or two years from the merchant company and the incorporated trades. 'By profession none ... are at all connected with letters, or ... in habits of communication of the learned.' He predicted accurately that if the Council exercised their newly confirmed authority, 'the downfal [sic] of the university may be confidently predicted'. The Royal College of Surgeons, which was independent of the University, would, as one of the incorporated trades, have authority over the University.[18]

The Royal commission, which the Senate had requested, was constituted in 1826 and the dispute simmered down until the commission reported in 1831. This long delay was due to the fact that the commission had been set up to enquire into the running of all the universities and colleges in Scotland and not, as the Senate had hoped, simply to look into its quarrel with the

Town Council. The commission's lengthy report made some sensible recommendations. It recognised that the Town Council was 'a body not well fitted for the due exercise of the patronage of the University,'[19] and recommended placing the control of the University in the hands of five curators, two appointed by the Crown, two by the Town Council and one by the Senate. However, a change of government meant that no action was taken on the recommendations.

The Town Council meanwhile, its confidence bolstered by favourable legal decisions, proceeded to exert its control over the University with increasing arrogance and lack of consideration. This had a devastating effect on the morale of the Senate and the University as a whole, and contributed to a fall in student numbers from 2300 in 1823 to 1550 in 1858. The medical faculty, which had suffered the greatest interference, halved its number of students during this period, although this was partly due to the establishment of more schools of medicine in the United Kingdom and America.

James Hamilton, who had started it all, had the satisfaction of achieving his objective in 1830, when midwifery was at last included in the medical curriculum, and by 1833 the MD examination began to be held in English. Now allowed to take part in the examination of students for their degree of Doctor of Medicine, the aggressive Hamilton was noted by Christison to be a kindly and sympathetic examiner.[20] Despite now being a member of the establishment, however, he still had a score to settle. In 1832 he took legal action against the Senate, demanding that all censorious comments concerning him in the minutes be deleted. This was eventually accepted and several pages were obliterated. Hamilton continued to occupy the Chair of Midwifery until his death in 1839, when he was succeeded by James Young Simpson who established respect for the specialty of midwifery beyond all doubt during his 30-year tenure in the post.

Duncan's humiliation

Andrew Duncan was to suffer another humiliation at the hands of the litigious Hamilton. In a speech to the Senate on 15 January 1825,[21] Duncan accused Hamilton of having 'published a false and calumnious libel against the Senatus Academicus, against the Institutions of Medicine ... and against the present Professor of Institutions of Medicine as an individual'. In his speech, Duncan repeated at length his grievances against Hamilton:

> *He asserts, in plain language, that all my labours in the University of Edinburgh, for more than 30 years, have been of no real use; and it follows, as an unavoidable conclusion, that I have been merely picking the pockets of*

the Students, and consuming their time, with useless, nay, with pernicious
theory. ... I cannot indeed say that I have sustained from this groundless
calumny any pecuniary injury. ... I can qualify [for] no damages. Dr
Hamilton's assertions ... have had no influence in diminishing the number
of my Pupils – 224 that winter session.

Duncan goes on to state that 'he who steals my purse steals trash. But he
who robs me of my good name, takes from me that which not enriches him,
but makes me poor indeed.' He pronounced Hamilton's original memorial
to the Town Council as 'one of the most singular productions that I have
ever known to come from the pen of any Professor'. He requested the Senate
to order Dr Hamilton to sign a palinode (recantation) in which he acknowledged his sins, apologised for his transgressions and entreated forgiveness,
failing which they should suspend him.

This speech and all the other speeches, reports and memoranda from
both antagonists were printed and widely circulated to the intense interest
and amusement of the students and the public at large. Duncan referred to
the matter in his printed lectures to his students, making derisory remarks
about Hamilton, and ending that 'he who has ventured to assert in print,
that, from the lectures on the Institutions of Medicine ... a student can
derive no knowledge which may enable him to cure disease, has proclaimed
himself to be, either an ignorant empiric, or an arrogant imposter'[22] (an
'empiric' in those days was a derogatory term implying a quack). He concluded another lecture with the remarks that 'the assertion with regard to my
lectures, is as false as it is calumnious and I flatter myself you will be able to
tell that, though now an octogenarian, I can still communicate to my hearers
much knowledge which may be useful in the cure of disease'.[23] Two hundred
and fifty printed copies of these lectures were circulated. Hamilton's reaction
was to declare to the Senate that 'you have now compelled me, after unexam-
pled forbearance, to institute legal proceedings against Dr Duncan Sr'.[24]

A successful action of scandal and defamation was raised by Hamilton
against Duncan 'for publishing and circulating aspersions and charges of a
most injurious and offensive nature and highly defamatory of the pursuer',
and Hamilton was awarded £50 damages and costs.[25] Duncan appealed,
but the Lord in Ordinary upheld the verdict of the Commissary Court and
Duncan was fined a further five guineas with expenses.[26] The frustrated
Duncan appealed again to the Court of Session. He was represented by
Francis Jeffrey, while Hamilton was represented by Henry Cockburn,
leaders of their profession who were to become distinguished judges. The
four Judges of the Inner House who heard this appeal again agreed (with
one dissension) that the original verdict was correct. They pointed out that
while Dr Hamilton had expressed himself improperly and was to some

extent to blame, Duncan was at greater fault in addressing himself to the students on this subject in language quite unjustifiable, and that he had allowed the matter to rankle too long in his mind.[27]

Thus concluded a sad episode which had clouded Duncan's later years. He wrote, 'although I may forgive any injury, yet I must candidly acknowledge, I am not always capable of forgetting it; particularly of forgetting false and scandalous calumnies, which, although they may never have hurt my pecuniary interest, have yet done irreparable injury to my mental feelings'. At the age of 81 his judgement was failing, and he had been unwise to make an intemperate tirade against a younger, wily adversary over a relatively minor issue affecting his pride.

The final outcome

Hamilton's action in appealing to Edinburgh Town Council over the heads of the University Senate had an unexpected sequel. It lit the fuse which started a chain of legal and parliamentary actions resulting in the Universities (Scotland) Act 1858 which transferred control of the University from Edinburgh Town Council to the University Court (in which the Council had representation). Thus a harmonious conclusion was brought to a bitter dispute between town and gown which had lasted 35 years. Alas, Andrew Duncan did not live to see this satisfactory outcome to the distressing events in which he had played such an active part.

Notes

1   Franklin (1964), p. 14.
2   Simpson (1994), vol. 3, pp. 131-41.
3   Christison (1885), vol. I, pp. 85-87. See also Young (1963), pp. 62-73.
4   Rosner (1999), p. 27.
5   This eulogy appeared in the preface of *Medical Commentaries* (1792), acknowledging Hamilton's contribution in no. 17 of a 272-page translation of a French paper, dated 1790.
6   Hamilton Jr (1793).
7   In another dispute involving Professor John Hope, who had accused Hamilton Jr of lying, Hamilton was awarded £500 damages which was reduced to one farthing on appeal. Christison, who also suffered provocation from Hamilton, chose to refrain from reacting as his colleagues had done, commenting that 'many a man has repented of acting, but devil a soul of forbearing'.
8   Christison (1861), p. 339.
9   Halford (1834).
10   Hamilton Jr (1824).
11   Christison (1861), pp. 25-26.
12   Hamilton Jr (1824).
13   Hamilton Jr (1824 and 1825).
14   Duncan (1824).
15   *Ibid.*
16   *Ibid.*
17   Hamilton Jr (1825).
18   Duncan Jr (1827), pp. 353-55.
19   Royal Commission Report, pp. 69-72.
20   Robert Christison was also involved in dispute with Hamilton in 1825 when Senate was discussing the status of the Chair of Medical Jurisprudence as well as Midwifery. Christison had maintained

that jurisprudence was even more important a subject than midwifery which
inevitably drew a long printed criticism
from Hamilton. Christison wrote: 'I was
highly provoked by his overstepping the
bounds of legitimate argument, and at
first premeditated retaliation. ... But I
cooled, and refrained; ... If only Duncan
had shown such restraint he might have
ended his days a happier man.'
21   Duncan (1825).
22   'Conclusion of lecture, 1824'.
23   'Observations on the office of a faithful
teacher ... (1823)'.
24   Hamilton Jr (1825).
25   Commissary Court, 5 July 1825, Dr James
Hamilton v. Dr Andrew Duncan.
26   Petition of Andrew Duncan Sr into the
Right Honourable, the Commissaries of
Edinburgh, Consistorial Court, 5 August
1825.
27   Cases decided in the Court of Session, no.
280, 2 February 1826.

CHAPTER XIV

Duncan and Sir Henry Raeburn

JOHN CHALMERS

Andrew Duncan and Sir Henry Raeburn were close friends, fellow members of the Harveian Society and golfing companions. In Duncan's oration to the Harveian Society, delivered in 1824 following the death of Raeburn, he records his first acquaintance with the artist:

> *Following the death of the young Charles Darwin [see page 117], I was anxious to retain some slight token in remembrance, of my highly esteemed young friend; and, for that purpose, I obtained a small portion of his hair. I applied to Mr Gilliland, at that time an eminent jeweller in Edinburgh, to have it preserved in a mourning ring. He told me, that one of his present apprentices was a young man of great genius, and could prepare for me in hair, a memorial that would demonstrate both taste and art. Young Raeburn was immediately called, and proposed to execute, on a small trinket, which might be hung at a watch, a Muse weeping over an urn, marked with the initials of Charles Darwin. This trinket was finished by Raeburn, in a manner which ... afforded manifest proof of very superior genius, and I still preserve it, as a memorial of the singular and early merit, both of Darwin and of Raeburn.*

Duncan then described Raeburn's progression from apprentice jeweller to portrait painter and suggested that the Harveian Society was to some degree responsible for bringing him to public notice, by commissioning some of his earliest works, including portraits of Alexander Wood and William Inglis (1712-92), one of the early captains of the Honourable Company of Edinburgh Golfers and Deacon of the Incorporation of Surgeons on three occasions. Duncan himself was one of Raeburn's subjects. He concluded by noting that Raeburn was distinguished also for his enjoyment of

> *... healthful and manly exercise and I am proud to say, that even in the 80th year of my age, I continued to be not only his fellow member in the Royal Company of Scottish Archers, in the Golfer's Company at Leith and in the*

*Society for the restoration of the Ludi Apollinares at Edinburgh ... but I was
his opponent in the last game at golf which he ever played. On Saturday the
7th of June 1823, I called at his painting rooms, after concluding the business
I had allotted for the day. After he had also finished his business, we walked
together to Leith Links. There, removed from the smoke of the city of Edinburgh, we conjoined, with pleasing conversation, a trial of skill at a salutary
and interesting exercise, to which we had both a strong attachment. ... I
may venture to say, that it will be difficult to find two men in Edinburgh,
who have attended more to the duties of their profession and, at the same
time, enjoyed a greater share of salutary recreation than we have done.*

After the game they enjoyed a temperate meal and a social glass at the
Golfer's Hall in the company of a few friends and returned to Edinburgh by
carriage; but 'in little more than the short space of a single month I had to
perform the melancholy duty of accompanying his dead body to a grave'.
Raeburn died aged 58, four years before his golfing companion.

An anonymous elegiac ode to Raeburn was subsequently submitted to
the Harveian Society:

*And yet, thou are not wholly lost! For still,
While taste and talent shall to me be dear,
Thy works shall shew thy genius and thy skill,
And future ages shall thy name revere;
We, who their equals in the race appear,
Shall one by one descend to kindred clay,
Our name shall perish like the leaf that's sear,
But thine shall flourish like the verdant bay,
Unscath'd amidst the storm, perchance to bloom for aye.*

Raeburn's portrait of Duncan was to become the subject of a bitter dispute between the Royal Public Dispensary and the Royal College of Physicians regarding ownership. In his Harveian Address on Sir Henry Raeburn,
Duncan stated:

*A third subject on which Raeburn at an early period employed his pencil
was a portrait of myself painted for the Royal Public Dispensary, to which
I had the happiness of giving a beginning in Edinburgh. On these pictures I
need hardly stop to say that he bestowed very peculiar attention; and indeed
hardly add, that, at an early period [of Raeburn's career], they attracted
very considerable notice in Edinburgh.*

This statement was confirmed by Richard Huie in his Harveian Oration of 1829: 'A portrait of the venerable founder was painted for the Dispensary some years ago, by the late Sir Henry Raeburn; and a bust is now about to be executed also, to be deposited in the Hall of the Institution.'

Alexander Bower stated in his *History of the University of Edinburgh*[1] that 'in [the Public Dispensary] there is a portrait of Dr Duncan, the founder of the Institution, painted for the Dispensary by the late Sir Henry Raeburn'. Bower, who was contemporary with Duncan and attended his lectures, published this, the third volume of his *History*, in 1830, but may have written it earlier. James Paterson, writing in *Kay's Edinburgh Portraits* published in 1838,[2] also states that Raeburn's portrait of Duncan was in the Dispensary Hall in West Richmond Street.

An engraving by E. Mitchell of the Raeburn portrait, made in 1819, is inscribed 'Painted for the Royal Dispensary of Edinburgh'.

The evidence from these various sources would appear to leave no doubt that a portrait of Duncan by Raeburn was painted for and placed in the Royal Dispensary. However, a letter dated 3 February 1829 suggests that this painting was then in the custody of the Royal College of Physicians. The letter, from a sculptor Lawrence Macdonald to the College Secretary, reads:

> *If you will permit me, I will beg through you a favour of the College of Physicians.*
>
> *My motive for so doing arises from being commissioned to execute in marble a bust of the late Doctor Duncan for the Royal Dispensary. The character of the work would be rendered more perfect should the college consent to allow me to have the possession for a few days of the portrait of the late Doctor, which I believe was painted by the late Sir Henry Raeburn.*
>
> *The portrait alluded to was painted before the natural force of his character had abated or the expression became undecided and as we are desirous to give a lasting representation of the late Doctor, the character, in order to do justice to the memory of the individual, and to posterity. ... the indulgence of the College in this matter would render the work more complete, and be doing a favour to the artist. ...*

The location of the original bust by Macdonald is unknown, but a plaster copy is held by the Royal College of Physicians.

No record has been found regarding the date and circumstances relating to the transfer of the portrait to the College, and these records with their conflicting dates do not help to clarify the matter. What is certain, however, is that by 1855 the painting was firmly in the possession of the College, for in that year the Dispensary commenced its appeal to the College to recover the painting which continued with interruptions until 1924. The history of this appeal is contained in entries in the minute books of the College and of the Dispensary.

The Royal College of Physicians council minute of 28 June 1855 records that the president had received a letter from the Royal Public Dispensary demanding on the part of its managers that a portrait of the late Dr Duncan, presently suspended in the reading room of the College, should be handed over to the Dispensary. The College Secretary was instructed to decline this request until the managers could prove legal right to its possession.

Presumably the required evidence could not be found, for no response from the Dispensary is recorded until 1912 when the Dispensary Manager's minute book on 9 July 1912 again raises the matter and reiterates 'that there was reason to believe that the Portrait by Sir Henry Raeburn of Dr Andrew Duncan, Founder of the Institution, which is in the possession of the Royal College of Physicians belongs to the Dispensary and not to the said College'. The secretary of the Dispensary was empowered to communicate with the College, suggesting a conference to put the matter finally to rest.

The College declined this proposal until the Dispensary submitted copies of any documents in their possession which appeared to them to justify a claim for the ownership of the picture. The Dispensary subsequently made a search of records 'at a cost not exceeding £5'. A College council minute of 28 January 1913 records that a 'Letter from the secretary of the Royal Public Dispensary along with the accompanying documents having been further considered, it was resolved that the president, Sir Robert Philip and the treasurer should be appointed to confer with the representatives of the Board of the Royal Public Dispensary regarding the ownership of the painting of Dr Duncan'.

As a result of this meeting the College decided, in its turn, to fund an 'expert search' of their records. A council minute of 9 June 1913 suggests that the evidence found was not convincing, although the 'Clerk expressed the opinion that the inference of ownership seemed to him to be distinctly in favour of the College'.

The Royal College of Physicians decided to seek legal opinions from the Dean of Faculty, Mr Charles Scott Dickson and Mr H. C. Macmillan KC. Their joint opinion of 28 October 1913 asked the following questions:

1. *Are Counsel of opinion that the Harveian Oration of Dr Duncan and the other documents and surrounding circumstances founded on by the Royal Public Dispensary give that Body good title to the Portrait?*

   We are of opinion in the negative. The Royal Dispensary, so far as appears, have never had possession of the Portrait and the evidence before us upon which they found, assuming it to be all admissible, is

*not in our opinion sufficient to establish in law that the Dispensary
ever owned the Portrait. The position of the Memorialists [the College]
appears to us to be much strengthened by the challenge of their rights
which the Royal Dispensary addressed to the Memorialists in 1855.
The Royal Dispensary took no steps to enforce the claim which they
then put forward and for fifty seven years they have acquiesced in the
continued possession of the Portrait by the Memorialists. In these
circumstances the Royal Dispensary are in our opinion effectually
barred from maintaining any right to delivery of the Portrait.*

2. *What course do Counsel recommend the College to follow?*

*We advise the Memorialists to decline to recognise any claim to the
Portrait on the part of the Royal Dispensary and, if necessary, to defend
any action which may be brought for its delivery. The question at issue
does not appear to us to be appropriate for determination either by
arbitration or by way of Special Case.*

The clerk was instructed to correspond with the representatives of the
Dispensary, proposing an exchange of legal opinions.

The Dispensary agreed to this and expressed the hope that the matter
should continue on the friendly footing hitherto followed. They obtained
separate opinions from Sheriff John Chisholm and Mr Charles D. Murray
KC which were both favourable to the Dispensary: 'In view of Counsel's
opinion on both sides being contrary, they suggested that the question at
issue be settled by Special Case to Court or, in the event of the College
declining to enter upon a Special Case, it was agreed … that the question
should be decided by raising an Action of Declarator and Delivery.'

On 28 October 1913 the College, having considered the documents
from the Dispensary, 'on the advice of the Clerk it was resolved that for the
present no further steps should be taken by the College in the matter'.

The Dispensary was not prepared to accept this. A minute of 14 April
1914 records that the secretary 'had made repeated enquiries as to whether
the College would agree to have the question tried by a friendly or Special
Case in the Court of Session. From the correspondence now submitted it
appeared that the Agent for the College had not given either an affirmative
or a negative reply to the enquiry and it was agreed that the correspondence
must be regarded as closed.'

After further consideration it was resolved on 22 April 1914 that as no
response had been received to the suggestion of a friendly petition in court,
'that a communication should now be addressed to the College, not through
their Law Agent, but through their president and council, proposing that

both parties should unite in having this matter definitely settled either by Arbitration or by a Special Case. ... failing such a proposal being agreed to it might be the duty of the managers to bring the question to the test of legal proceedings ...'.

By 13 October 1914 no further consideration from the College had been received, but the Dispensary decided that 'in view of the present national crisis it is also resolved to defer actual proceedings until further instructions from the Board'. There the matter rested until 11 April 1922 when the visiting committee of the Dispensary recommended that 'the question of ownership of the portrait of Dr Duncan, ... should be taken up again, the matter having been interrupted by the outbreak of the War when being specially considered'.

Repeated approaches were subsequently made to the College which were largely ignored. On 4 July 1922 the Dispensary made a concession that the College might retain the portrait if they conceded that ownership rested with the Dispensary, but again the College failed to respond.

On 15 January 1924 the Dispensary drew to the College's attention the fact that recent cleaning and restoration of the portrait had 'brought to light in the background the frontage building of the Edinburgh Dispensary which again accentuated the fact that the portrait is ... painted by Raeburn ...'.

At the College council meeting of 24 April 1924, it was reported:

Some months ago the council received from the Directors of the Royal Public Dispensary a request that a plate be attached to the portrait of Andrew Duncan by Sir Henry Raeburn in the College Hall, stating that that portrait had been painted for the Royal Public Dispensary. As the council was not satisfied that this was the case a committee was appointed to investigate the matter.

As a result of its enquiries the committee has come to the conclusion that the portrait of Duncan in the College Hall is not the portrait painted for the Dispensary. The main ground for this conclusion is the following extract from Dr Andrew Duncan's Harveian Oration on Sir Henry Raeburn delivered in 1824, the year after Raeburn's death.

A third subject on which Raeburn at an early period employed his pencil was a portrait of myself [Dr Andrew Duncan] painted for the Royal Public Dispensary to which I had the happiness of giving a beginning in Edinburgh. On these pictures (Wm Inglis, esq., Dr Alex. Wood, and myself) I need hardly stop to say that he bestowed very peculiar attention; and indeed hardly add, that, at an early period, they attracted very considerable notice in Edinburgh.

> *Considering that the portrait in the hall of the College was admittedly painted about 1818, long after Raeburn had attained an European reputation, it cannot, in the opinion of the committee, be the picture which Duncan stated was commissioned to be painted for the Royal Public Dispensary. The committee believes that there must be a portrait of Duncan by Raeburn somewhere, which would correspond to the period mentioned in the Oration, though it cannot for the present be traced.*

This report, which is the last reference to the dispute in either the College or Dispensary records, is extraordinary in several respects. No evidence is given to support the opinion that the portrait was painted about 1818. The portrait is of Duncan in his prime – not that of an old man aged 74, as he would have been in 1818. Raeburn set up his studio in Edinburgh in 1787, at which time Duncan would have been aged 43. It is entirely possible that Duncan should have arranged for Raeburn to be given the commission to paint his portrait and those of his associates William Inglis and Alexander Wood at that time, in order to help to establish the reputation of his friend, as he claimed. Duncan further states that these portraits were painted before those of William Robertson, Adam Ferguson and Thomas Elder which, according to Talbot Rice and Peter McIntyre,[3] were painted in 1792, c.1790 and 1797 respectively. The report ignores the very convincing evidence of the depiction of the Dispensary building in the background which surely establishes beyond doubt that this is the portrait done by Raeburn on behalf of the Dispensary. There is no record of a second portrait of Duncan by Raeburn.[4]

However, no one would dispute that the Royal College of Physicians, of which Duncan was twice president, is an appropriate location for his portrait, particularly as the Royal Public Dispensary no longer exists. It was absorbed into the General Practice Teaching Unit of the University in 1963.

Addendum: modern legal opinion

An eminent contemporary Counsel, Sir Frederick O'Brien QC, reviewed the legal aspects of the case in 2008 and his opinion reads:

> *The earliest surviving evidence of the close connection between the Royal Public Dispensary and the portrait of its founder, Dr Andrew Duncan, are the two Harveian addresses of 1824 and 1829. In the first Dr Duncan referred to a portrait of himself painted by Raeburn for the Dispensary; and in the second Richard Huie spoke similarly of 'a portrait of the venerable founder which was painted for the Dispensary some years ago by the late Sir Henry Raeburn'.*

This is historical rather than legal evidence of how the Dispensary came into possession of the painting, and it is not surprising that in their joint opinion Mr Scott Dickson and Mr Macmillan held it to be insufficient to establish that the Dispensary had ever owned the portrait.

Ironically, I suspect that the Royal College of Physicians would have a similar difficulty in proving ownership as distinct from possession. I note that the two learned King's Counsel upheld the College's right to the portrait, not because there was proof of purchase by them, or gift to them, but because 57 years had passed between the first attempt by the Dispensary to recover the painting in 1855 and the next in 1912. The concept of an owner being 'barred' from insisting in his right if he has acquiesced in someone else keeping his property for a lengthy period of time is well known in the laws of Scotland and England, but in the last century the courts have been less inclined to uphold a plea of 'bar' on the basis of lengthy delay alone. Some credible explanation for the delay would still have to be put forward.

In any event all this is academic. Since the Dispensary ceased to exist in 1963 no one could now have a title to sue on its behalf. As the College has nothing to fear in the way of legal challenge to their claim to the portrait, ... it would be magnanimous of them to put on record that the Royal Public Dispensary was probably the original owner of the portrait of its founder.[5]

ANDREW DUNCAN
Engraving of the Henry Raeburn portrait of Andrew Duncan by E. Mitchell. The engraving is subtitled:

'Andw. Duncan Senr. M.D. & Profer.
Physician to the King & the Prince Regent
1st Jany. 1819
Painted for the Royal Dispensary of Edinb.
H. Raeburn Pixt. E. Mitchell Sculpt.'

There are a number of copies of the engraving, including one owned by the Royal College of Physicians of Edinburgh.

Notes

1 Bower (1830), vol. III, p. 287.
2 Paterson (1838), vol. II, pp. 52-56.
3 Talbot, Rice and McIntyre (1957).
4 The portrait of Duncan painted for the Royal Medical Society and now in the Scottish National Portrait Gallery has been attributed to Raeburn by R. A. T. Mackie, *Raeburn Life and Art*, PhD Thesis, Edinburgh University (1993), but is clearly documented as being by Sir John Watson Gordon.
5 Personal communication to author.

CHAPTER XV

Memorials to the Dead

JOHN CHALMERS

Remember Man, as thou goes by,
As thou art now, so once was I.
As I am now, so shalt thou be;
Remember Man, that thou must die.

Inscription at entry to Greyfriars Churchyard,
quoted by Duncan

Andrew Duncan had an absorbing interest in graves and their epitaphs. In his booklet on the subject '*Elogiorum Sepulchralium Edinenisium Delectus* "Monumental Inscriptions" selected from burial-grounds in Edinburgh' (1815), he records a random selection of these. In his dedication he explains his objective: 'I trust, … that the examples here recorded, of men eminently distinguished and useful, will have some influence on their posterity, even on many who are yet unborn.' In the preface he writes:

> *Since the death of an amiable son* [Henry Francis, aged 13], *the Editor has made it a religious duty to pay a visit to his Grave every Christmas Day, the period of his death. This visit he has also extended to other Churchyards, where the dust of several of his best Friends is now deposited. His meditates during these mournful visits, have led him to imagine that he was invited by the calls of Gratitude, to take this method of promulgating commemo-ration of departed worth.*

Duncan gives examples of epitaphs from the cemeteries of the Chapel of Ease of St Cuthberts (now the Buccleuch Cemetery), Greyfriars, Canongate and Calton (now Old Calton). His choice seems random, although it includes some doctors and medical students. Many are individuals who are no longer 'eminently distinguished' or memorable – presumably friends or acquain-tances of Duncan. The inscriptions are also mostly in Latin, which makes it more difficult for the modern reader. One of interest is that of Dr Archibald

Pitcairne in Greyfriars Churchyard, whose grave was restored by the intervention of Duncan.

Archibald Pitcairne (1652-1713) graduated MA from the University of Edinburgh in 1671. He started with law, but changed course to study medicine both in France and Edinburgh. He obtained his MD at Rheims and returned to Edinburgh to set up practice. Pitcairne was one of the founding Fellows of the Royal College of Physicians, but failed in his efforts to start a medical faculty in the University of Edinburgh.[1] He was invited to become Professor of Medicine at Leyden in 1692, and Hermann Boerhaave, who was one of his students, acclaimed him as his master. Boerhaave (1668-1738) was to become the leading physician in Europe for a generation. The Leyden Medical School under his guidance was the model on which the Edinburgh Medical School was based.

At the insistence of his second wife, Pitcairne had to return to Edinburgh, where he once more became established as a very successful physician. He met his patients in a tavern opposite St Giles Cathedral, the Greping-Office (or Grape-Wine Office), starting at 6.30am and sometimes remaining there for several days at a time, his servant bringing him a clean shirt each day. He published many medical papers, composed poetry in Latin which was highly regarded, and wrote a comedy entitled 'The Assembly'. His prescriptions, however, made the witches' brew in 'Macbeth' seem almost palatable by comparison; for example, his treatment for juvenile epilepsy contained 13 ingredients including a broth of earthworms, pigeon's dung, powder of human skull, shavings of elk's hoofs and a variety of herbals. He was very outspoken and, as was the custom of his time, he became involved in a controversy leading to his temporary expulsion from the College of Physicians. He was then admitted to the Incorporation of Surgeons where he was instrumental in the introduction of public anatomical dissections. A dissection carried out by Pitcairne in 1702 can still be seen in the College museum. Pitcairne was charged with treason for expressing his loyalty to the Jacobite cause and was bound over under penalty of £200. At his death his extensive library was bought by the Russian Tsar Peter the Great. A great lover of wine, he bequeathed a jeroboam, to be drunk on the restoration of the Stuart kings.

In 1800 Archibald Pitcairne's grave in Greyfriars Churchyard was in a state of neglect, the tombstone lying flat on the ground and largely covered by earth. With the agreement of Pitcairne's grand-daughter, Lady Ann Erskine, Andrew Duncan prevailed upon the Aesculapian and Harveian Societies to fund the necessary repairs. Forty-nine members contributed half a guinea each. As reward for their efforts,

> *a meeting of the Subscribers, … is to be held at his Tombstone … on the 25th of December, on business of very great importance. It is proposed,*

that, immediately after the meeting, an adjournment shall take place to the Grapine alias Grape-wine Office, (at Keggie's under the pillars in the entrance to the Parliament Square,) where those who attend will have an opportunity of partaking of a Jeroboam left by Dr Pitcairne, with directions that it should be opened at the Restoration.

As the restoration of the Stuart monarchy, which Pitcairne had hoped for, now seemed unlikely, the restoration of his grave was used as the justification to broach the jeroboam, and the malmsey was found to be in excellent condition. Further repair of Pitcairne's gravestone was carried out by the Royal College of Physicians in 1952, the tercentenary of Pitcairne's birth.

The inscription on Pitcairne's memorial is in Latin, which in translation reads: 'Behold this little urn contains the great Pitcairne, a mathematician, poet, physician and sage. Farewell then, light of Scotland and prince of physicians! O pillar and darling of the Muses farewell!' The stone is also inscribed with the names of his wife, Elizabeth Stevenson, his daughter Janet who became Countess of Kellie in Fife, and his grand-daughter Lady Ann Erskine who died unmarried. The 5th Earl of Kellie, whom Janet married, was described as an amiable sociable drunk of limited intelligence. A keen Jacobite, like all the Erskines, he joined the '45 rebellion and was present at the battle of Culloden after which, like Charles II, he hid for a time in a tree, lowering a rope for food. He eventually gave himself up and was imprisoned in Edinburgh Castle from 1746-49 when he was released by his captors who had concluded that he was little threat. His name does not appear in the list of members of the Beggar's Benison, but his eldest son Thomas, who became the 6th Earl, was a fellow member with Duncan. Thomas was a talented musician and composer who organised and conducted regular St Cecilia's Day concerts, but he was also a drunk who had a coarse wit and lived beyond his means. He eventually had to sell most of his estates, leaving only Kellie Castle for his brother who succeeded him.

Following the restoration of the gravestone, the following inscription was added in Latin, which translated reads: 'The Edinburgh Aesculapian Club instituted in 1773 caused this monument to be restored on the 12th June 1800, Alex Wood, late Deacon of the Royal College of Surgeons being president, and Andrew Duncan, Doctor of Medicine and professor being secretary.' The Aesculapian Club also restored the memorial of John Barnet, a medical student, in Greyfriars, and more notably the stone of Robert Fergusson in Canongate.

The poet Robert Fergusson (1750-74) was educated in University of St Andrews where he was befriended by Duncan's uncle, Professor Nicholas Vilant. Duncan attended Fergusson during his final illness in Edinburgh's

Bedlam and was so distressed by the conditions there that he was moved to found the Edinburgh Lunatic Asylum (see chapter IV).

Fergusson's fellow poet Robert Burns acknowledged the debt which he owed to Fergusson and refers to him as 'my elder brother in Misfortune; by far my elder Brother in the muse'. Burns financed the erection of a headstone to mark Fergusson's grave in the Canongate Churchyard, which he had inscribed with this verse:

> *No sculptur'd marble here, nor pompous lay,*
> *No storied Urn, nor animated Bust;*
> *This simple stone directs pale Scotias way,*
> *To pour her sorrows o'er her Poet's dust.*

and on the reverse :

> *By special grant from the Managers to Robert Burns this stone is to remain for ever sacred to the Memory of Robert Fergusson.*

Andrew Duncan wrote that 'from inattention in the mason employed to erect the monument, the foundation soon gave way, and it was in danger of falling. … Some members of the Aesculapian Club, animated by pious zeal for departed worth, which had before led them to prevent some other Sepulchral Monuments from going to ruin, applied for the liberty to repair this tribute from one poet to another, and permission being granted, they took that opportunity of offering to it an additional inscription, commemorating the genius of Burns'. Duncan was a great admirer of Burns and was one of the subscribers to the first edition of Burns' poems. This additional inscription was not, however, added to the restored stone. Since Duncan's time the headstone was further restored by Robert Louis Stevenson, and Fergusson's grave is currently undergoing yet another restoration.

Andrew Duncan's vault

Duncan's own family vault is in Buccleuch Churchyard, situated in Chapel Street in the shadow of the Appleton Tower of the University of Edinburgh. Buccleuch Church started life as an extension of St Cuthbert's Parish Church which had become overcrowded. Four hundred pounds was raised by March 1755 and the building was finished and opened for service with seating for 1200 by January 1756. It was known as St Cuthbert's Chapel of Ease (hence Chapel Street) and it was built on the site of an old windmill which was used to pump water from the Borough Loch on the Meadows to supply breweries (hence Windmill Street which runs alongside the graveyard).

During its first year as a burial ground there were 51 interments, 36 being of children under ten. The burial ground was closed in 1819 except to those who had relatives there, and in 1873 it was closed completely. Between 1764 and 1828 there were 1700 interments. Only about 70 graves remain identifiable today with memorials. The church itself was closed in 1969 and is now used by the University of Edinburgh for storage.

Many famous people are buried there, including Flora MacLeod of Raasay who married Mure Campbell of Rowallan who became the Earl of Loudoun. She died in childbirth in 1780, but her daughter, also Flora, survived to become the wife of Francis Hastings who became Governor General of Bengal and a marquis. There are also many distinguished divines including Rev. Robert Hamilton DD (1707-87), Professor of Divinity and Moderator of the General Assembly, and Rev. Nicholas Vilant who was certainly a relative of Duncan.

Mrs Alison Rutherfurd or Cockburn (1713-94) is remembered as the writer of the words of the 'Flowers of the Forest' and other songs. Burns was one of her admirers and she was a notable hostess of the Enlightenment. (She is the only occupant of the graveyard who is commemorated by a plaque on the outside wall.) Buried adjacent to the above, in an unmarked grave, is the notorious Deacon William Brodie. On the other side of Brodie lies Dr Alexander Adam (1741-1809) who became a renowned rector of the High School and a distinguished Latin scholar. He came from a very humble home and sustained himself on four guineas a year during his university days. The Latin inscription on his memorial was composed by James Gregory – a tribute to his classical scholarship. Adam is described in Grant as being 'among the last who adhered to the old-fashioned dress, breeches and silk stockings, with knee and shoe-buckles and the queue, though he had relinquished the use of hair-powder'. There are memorial windows in the church to Alexander Adam and Flora Macleod. Duncan erected a memorial to his forebear, Nicholas Vilant, the founder of the founder of the Vilant dynasty, who lived to be 106, but this memorial no longer survives.[2]

The most interesting vault in the churchyard is that of Andrew Duncan himself. This was his parish church in which he took considerable interest. He was responsible for restoring several of the memorials there, including those of the author David Herd and Dr Robert Hamilton. Ever interested in the welfare of his medical students, he allowed several who died while in Edinburgh to be buried in his own vault, including Jacob Pattison of Witham who died 1782 aged 23, Francis Foulke of Trinity College Dublin, George Mulvihill of County Clare Ireland (died 1800 aged 23), and Charles Darwin, the eldest son of Erasmus Darwin and uncle of the more famous Charles.

Charles Darwin (1758-78) was the second of seven members of the Darwin family to have studied medicine in Edinburgh.[3] He assisted Duncan in the running of the Edinburgh Dispensary and undertook the care of the sick poor of the parish of Waterleith [*sic*]. He died of poisoning, contracted while dissecting the brain of a child who had died of hydrocephalus. Clearly an outstanding student, he was awarded in 1777 the first gold medal to be presented by the Aesculapian Society. His father, Erasmus, wrote to Duncan that 'he might have been, had Heaven assented, an ornament to medicine, to philosophy and to mankind'. Darwin's Aesculapian Society's Prize essay, and his proposed MD thesis, translated into English by his father, were published by his father in 1780.[4]

The medical students buried in his vault were all members of the undergraduate Royal Medical Society, with which Duncan was closely associated. The memorials of Darwin (*fig.* 31) and Mulvihill are still clear and legible, but that of Foulke is missing and Pattison's is destroyed, although the Latin inscriptions of both are recorded in Duncan's book. Both Pattison and Foulke were presidents of the Royal Medical Society. Francis Foulke's death from a wound sustained in a duel is recorded in chapter VIII. Duncan mentions the burial of other medical students, but does not make clear whether these were buried in his vault.

In 1891 the Aesculapian Club found that Andrew Duncan's vault was 'a mass of rank and mouldering vegetation' and had it completely restored. Contributions towards the restoration were made by the Aesculapian and Harveian Societies, the Royal College of Physicians, the Royal Dispensary and the Royal Edinburgh Asylum. The relettering of the Darwin tablet was paid for by his existing relatives.[5]

Andrew Duncan's own memorial reads:

Sacred to the memory of Andrew Duncan M.D. Fellow of the Royal College of Physicians and Professor of the Theory of Medicine in the University of Edinburgh, who has left behind him in the Royal Public Dispensary, the Edinburgh Lunatic Asylum, the Caledonian Horticultural Society and other institutions of which he was the founder a more lasting memorial than this tablet will present of the activity of his mind and the benevolence of his heart. Born 17th October 1744, he died 5th July 1828 aged 83 years. Also in memory of Elizabeth Knox his widow who died 26th of January 1829 aged 88 years, also in memory of their daughter Elizabeth Duncan born 26th January 1777 died 22nd February 1864. Catherine Duncan born 11th April 1785 died 5th April 1855. Anne C. D. Duncan born 2nd February 1796 died 2nd March 1856.

This central panel is flanked by two others. On the left:

Here also lie the remains of a beloved grandson William Toone Duncan,

*youngest son of Major Genr Duncan on East India Company Service. A
youth of great promise who died 22nd June 1837 in his 18th year.*

On the right:

*To the memory of Henry Francis Duncan, youngest son of Andrew Duncan
M.D. who died on the 24th December 1805 in the 14th year of his age.*

It was to this grave that Duncan made a pilgrimage each Christmas. Henry
was the son who, at the age of five, partnered his father in a golf match
against Sandy Wood and his grandson, recorded on page 130.

* * *

After Duncan's death in July 1828, his funeral was reported thus in the
Edinburgh Evening Courant of 12 July 1828:

*A large deputation of the Caledonian Horticultural Society the Right
Honourable Sir Robert Liston GCB as Vice President in the rear
The Hunterian Society
The Plinian Society
The Royal Physical Society
The Royal Medical Society, with their respective Presidents in the rear.
The Medical Officers of the Royal Public Dispensary
The Royal College of Physicians, the Presidents in the rear
Janitor of the College with the Mace
The Senatus Academicus the Rev Dr Brunton as Principal in the rear
The Town Council of Edinburgh in their robes
The Sword and Mace
The Right Honourable the Lord Provost
Two Mutes
The Body*

*Then followed the private friends of the deceased. The procession which
was on foot was followed by a number of gentlemen's carriages. On
arriving at the churchyard the different societies ranged themselves on
one side and the Senatus Academicus and Magistrates on the other while
the body and the friends moved up the centre to the grave. There was a
large concourse of spectators in the different streets through which the
procession passed.*

Civic funerals such as this were accorded only to outstanding citizens. Others who received this honour include James Gregory, Thomas Chalmers the distinguished cleric and James Young Simpson.

In the Introduction we expressed the opinion that Andrew Duncan might be regarded as one of the great men of the Scottish Enlightenment. A common theme linking the intellectuals of this period was a desire to improve the wellbeing of mankind. Duncan was not one of the great thinkers, who contributed so much in the fields of philosophy, economics, science and the arts, although he was intimate with many of these men in the clubs and societies which formed such an important part of his life. Duncan's contribution was made in practical ways, such as the founding of institutions for the benefit of the disadvantaged and promoting his love of gardening. For his own profession of medicine, the establishment of a ground-breaking medical journal and his promotion of public health were significant innovations. Having read the book we hope that readers might agree that Duncan merited a place among the panoply of Enlightenment figures.

The genial, kind-hearted nature of the man is well expressed in the following tribute from the students' Hunterian Medical Society, which was typical of the many received after his death:

We have fully appreciated the public virtue, the private worth, the literary attainments, the splendid talents, the modest benevolence, the genuine philanthropy of the much-lamented deceased. In him science has lost a devoted zealot, – the University of Edinburgh a most distinguished orna-ment, – the inhabitants of Edinburgh a first-rate citizen, – the poor a liberal and unostentatious donor, – and the medical students a warm hearted friend. ...[6]

Duncan had his faults – vanity, intolerance of criticism and excessive pride in his longevity, which led him to continue his teaching and committee activities after his mental facilities had declined, but few have left so many and such varied contributions to the common good. His favourite poet, Robert Burns, in another context, wrote two lines which might justly be Andrew Duncan's epitaph:

If there's another world he lives in bliss,
If there be none he made the best of this.

Notes

1   Thin (1928), pp. 368-82.
2   An article on Duncan's vault in *The Scotsman* on 22 October 1892 states that this Nicolas Vilant was Duncan's great-grandfather, the French protestant refugee who died aged 106, but he died long before the Buccleuch Churchyard was created.
3   Morgan (1936/7), pp. 221-26.
4   Darwin and Darwin (1780).
5   *The Scotsman* article referred to in note 2 above.
6. Letter to Andrew Duncan Jr in Duncan Archive. The Hunterian Society was an Edinburgh medical students' society which existed from 1824-68. Andrew Duncan was appointed an Honorary Member two years after his death! Richard Owen (1804-92) was a founder member and its first president. Owen subsequently became the Hunterian Professor of the Royal College of Surgeons of England and was the driving force behind the establishment of the Natural History Museum in South Kensington.

ARTHUR'S SEAT, EDINBURGH

Duncan enjoyed climbing Arthur's Seat in Edinburgh with friends and family well into his eighties.
(GRANT: *OLD AND NEW EDINBURGH*)

The Writings of
Andrew Duncan Senior

In this appendix an attempt has been made to include all of Duncan's accessible writings. No discrimination has been made between his major works and the many apparently trivial papers, which were often intended for local or family circulation, for some of these contain a detail of value in compiling this biography. All of these publications have been located in one or more of the following sources:

Royal Colleges of Physicians and Surgeons
    of Edinburgh (RCPE, RCSE) – Libraries
University of Edinburgh and Edinburgh Univer-
    sity Library (EUL)

National Library of Scotland (NLS)
British Library (BL)
Wellcome Library (WL)
Edinburgh Central Library (ECL)

In many of the lesser papers no printer or publisher is mentioned, but in general Duncan's good friend Patrick Neill in Edinburgh was the chosen printer. Neill also worked for two Edinburgh-based firms: A[dam] Neill & Co. and A[rchibald] Constable & Co. Multiple publishers are frequently listed in the more important works, but one was usually the principal publisher and the others just retailers.

1769   *'De Purgantium Natura et Usu'* (MD thesis) (Edinburgh: Balfour, Auld and Smellie).

1770   *Elements of Therapeutics, or first Principles of the Practice of Medicine* (2nd edition, 2 vols, 1773) (Edinburgh: W. Drummond; London: John Murray).

1771   'Introductory address to the Medical Society of students at Edinburgh'.

–   Section on 'Medicine' in the first edition of *Encyclopaedia Britannica*.

1772   'Observations on the operation and use of mercury in the venereal disease' (London: T. Cadell and John Murray; Edinburgh: A. Kincaid and W. Creech).

–   'Introductory address to the Medical Society of Students at Edinburgh'.

1773-1795   *Medical and Philosophical Commentaries,* by a society in Edinburgh. (See notes for chapter II.)

–   *Elements of Therapeutics, or first Principles of the Practice of Physic.*

c.1775   (undated) 'A short account of the commencement, progress and present state of the buildings belonging to the Royal Medical Society of Edinburgh'.

1776   'An address to the students of medicine at Edinburgh; introductory to a course of lectures on the theory and practice of physic' (delivered 1 November 1776).

–   Heads of lectures on theory and practice of medicine. (Subsequent editions 1780 and 1790.)

1777   'Observations on a proposal for establishing at Edinburgh, a Public Dispensary for the Relief of the Poor'.

1778   'Medical Cases, selected from the Records of the Public Dispensary at Edinburgh; with remarks and observations being the Substance of Case Lectures, delivered during the years 1776-77' (Edinburgh: Charles Elliot; London: John Murray). (Subsequent editions 1781, 1784 and 1790;

translated into Latin in Leyden 1785 and French 1797.)

- 'De laudibus Gulielmi Harvei oratio' (Edinburgh: Charles Elliot).

1780 'An account of the Life and Writings of the late Alexander Monro Sr delivered as the Harveian oration at Edinburgh, for the year 1780' (Edinburgh: Charles Elliot).

- 'Address to the Students of Medicine on delivering the Prize for 1780 to Dr Arthur Broughton'.

- 'Heads of Lectures on Materia Medica' (and subsequent editions).

1781 'Heads of Lectures on the Theory and Practice of Medicine' (2nd edition and subsequent editions 1785 and 1789) (Edinburgh: Charles Elliot).

1782 'Heads of lectures on pathology' (Edinburgh: Charles Elliot).

- 'A letter to Dr Robert Jones of Caermarthenshire, in answer to the account which he has published of the case of Mr John Braham Isaacson student of Medicine, and to the Injurious Aspersions which he has thrown out against the physicians who attended Mr Isaacson' (Edinburgh: Charles Elliot).

1783 'A system of the Practice of Medicine; from the Latin [Medicina rationales systematica] of Dr Hoffman (revised and completed by Andrew Duncan', (in 2 vols) (London: John Murray).

1784 'An alphabetical list of the materia medica; intended as a synopsis of lectures on that subject'.

- Transactions of the Royal Society of Edinburgh I.

1786 'A short account of the late Dr John Parsons, … Dr Richard Huck Saunders, … Dr Charles Colignon, … and Sir Alexander Dick' from Medical Commentaries 10 (London: John Murray).

- 'Heads of lectures on materia media' (London: John Murray).

1789 The Edinburgh New Dispensatory (2nd edition; subsequent editions 1791 and 1797) (Edinburgh: William Creech).

- 'An account of the life, writings and character of Dr J. Hope', Harveian Oration 1788 (Edinburgh: Charles Elliot).

- 'Account of Sir Alexander Dick', Transactions of the Royal Society of Edinburgh II, pp. 58-62.

1792 'Letter on the chirurgical attendance at the Royal Infirmary of Edinburgh'.

1794 'Head of lectures on therapeutics'.

1795 'Clinical Reports and Commentaries, February to April 1795' (Mss RCPE).

- 'Heads of lectures on medical jurisprudence, or the institutiones medicinae legalis' (Edinburgh: G. Mudie & Sons).

1796 'Heads of lectures on pathological philosophy'.

1796-1802 Joint editor with Andrew Duncan Jr of Annals of Medicine (5 vols).

1798 'A short view of the extent and importance of Medical Jurisprudence, considered as a branch of education: Memorial to the Patrons of the University of Edinburgh'.

1800 'Poems on various occasions written either by myself or by intimate friends to whom I [Duncan] gave some assistance' (Ms in RCPE).

- 'Account of the reparation of Dr Pitcairn's monument in Greyfriars Churchyard in Edinburgh, with a list of medical practitioners residing in Edinburgh, who agreed to pay each an equal share of the expence [sic] of that reparation' (Edinburgh: A. Neill & Co.).

1801 Heads of lectures on medical police (Edinburgh: A. Neill & Co.).

- 'Heads of lectures on the institutions of medicine'.

- 'Heads of lectures on juridical medicine or the Institutiones Medicinae Forensis'.

1803 'Letter to the right honourable Neil Macvicar, Lord Provost of Edinburgh, 11 October 1803'.

1805 'Question proposed by Dr Duncan Sr to the RCPE respecting the law passed on 11 April 1754'.

1807 (with others*) 'Address to the public respecting the establishment of a lunatic asylum at Edinburgh'(Edinburgh: James Ballantyne).

- 'Meditation on the top of Arthur's Seat, …, soon after sunrise, 1 May 1807'.

- 'Case of gout in an African Negro', in Edinburgh Medical Surgical Journal 3, pp. 9-12.

1808 'Opinion delivered by Dr Duncan Sr in the RCPE on 13 September 1808 upon a charge against Dr Gregory'.

1809 Major revision of Duncan's section on 'Medicine', 4th edition of the *Encyclopaedia Britannica*.

– 'General view of the method of conducting a clinical course'.

– (with others*) 'Observations on the structure of hospitals and the treatment of lunatics, and on the general principles on which the cure of insanity may be most successfully conducted. To which is annexed, an account of the intended establishment of a lunatic asylum at Edibnrugh [*sic*]' (Edinburgh: James Ballantyne).

1810 'A short account of a method of preparing a Soporific Medicine from the inspissated white juice of the common garden lettuce or *Lactuca sativa of Linnaeus*. Address to Caledonian Horticultural Society of Edinburgh' (EUL SB6104/6).

– 'Report presented to the Royal College of Physicians of Edinburgh respecting the contagious Epidemic Diseases which have prevailed in the City and its neighbourhood during the year 1810' (EUL SB6104/6).

1811 'Letter to Dr James Gregory in consequence of certain printed papers entitled 'The Viper and File', 'There is Wisdom in Silence', 'An old story', etc., lately distributed by him' (with five appendices).

1812 (with others*) 'A short account of the rise, progress, and present state of the Lunatic Asylum at Edinburgh, with some remarks on the general treatment of lunatics, pointing out the advantages of avoiding all cruelty. To which will be annexed, a complete list of the contributions received, whether from towns, parishes, or individuals, for erecting a building much wanted in the metropolis of Scotland' (Edinburgh: P. Neill).

1813 'Observations on the distinguishing symptoms of three different species of Pulmonary Consumption; the catarrhal, the apostematous and the tuberculous' (further editions 1816 and 1819) (Edinburgh: A. Constable & Co.).

– '*Carminum Rariorum Macaronicorum delectus, in usum Ludorum Apollinarium*' (Edinburgh: Peter Hill).

1814 'Observations on the preparation of soporific medicines from the common garden lettuce', in *Memoirs of the Caledonian Horticultural Society*, vol. I, pp. 160-68.

– 'Contemplations on the top of Arthur's Seat, 1 May 1814'.

– 'Observations on the propagation by cuttings of the Original, the Mother, the Oslin or the Bur-knot Apple Tree', in *Memoirs of the Caledonian Horticultural Society*, vol I, pp. 237-45.

– 'A discourse read at the quarterly meeting of the Caledonian Horticultural Society in the Hall of the RCPE, 13 December 1814'.

– 'A Report respecting can-flues in the hot-house', in *Memoirs of the Caledonian Horticultural Society*, vol. I, pp. 353-55.

1815 '*Elogiorium sepulchralium Edinensium delectus* "Monumental Inscriptions" selected from the burial grounds at Edinburgh' (Edinburgh: P. Neill).

– 'Conclusions of a clinical lecture at Edinburgh, 7 March 1815'.

– 'Copy of a Letter to the right honourable Neil MacVicar, Lord Provost of Edinburgh, dated 11 October 1803, recommending the establishment of a lunatic asylum in the metropolis of Scotland, to which is now added a postscript to the present Lord Provost re. appropriation of the money left by John Watson Esq. for pious and charitable purposes at Edinburgh' (Edinburgh: A. Neill & Co.; A Constable and Co.).

1815/16 'Discourses to the Caledonian Horticultural Society on 4 December 1815 and 3 December 1816', in *Memoirs of the Caledonian Horticultural Society*, vol. III, pp. 331-43 and 344-54.

1816 'To the Vice-President of the Caledonian Horticultural Society'.

– 'Contemplations on the top of Arthur's seat by a gentleman far advance in life, 1 May 1816, on the approaching marriage of the Princess Charlotte' (Edinburgh: A. Neill & Co.)

1817 'Exchange of correspondence with Rev. D. Ritchie regarding church collections for New Town Dispensary' (NLS).

1818 'Further communications respecting *lactucarium*', in *Memoirs of the Caledonian Horticultural Society*, vol. II, pp. 312-319.

– Invitation: 'A fish dinner will be provided at the Golf House, Leith for some social medical men, on Tuesday 29 December'.

– 'An Account of the Life, Writings and Character of Dr A. Monro, *secundus*. Harveian Oration for the year 1818' (Edinburgh: A. Constable & Co.).

– 'A letter to His Majesty's Sheriffs-Depute in Scotland, recommending the establishment of four national asylums for the reception of criminal and pauper lunatics' (Edinburgh: P. Neill).

– 'Meditation on top of Arthur's Seat occasioned by the death of the Princess Charlotte of Wales, 1 May 1818' (Edinburgh: P. Neill).

– 'Miscellaneous poems, extracted from the records of the Circulation Club at Edinburgh' (Edinburgh: Peter Hill).

– 'A discourse read at a meeting of the Caledonian Horticultural Society, 10 March 1818'.

– 'Presenting the gold medal for 1817 to P. Neill and proposing the establishment of a Royal Horticultural Garden in Edinburgh' (Edinburgh: A. Neill & Co.).

– 'A discourse read at the annual election meeting of the Caledonian Horticultural Society, 8 December 1818, upon delivering the prize medal [to J. Macdonald] for experiments on the culture of onions'.

– 'Letter to Rt Hon. Kincaid Mackenzie, Lord Provost, 10 June 1818, with ideas on the development of the Princes Street Gardens'.

1819 'Meditation on the top of Arthur's Seat on 1 May 1819 by A. D. *aetat* 75, when attended by seven grandchildren, seven others being absent' (Edinburgh: P. Neill).

– 'Chronological list of the Royal Company of Scottish Archers, compiled by Andrew Duncan' (Edinburgh: P. Neill).

– 'Letter to the right honourable William Dundas ... suggesting the establishment of a Royal Experimental Garden at Edinburgh, for the improvement of horticulture'.

– 'A discourse read at the annual election meeting of the Caledonian Horticultural Society, 2 December 1819, upon delivering the prize medal [to S. Parkes] for a memoir on the employment of sea-salt for the purposes of horticulture' (Edinburgh: A. Constable & Co.).

1820 'Inscriptions in a small garden [*Hinc Sanitas*] at the foot of St Leonard's Hill, Edinburgh'.

– 'An humble apology for the father of our College, Dr Duncan Sr' (Balfour and Clark).

– 'Account of the first meeting in the New College Hall, lately built for the University of Edinburgh on 1 August 1820'.

– 'Invitation for a gymnastic meeting, to celebrate the *Ludi Apollinares* at Leith Links'.

– 'A discourse read at the annual election meeting of the Caledonian Horticultural Society, 7 December 1820, delivering a prize medal to William Harrison of Edinburgh' (Edinburgh: P. Neill).

– 'Additional observations on the use of *lactucarium*, or lettuce opium, particularly in a case of *cynanche laryngea*'.

– 'Alphabetical list of the Caledonian Horticultural Society from the commencement 5 December 1809 until 1 December 1820'.

1820? 'The Lord's Prayer, with a paraphrase, commonly denominated the universal prayer, written by Alexander Pope Esq.' (Edinburgh: P. Neill).

1821 'At a convivial meeting of the Royal Company of Scottish Archers, held in their hall on Saturday 27 October 1821, the Company drank a bumper [toast] to the health of Dr Duncan, who had completed the fiftieth year of his being a member of the Corps, and who had gained a prize at the butts, the pagoda medal, on that day'.

– 'Duncan's grand panacea, an infallible cure for all diseases, translated into Pindaric rhyme by Dr Barclay; and published at the fortieth anniversary of the Edinburgh Harveian Festival, 14 April 1821' (Edinburgh: P. Neill).

1821   'A short account of the life of the right honourable Sir Joseph Banks KB, President of the Royal Society of London. Read at the 40th anniversary festival of the Harveian Society of Edinburgh, on the 12 April 1821' (Edinburgh: A. Constable & Co).

–   'Tribute of veneration addressed to the first meeting of the Loyal Edinburgh Association, for commemorating the reign of George III'. Appendix contains poems delivered on the top of Arthur's Seat, 1 May 1817 and 1821 (Edinburgh: P. Neill for A. Constable & Co.).

1821   'A discourse read at the annual election meeting of the Caledonian Horticultural Society, 6 December 1821, upon delivering to Patrick Neill Esq. their annual premium for the most interesting communication, in *Journal of a horticultural tour through Flanders, etc.*' (Edinburgh: A. Constable & Co.).

1822   'Heads of lectures on the institutions of medicine'.

–   'Advice given to the rich and great by a physician, who has very nearly arrived at the 80th year of his age, from the top of Arthur's Seat on the 1 May 1822' (Edinburgh: P. Neill).

–   'Verses on the marriage of Captain Duncan to Miss Hill[;] addresses to a large company setting out to witness that ceremony, by a boy, in the eighth year of his age ... written by his grandfather, a man in his seventy-eighth year'.

–   'A discourse read at the annual election meeting of the Caledonian Horticultural Society, 5 December 1822, upon delivering the prize medal to Mr Walter Henderson for his memoir on the culture of orange-trees in Scotland' (Edinburgh: Bell and Bradfute).

1823   'Observations on the office of a faithful teacher, and on the duty of an attentive student of medicine, delivered as an introductory lecture to the institutes of medicine ... on 29 October 1823' (Edinburgh: Bell and Bradfute).

–   'A discourse read at the annual election meeting of the Caledonian Horticultural Society, 4 December 1823, stating the advantages which would accrue to the Church of Scotland from the professorship of horticulture in the University of Edinburgh' (Edinburgh: Bell & Bradfute).

–   'Contemplations on the top of Arthur's Seat by the oldest physician in Edinburgh'.

–   'Extract of a letter from a medical practitioner in Edinburgh, to a brother doctor in London'.

–   'Letter to William Wood, President of the Royal College of Surgeons of Edinburgh'.

–   'Letter to Rev. Andrew Brown, Professor of Rhetoric at Edinburgh University'.

–   'Thanks returned by an octogenarian physician to his friends in the County of Fife, particularly the ancient City of St Andrews'.

–   'A letter to John Waugh Esq., preses of a committee of the Town Council, respecting a new High School at Edinburgh'.

1824   'Letter to the Editor of the *Advertiser* regarding the High School, 4 August 1824'.

–   'A discourse read at the annual election meeting of the Caledonian Horticultural Society, 2 December 1824'.

–   'Conclusion of a lecture on pathology of respiration'.

–   'A speech delivered at a meeting of the *Senatus Academicus* of the University of Edinburgh on the 20 November 1824, respecting a proposal for new regulations in granting the degree of Doctor of Medicine'.

–   'A tribute of regard to the memory of Sir Henry Raeburn RA, portrait painter to the King for Scotland read at the 43rd anniversary meeting of the Harveian Society Edinburgh 1824, with appendix consisting of verses by Sir A. Boswell and others' (Edinburgh: P. Neill).

1825   'As the observation which Dr Duncan senior concluded his lecture on the subject of human blood, delivered during the winter course, on the institutions of medicine ... on 15 December 1824, may perhaps be incorrectly reported by some of his hearers, he has thought it right to put them in print, in the words in which they were delivered by him, that each of his students may be enabled to give a fair report of them'.

- 'Speech delivered by Andrew Duncan Sr at a quarterly statutory meeting of the *Senatus Academicus* of the University of Edinburgh on 15 January 1825', accusing Dr James Hamilton, Professor of Midwifery, of having published a false and calumnious libel against the *Senatus Academicus*; … against the institutions of medicine; …and against the present professor of institutes of medicine as an individual'.

- 'Testimony of veneration for the memory of Dr Mathew Baillie, of London. Read at the forty-fourth anniversary festival of the Harveian Society of Edinburgh on the 12 April 1825'.

1825 'Memorial for, in the action of damages at the instance of Dr James Hamilton'.

- 'Letter to Sir William Fettes, Bart, affording demonstrative evidence, that much greater benefit will arise to those who have at once to struggle both with poverty and disease, from improving the Royal Infirmary by the establish-ment of a lock hospital, and an hospital for incurables, than by beginning a new rival infirmary, which may be productive of many evils' (Edinburgh: printed by P. Neill for Bell and Bradfute).

- 'Observations on the preparation and use of *lactucarium*, or lettuce opium', in *Memoirs of the Royal Caledonian Society*, vol. III, pp. 352-370.

- 'A discourse read at the annual general meeting of the Caledonian Horticul-tural Society, 1 December 1825, upon awarding to Mr John Hay, garden architect, their annual premium for the most interesting communication' (Edinburgh: P. Neill).

1826 'A letter to the Royal Colleges of Physicians of London, Dublin and of Edinburgh, respecting a proposal for the improvement of medicine by publishing annually under the authority of these three Royal Colleges a *Pharmacopoeia Britannica*'.

1827 'Dr Duncan senior of Edinburgh, in the eighty third year of his age, has addres-sed the following letter to a friend, on the death of Alexander Duke of Gordon'.

1829 'Observations on the culture of onions', in *Memoirs of the Caledonian Society*, vol. IV, pp. 305-309.

(with others *) A series of anonymous pamphlets regarding the planning of Edinburgh's Lunatic Asylum was undoubtedly compiled and partly written by Andrew Duncan Sr.

Also:
'Duncan's Miscellanies', 3 volumes are held in the RCPE Library (Str. Ms. Duncan, Andrew 7).

One hundred volumes of 'Practical Observations in Medicine', which consist of his case records used in teaching, handwritten mostly by Duncan, are held in the RCPE Library (two volumes are missing).

APPENDIX II

The Children of Andrew Duncan Senior

Katharine Elisa 25/02/1772-02/03/1776

Andrew 01/08/1773-13/05/1832
Professor of Medicine
Married Mary McFarquhar, 20/06/1800
Two children

John 19/03/1775-04/12 1776

Elizabeth Katharine 20/01/1777-22/02/1864
(Bess/Betsy)

Janet 24/07/1778-07/12/1782

Alexander (Sandy) 30/03/1780-14/05/1859
General in Bengal Infantry
Married Mary Lanigan, 05/02/1802
Twelve children, all born in India

Margaret 07/03/1783-13/11/1852
Married William Scott WS, 09/10/1816
Five children

Katharine (Catherine) 11/04/1785-05/04/1853
['Katharine' is the spelling in the baptismal records.
However, 'Catherine' is more commonly used in family correspondence.]

John 25/03/1787-28/10/1856
Colonel in Bengal Infantry
Married Mary Hill, 14/05/1822
No children

Henrietta Francis 28/12/1789-26/02/1792

Henry Francis 17/04/1792-24/12/1805

Ann Calderwood 02/02/1796-02/03/1856

Bibliography

Abraham, J. J. (1933): *Lettsom, his life, times, friends and descendants* (London: William Heinemann).

Anderson, J. M. (ed) (1905): *The Matriculation roll of the University of St Andrews 1747-1897* (Edinburgh and London: William Blackwood & Son).

Anderson, W. P. (1931): *Silences that Speak* (Edinburgh: Brunton).

Anon (1795): 'Andrew Duncan Sr clinical reports and commentaries, Feb-Apr 1795, presented by Alexander Blackhall Morison, Edinburgh', MSS Collection, Royal College of Physicians Edinburgh.

Anon (1817a): *Observations by the Managers of the New Town Dispensary on the Report to the Quarterly Meeting of Managers to the Public Dispensary, 7 August 1817* (Edinburgh: printed at the Caledonian Mercury Press).

Anon (1817b): *Report of the First Annual General Meeting of the Governors of the New Town Dispensary, 4 March 1817* (Edinburgh: printed by Caw & Elder) [subscribers' names appear on pp. 21-31].

Anon (1822): *Transcript of The Trial of James Stuart Esq. Younger of Dunearn* (Edinburgh: Archibald Constable & Co).

Anon (Duncan, A.?) (1823): 'Extract of a letter from a medical practitioner in Edinburgh, to a brother doctor in London.'

Anon (1831): *Fifty-Fourth Annual Report of the Edinburgh Royal Public Dispensary and Vaccine Institution of Edinburgh*, January 1831, Instituted A.D. 1776 (Edinburgh: printed by A. Neill & Co.).

Anon (1840): *Public meeting respecting the Edinburgh Lunatic Asylum Report*, Edinburgh City Library (ECL), Edinburgh Room, Quarto RC 503.

Anon (1843a): *Annual Report of the New Town Dispensary, No. 17, East Thistle Street, Instituted in September 1815, for affording gratuitous medical assistance to the sick and diseased poor. Supported entirely by voluntary annual subscriptions and donations. For the year MDCCCXLII* (Edinburgh: printed for the Institution).

Anon (1843b): *Report of the Treasury Committee regarding the pauper lunatics of the City and the proposal to transfer them to the New Asylum at Morningside* (Edinburgh: A. Neill & Co.).

Baumgartner, L. and E. M. Ramsey (1933/4): Johan Peter Frank and his 'System Einer Vollständigen Medicinischen Polizey', *Annals of Medical History New Series*, vol. 5, pp. 525-34; vol. 6, pp. 69-90.

Baron, J. H. (2006): 'Medical Police and the Nanny State: Public Health versus Private Autonomy', *Mount Sinai Journal of Medicine* 73, pp. 708-15.

Black, W. (1781): *Observations medical and political on the small-pox and inoculation* (London: Johnson).

Blair, J. S. G. (1982): *History of Medicine in the University of St Andrews* (Edinburgh: Scottish Academic Press).

Blane, G. (1785): *Observations on the diseases incident to seamen* (London: Cooper).

Boswell, Sir A. (1871): *The Poetical Works* (Smith, R. H. [ed]) (Glasgow: Maurice Ogle & Co.).

Boucé, P-G. (ed) (1982): *Sexual Mores in Enlightenment Scotland in Sexuality in eighteenth-century Britain* (Manchester: Manchester University Press).

Bower, A. (1817-30): The History of the University of Edinburgh, 3 vols (Edinburgh: Oliphant, Waugh and Innes; London: John Murray).

Bristed, J. (1803): *A pedestrian tour through part of the Highlands of Scotland in 1801*, 2 vols (London: T. Walles).

Brown, J. (1795): *The elements of Medicine*, trans. from Latin, 2 vols (London: J. Johnstone).

Brown, T. (1809): A letter in reply to the report of the surgeons of the Vaccine Institution (Edinburgh: J. Ballantyne).

Bryce, W. M. (1917/8): The Burgh Muir of Edinburgh, *Book of the Old Edinburgh Club* X, pp. 206-10.

Buchan, J. (2003): *Crowded with Genius. The Scottish Enlightenment: Edinburgh's Moment of the Mind* (New York: Harper Collins).

Buchan, W. (1772): *Domestic Medicine: A Treatise on the Prevention and Cure of Diseases by Regimen and Simple Medicines* (Edinburgh: W. Creech and J. Balfour).

Burnett, J. (2000): *Riot, Revelry and Rout, Sport in Lowland Scotland before 1860* (East Linton: Tuckwell Press).

Butterfield, L. H. (ed) (1951): *Letters of Benjamin Rush* (Princeton: Princeton University Press).

Bynum, W. F. and R. Porter (eds) (1988): 'Brunonianism in Britain and Europe', *Medical History*, supplement no. 8 (London: Wellcome Institute).

Bynum, W. F., S. Lock and R. Porter (eds) (1992): *Medical Journals and Medical Knowledge* (London: Routledge, Wellcome Institute).

Byrom, C. (1998): 'Certificate of Merit – a fascinating insight into an aspect of the Caley's early history', *Caledonian Gardener*, pp. 9-15.

Byrom, C. (1999): 'Dr Andrew Duncan, Senior (1744-1828), Father of the Caledonian Horticultural Society', *Caledonian Gardener*, pp. 5-14.

Byrom, C. and G. Dalgleish (1991): 'A massive and handsome silver vase', *Royal Caledonian Horticultural Society Journal*, pp. 32-34.

Byrom, C. and G. Dalgleish (2001): 'All that Glitters. Part I; The Early Years', *Caledonian Gardener*, pp. 20-36

Byrom, C. and G. Dalgleish (2003): 'All that Glitters. Part 2', *Caledonian Gardener*, pp. 47-61.

Caird, F. M. (1921-22): *Transactions of the Medico-Chirurgical Society of Edinburgh*, new series 36.

Cameron, J. R. J. (1971): 'Sir James Young Simpson: The Man and his Discoveries', *Journal of the Royal College of Surgeons of Edinburgh* 16.

Campbell, N. and R. M. S. Smellie (1983): *The Royal Society of Edinburgh (1783-1983)* (Edinburgh: Royal Society of Edinburgh).

Cant, R. G. (1992): *The University of St Andrews, a Short History*, 3rd edition (St Andrews: St Andrews University Library).

Chalmers, I. and U. Tröhler (2000): 'Helping Physicians To Keep Abreast of the Medical Literature: Medical and Philosophical Commentaries, 1773-1795', *Annals of Internal Medicine* 133.

Chalmers, J. (2003): *Audubon in Edinburgh* (Edinburgh: NMS Enterprises Limited – Publishing).

Chambers, R. (1869): *Traditions of Edinburgh* (Edinburgh: W. & R. Chambers).

Chitnis, A. C. (1976): *The Scottish Enlightenment: A Social History* (London: Croom Helm).

Christison, R. (1861): *Graduation under the Medical and Scottish Universities Acts* (Edinburgh: Adam and Charles Black).

Christison, R. (1885): *The Life of Sir Robert Christison, Bart*, edited by his sons (Edinburgh: Blackwood).

Clark, J. (1773): *Observations on the diseases in long voyages to hot countries* (London: Wilson).

Cockburn, H. (1874): *Journal 1831-1854* (Edinburgh: Edmonston & Douglas).

Cockburn, H. (1909): *Memorials of his Time* (Edinburgh: T. N. Foulis).

Cockburn, H. A. (1910): An account of the Friday Club written by Lord Cockburn, together with notes on certain other social clubs in Edinburgh, *The Book of the Old Edinburgh Club* III, pp. 135-41.

Colman, E. (1999): 'The first English medical journals: Medicina Curiosa', *Lancet*, p. 354.

Comrie, J. D. (1927): *History of Scottish Medicine to 1860* (London: Baillere, Tindall, & Cox).

Comrie, J. D. (1932): *History of Scottish Medicine*, 2nd edition (London: Baillere, Tindall & Cox).

Comrie, J. D. (1936/7): 'John and James Gregory', *University of Edinburgh Journal*, no. 8, pp. 126-30.

Cormack, J. J. C. (1997): *After Dinner Speech to Medico-Chirurgical Society of Edinburgh*.

Cosh, M. (2003): *Edinburgh the Golden Age* (Edinburgh: John Donald).

Cousland, C. J. (1946): *Honoured in Scotland's Capital 1459-1946. Freemen or 'Burgesses* and Gild Brothers Gratis' of the City of Edinburgh (Edinburgh: C. J. Cousland).

Cowan, D. L. (1957): 'The Edinburgh Pharmacopoeia', Medical History I, pp.123-39.

Cozens-Hardy, B. (ed) (1950): The Diary of Sylas Neville, 1767-1788 (Oxford: Oxford University Press).

Craig, W. (1883-84): 'On the early publications of the Medico-Chirurgical Society of Edinburgh', Transactions of the Medico-Chirurgical Society of Edinburgh, new series 3.

Craig, W. S. (1976): History of the Royal College of Physicians of Edinburgh (Oxford, London & Edinburgh: Blackwell Scientific Publisher).

Creswell, C. H. (1926): The Royal College of Surgeons of Edinburgh. Historical Notes from 1505 to 1905 (Edinburgh: Oliver & Boyd).

Cullen, W. (1783): 'Memorial of the Philosophical Society of Edinburgh', Scots Magazine 45, appendix, p. 676.

Daiches, D. (1982): Robert Fergusson (Edinburgh: Scottish Academic Press).

Darwin, C. and E. Darwin (eds) (1780): Experiments establishing a criterion between mucaginous and purulent matter. And an account of the retrograde motions of the absorbent vessels of animal bodies in some diseases. (Lichfield: printed for J. Jackson; London: T. Cadell; Edinburgh: W. Creech).

Dawson, T. (1776): Cases in the acute rheumatism and the gout; with cursory remarks, and the method of treatment, 3rd edition, with considerable additions (London: printed for J. Johnson & P. Elmsly).

Dingwall, H. M. (2003): A History of Scottish Medicine: themes and influences (Edinburgh: Edinburgh University Press).

Dingwall, H. M. (2005): 'A Famous and Flourishing Society' The History of the Royal College of Surgeons of Edinburgh, 1505-2005 (Edinburgh: Edinburgh University Press).

Dobson, D. (2008a): The Shipping of Anstruther and the East Neuk of Fife 1742-1771 (private publication).

Dobson, D. (2008b): A Directory of Seafarers of the East Neuk of Fife 1589-1800 (private publication).

Dobson, M. (1779): A medical commentary on fixed air (Chester: Monk).

Doig, A., et al. (eds) (1993): William Cullen and the 18th century medical world (Edinburgh: Edinburgh University Press).

Duncan, A. (1770): Elements of Therapeutics, or first Principles of the Practice of Medicine (Edinburgh: printed by Balfour, Auld & Smellie for W. Drummond).

Duncan, A. (1772): 'Observations on the operation and use of mercury in the venereal disease' (London: T. Cadell and John Murray; Edinburgh: A. Kincaid and W. Creech).

Duncan, A. (1778): 'Medical Cases, selected from the Records of the Public Dispensary at Edinburgh; with Remarks and Observations; being the Substance of Case Lectures, delivered during the years 1776-77' and two subsequent editions published in 1781 and 1784 (Edinburgh: Charles Elliot; London: John Murray).

Duncan, A. (1782): 'A letter to Dr Robert Jones of Caermarthenshire, in answer to the account which he has published of the case of Mr John Braham Isaacson, student of Medicine, and to the Injurious Aspersions which he has thrown out against the Physicians who attended Mr Isaacson' (Edinburgh: Charles Elliot).

Duncan, A. (1784): Transactions of the Royal Society of Edinburgh I, p. 27.

Duncan, A. (1789): 'Account of Sir Alexander Dick', Transactions of the Royal Society of Edinburgh II, pp. 58-62.

Duncan, A. (1801a): 'Heads of lectures on medical police' (A. Neill & Co.).

Duncan, A. (1801b): Heads of lectures on the institutions of medicine.

Duncan, A. (1801c): 'Heads of lectures on juridicial medicine or, the Institutiones Medicinae forensis'.

Duncan (and others) (1807): 'Address to the public respecting the establishment of a lunatic asylum at Edinburgh' (Edinburgh: James Ballantyne).

Duncan (and others) (1809): 'Observations on the structure of hospitals and the treatment of lunatics, and on the general principles on which the cure of insanity may be most successfully conducted. To which is annexed, an account of the intended establishment of a lunatic asylum at Edibnurgh [sic]'. (Edinburgh: James Ballantyne).

Duncan, A. (1810): 'A short account of a method of preparing a Soporific Medicine from the inspissated white juice of the common garden lettuce or Lactuca sativa of Linnaeus'. Address to Caledonian Horticultural Society (EUL SB6104/6).

Duncan, A. (1811): 'Letter to Dr James Gregory in consequence of certain printed papers entitled 'The Viper and File', 'There is Wisdom in Silence', 'An old story', etc., lately distributed by him (with five appendices)'.

Duncan (and others) (1812): 'A short account of the rise, progress, and present state of the Lunatic Asylum at Edinburgh, with some remarks on the general treatment of lunatics, pointing out the advantages of avoiding all cruelty. To which will be annexed, a complete list of the contributions received, whether from towns, parishes, or individuals, for erecting a building much wanted in the metropolis of Scotland' (Edinburgh: P. Neill).

Duncan, A. (1818a): 'A letter to His Majesty's Sheriffs-Depute in Scotland, recommending the establishment of four national asylums for the reception of criminal and pauper lunatics' (Edinburgh: P. Neill).

Duncan, A. (1818b) 'Miscellaneous poems, extracted from the records of the Circulation Club at Edinburgh' (Edinburgh: Peter Hill).

Duncan (1820): 'Additional observations on the use of *lactucarium*, or lettuce opium, particularly in a case of *cynanche laryngea*' (RCPE Library).

Duncan, A. (1824): 'Speech delivered at a meeting of the *Senatus Academicus* of the University of Edinburgh on the 20 November 1824, respecting a proposal for new regulations in granting the degree of Doctor of Medicine' (EUL).

Duncan, A (1825): 'Speech delivered by Andrew Duncan Sr at a quarterly statutory meeting of the *Senatus Academicus* of the University of Edinburgh on 15 January 1825' (EUL).

Duncan Jr, A. (1803): 'Letter containing Experiment and Observations on Cinchona', *Nicholson's Journal* VI.

Duncan Jr, A. (1818): 'Reports on the Practice in the Clinical wards of the Royal Infirmary of Edinburgh' (RCPE Library).

Duncan Jr, A. (1827): 'Medical Education', *Edinburgh Medical Surgical Journal* 27.

Dunlop, D. (1974): 'An Edinburgh Bicentenary: Aesculapian Club 1773-1973', *Journal of the Royal College of Surgeons of Edinburgh*.

Farrington, A. (1999): *Catalogue of the East India Company. Ships Journals and logs 1600-1834* (London: British Library).

Fletcher, H. R. and W. H. Brown (1970): *The Royal Botanic Garden Edinburgh 1670-1970* (Edinburgh: HMSO).

Fowler, T. (1785): *Medical reports on the effects of tobacco in the cure of dropsies and dysenteries* (London: for the author).

Fowler, T. (1786): *Medical reports on the effects of arsenic in the cure of agues, remittent fevers, and periodic headaches* (London: Johnson).

Fowler, T. (1795): *Medical reports on the effects of blood letting, sudorifics, and blistering in the cure of the acute and chronic rheumatism* (London: Johnson).

Franklin, B. (1964): *The Autobiography of Benjamin Franklin* (London: Everyman's Library).

Grant, A. (1884): *The story of the University of Edinburgh during its first three hundred years*, 2 vols (London: Longmans, Green).

Grant, J. (1881-83): *Old and New Edinburgh*, 3 vols (London: Cassell & Co.).

Gray, J. (1952): *History of the Royal Medical Society 1737-1937* (D. Guthrie, ed.) (Edinburgh: Edinburgh University Press).

Gregory, James (1800): *Memorial to the Managers of the Royal Infirmary* (Edinburgh: Murray and Cochrane).

Gregory, James (1803): *Additional Memorial to the Managers of the Royal Infirmary* (Edinburgh: W. Creech).

Gregory, John (1772): *Lectures on the Duties and Qualifications of a Physician* (Edinburgh: W. Strachan and T. Cadell).

Guthrie, D. (1945): *A History of Medicine* (Edinburgh and London: Thos Nelson & Son).

Guthrie, D. (1959): *The Medical School of Edinburgh* (Edinburgh: printed by G. Waterston).

Guthrie, D. (1965): *Extramural Medical Education in Edinburgh and the School of Medicine of the Royal Colleges* (Edinburgh: E. and S. Livingstone).

Haakonssen, L. (1997): *Medicine and morals in the enlightenment: John Gregory, Thomas Percival and Benjamin Rush* (Amsterdam: Rodopi).

Halford, H. (1834): *On the education and conduct of a physician* (London: John Murray).

Hamilton Jr, J. (1793): Reply to Dr Gregory, Edinburgh (CRC, EUL).

Hamilton Jr, J. (1824): Memorial from Dr Hamilton, Professor of Midwifery to the Right Honourable the Lord Provost, Magistrates and Town Council of Edinburgh, 17 January 1824 (EUL).

Hamilton Jr, J. (1824 and 1825): Letters from Dr Hamilton to the Members of the Senate Academicus of the University of Edinburgh 27 September 1824, 18 November 1824 and 7 February 1825 (EUL).

Hamilton Jr, J. (1825): An account of the conduct of the Senate Academicus of the University of Edinburgh in regard to the claim of the Professor of Midwifery addressed to the Rt Hon. Alexander Henderson, Lord Provost of the City of Edinburgh by James Hamilton on 6 June 1825 (EUL).

Handyside, P. D. (1874): 'Valedictory Address to the Medico-Chirurgical Society of Edinburgh', *Edinburgh Medical Journal* 19.

Hay, I. (1951): *The Royal Company of Archers* (Edinburgh: Blackwood).

Henderson, D. K. (1964): *The Evolution of Psychiatry in Scotland* (Edinburgh: E. & S. Livingstone).

Home, F. (1782): *Clinical Experiments, Histories and Dissections*, 2nd edition (Edinburgh: William Creech).

Houston, R. A. (2000): *Madness and Society in Eighteenth-Century Scotland* (Oxford: Clarendon Press).

Houston, R. A. (2003): 'Care of the Mentally disabled in and around Edinburgh c.1680-c.1820', *Journal of the Royal College of Physicians of Edinburgh* 33, supplement 2, pp. 12-20.

Huie, R. (1829): *Harveian Oration: being a Tribute of Respect for the memory of Andrew Duncan Sr MD* (P. Neill).

Hutchison, R. (1913): 'The Function of the Royal Medical Society in Medical Education', *Edinburgh Medical Journal*, new series X.

Innes, J. (1983): 'The Harveians of Edinburgh – their first two hundred years', *Scottish Medical Journal* 28, pp. 285-89.

Ismay, T. (1936/7): 'Letter from Thomas Ismay, student of medicine at Edinburgh, to his Father, 1771', *University of Edinburgh Journal* VIII, pp. 57-61.

Jardine, W. (1833-43) *The Naturalist's Library*, 40 vols. (Edinburgh: W. H. Lizars).

Jenkinson, J. (1993): *Scottish Medical Societies 1731-1939; their history and records* (Edinburgh: Edinburgh University Press).

Jenner, E. (1798): *An inquiry into the causes and effects of variolæ vaccinæ ... a disease known by the name of cowpox* (London: Sampson Low).

Johnson, J. (pseudonym) (1792): *A Guide for gentlemen studying medicine at the University of Edinburgh* (London: J. Robinson).

Johnstone R. W., J. D. S Cameron, C. McNeil, D. M. Dunlop, K. Paterson Brown, J. Sturrock (1954): *Edinburgh Medical Journal* 61, pp. 389-90.

Jones, R. (1781): *An inquiry into the state of medicine, on the principles of inductive philosophy. With an appendix; containing practical cases and observations* (Edinburgh: Charles Elliot).

Kaufman, M. H. (1997): 'The First and Second Halls of the RMS', *Book of the Old Edinburgh Club*, new series 4, pp. 119-29.

Kaufman, M. H. (2003a): *Medical Teaching in Edinburgh during the 18th and 19th centuries* (Edinburgh: RCSE).

Kaufman, M. H. (2003b): 'The Royal Medical Society's Library', *Journal of the Royal College of Physicians of Edinburgh* 33, supplementary 12, pp. 56-63.

Kaufman M. H. (2005): 'The excoriation of Benjamin Bell: Who was "Jonathan Daw-plucker"?', *Journal of the Royal College of Physicians of Edinburgh* 35, pp. 356-64.

Kaufman M. H. (2007): 'Origin and history of the Regius Chair of Medical Jurisprudence and Medical Police established in the University of Edinburgh in 1807', *Journal of Forensic and Legal Medicine* 14, pp. 121-30.

Kay, J. (1837): *A series of original portraits and caricature etchings by the late John Kay*, 2 vols (Edinburgh: Hugh Paton, Carver and Gilder).

Kerr, H. F. (1922): 'Map of Edinburgh in mid-18th Century', *Book of Old Edinburgh Club* XI, pp. 1-19.

Le Fanu, W. R. (1984): *British Periodicals of Medicine 1640-1899* (Oxford: Wellcome Unit for the History of Medicine).

Lettsom, J. C. (1774): *Medical memoirs of the General Dispensary in London* (London: Dilly).

Lind, J. (1772): *A treatise on the scurvy*, 3rd edition (London: Crowder, et al.).

McDougall, W. (2002): *Science and Medicine in the Scottish Enlightenment* (C. W. J. Withers and P. Wood, eds.) (East Linton: Tuckwell Press), pp. 215-54.

McDougall, W. (2002): 'Charles Elliot's Medical

Publications and the International Book Trade', *Science and Medicine in the Scottish Enlightenment* (C. W. J. Withers and P. Wood, eds.) (East Linton: Tuckwell Press).

McElroy, D. D. (1952): *The Literary Clubs and Societies in Eighteenth-Century Scotland* (University of Edinburgh, Ph.D. Thesis).

McElroy, D. D. (1969): *Scotland's Age of Improvement. A Survey of 18th Century Literary Clubs and Societies* (Pullman: Washington State University Press).

Macintyre, I. and I. MacLaren (eds) (2005): *Surgeons' Lives* (Edinburgh: RCSE).

Mackenzie, D. (1935): 'The History of the Royal Caledonian Horticultural Society', *Transactions of the Royal Caledonian Horticultural Society* 5, pp. 64-83.

Mackie, R. A. T. (1993): *Raeburn Life and Art*, PhD Thesis, Edinburgh University.

Maclagan, D. (1873): 'Centenary of the Aesculapian', *Edinburgh Medical Journal* XIX, 2nd series.

McLaren, M. (ed) (1949): *The House of Neill 1749-1949* (A. Neill & Co. Ltd).

Macmillan, D. (1990): *Scottish Art 1460-1990* (Edinburgh: Mainstream Publications).

McCrae, M. (2003): Andrew Duncan and the Health of Nations, *Journal of the Royal College of Physicians of Edinburgh* 33; History supplement 12, pp. 2-11.

McRae, M. (2007): *Physicians and Society: a History of the Royal College of Physicians of Edinburgh* (Edinburgh: Donald).

Maehle, A.-H. (1999): *Drugs on trial: Experimental pharmacology and therapeutic innovation in the eighteenth century* (Amsterdam-Atlanta: Rodopi).

Marshall, J. (1846): *A Winter with Robert Burns*, (re-published 2002) (Edinburgh: Masonic Publishing Co.).

Masson, A. H. B. (1995): *Portraits, Paintings and Busts in the Royal College of Surgeons of Edinburgh* (Edinburgh: RCSE).

Miles, A. (1918): *The Edinburgh School of Surgery before Lister* (London: A & C Black).

Millar, J. (1777): *Observations on the practice in the Medical Department of the Westminster General Dispensary* (London: by order of the Governors).

Millar, J. (1778-79): *Observations on the management of diseases in Army and Navy* (London: for the author).

Mitchell, A. (1864): *The insane in private dwellings* (Edinburgh: Edmonton and Douglas).

Mitchell, J. F. (1961): Some Edinburgh Monumental Inscriptions, Ed Room MS YCS 436.

Morgan, A. (1936/7): 'The Darwins as students of medicine', *University of Edinburgh Journal* 8, pp. 221-26.

Mowat, I. R. M. (2002): 'Adam Square: an Edinburgh architectural first', *Book of the Old Edinburgh Club*, new series, vol. 5, pp 93-101.

Neill, P. (1823): *Journal of a Horticultural tour through some parts of Flanders, Holland and the North of France in the Autumn of 1817* (Edinburgh: Bell and Bradfute).

Nicolson, M. (2000): 'The Continental Journeys of Andrew Duncan Junior: a physicians's education and the international culture of eighteenth-century medicine', pp. 89-119 in R. Wrigley, and G. Revill (eds): *Pathologies of Travel* (Amsterdam: Rodopi).

Omond, R. (1874): 'Harveian Address 1874', *Edinburgh Medical Journal* 20, pp. 97-104.

Passmore, R. (2001): *Fellows of the Edinburgh College of Physicians during the Scottish Enlightenment* (Edinburgh: RCPE).

Paterson, J. (1838): *Kay's Edinburgh Portraits* (London: Hamilton, Adams & Co.; Edinburgh: Hugh Paton).

Paul, J. B. (1875): *The History of the Royal Company of Archers* (Edinburgh: Wm Blackwood and Sons).

Percival, T. (1767): *Essays medical and experimental*, 1st series (London: Johnson).

Pettigrew, T. J. (1817): *Memoirs of the life and writings of the late John Coakley Lettsom*, vol. 2 (London: Longman, *etc.*).

Pitcairn, C. (1905): *History of the Fife Pitcairns* (Edinburgh: Blackwood & Sons).

Pitman, J. (1988): The Richard Poole Collection, *Proceedings of the Royal College Physicians Edinburgh* 18, pp. 300-305.

Pottinger, G. (1972): *Muirfield and the Honourable Company* (Edinburgh: Scottish Academic Press).

Power, D'Arcy (1939): *British Medical Societies* (London: Medical Press).

Presley, A. S. (1983): 'From madhouses to mental hospital', *Scottish Medical Journal* 28, pp. 71-74.

Risse, G. B. (1986): *Hospital life in Enlightenment Scotland. Care and teaching at the Royal*

Infirmary Edinburgh (Cambridge: Cambridge University Press).

Risse, G. B. (2005): *New medical challenges during the Scottish Enlightenment* (Amster-dam: Rodopi).

Roddis, L. H. (1936) in 'William Withering and the introduction of digitalis into medical practice', *Annals of Medical History* VIII, pp. 107-108.

Rosner, L. M. (1981): *Scottish Men of Medicine. Andrew Duncan MD FRSE (1744-1828)* (Edinburgh: History of Medicine and Science Unit).

Rosner, L. M. (1991): *Medical Education in the Age of Improvement. Edinburgh Students and Apprentices 1760-1826* (Edinburgh: Edinburgh University Press).

Rosner, L. M. (1999): *The Most Beautiful Man in Existence. The Scandalous Life of Alexander Lesassier* (Philadelphia: University of Pennsylvania Press).

Russell, B. (1759): *Dissertatio medica inauguralis, de cupro, …* (Edinburgh: Hamilton, Balfour & Neill).

Sachse, W. L. (1956): *The Colonial American in Britain* (Madison: University of Wisconsin Press).

Shapin, S. (1974): 'Property, Patronage and the Politics of Science: The Founding of the Royal Society of Edinburgh', *British Journal for the History of Science* VII, pp. 1-43.

Shepherd, T. H. (1831): *Modern Athens* (London: Jones).

Sher, R. B. (2006): *The Enlightenment and the Book: Scottish Authors & their Publishers in Eighteenth-Century Britain, Ireland & America* (Chicago: University of Chicago Press).

Simpson, A. D. C. (1994): 'James Hamilton's Lying-in Hospital', *Book of the Old Edinburgh Club*, new series 3, pp. 131-41.

Smellie, W. (1800): *Literary and Characteristic Lives of Gregory* (Edinburgh: Kames, Hume & Smith), pp. 161-62.

Smith, C. J. (1978-88): *Historic South Edinburgh*, 4 vols (Edinburgh: Charles Skilton Ltd).

Smith, F. B. (2004): 'Mackenzie, Sir James (1853-1925), physician and medical researcher', in *Dictionary of National Biography* 35 (Oxford: Oxford University Press)

Smith J. (1908): *Epitaphs in Buccleuch Church-yard 1908*, Edinburgh Room, ECL, MSYCS 436 B91.

Smith N. (1982): 'Sexual mores in enlightenment Scotland', in P.-G. Boucé (ed) *Sexuality in eighteenth century Britain* (Manchester University Press), pp. 47-73.

Smith, S. G. (ed) (1952): *Robert Fergusson 1750-1774* (Edinburgh: Nelson).

Spens, T. and J. Hope (1805): Letter to James Gregory, 29 January 1805.

Stevenson, D. (2001): *The Beggar's Benison, Sex Clubs of Enlightenment Scotland and their rituals* (East Linton: Tuckwell Press).

Stevenson, S. (1989): *Anstruther a History* (Edinburgh: Donald).

Stewart, A. G. (1901): *The Academic Gregories* (Edinburgh: Oliphant, Anderson & Ferrier).

Storer, J. and H. S. Storer (1820): *Views in Edinburgh and its Vicinity; drawn and engraved by J. & H. S. Storer, Exhibiting remains of Antiquity, Public Buildings, and Picturesque Scenery*, 2 vols (Edinburgh: A. Constable & Co).

Stuart, M. W. (1952): *Old Edinburgh Taverns* (London: Hale).

Stuart, W. J. (undated, c.1958): *The History of the Aesculapian Club* (privately published).

Talbot Rice, D. and P. McIntyre (1957): *The University Portraits* (Edinburgh: Edinburgh University Press).

Thin, R. (1928): 'Archibald Pitcairne 1652-1712', *Edinburgh Medical Journal* 35, pp. 365-82.

Thomson, D. M. (1984): 'General practice and the Edinburgh Medical School: 200 years of teaching, care and research', *Journal of the Royal College of General Practitioners* 34, pp. 9-12.

Thomson, J. (1859): *An Account of the Life, Lectures, and Writings of William Cullen, M.D., Professor of the Practice of Physic in the University of Edinburgh*, 2 vols (Edinburgh & London: W. Blackwood & Sons).

Thomson, St C. (1918): *John Coakley Lettsom and the foundation of the Medical Society Presidential address* (London: Harrison & Sons).

Tröhler, U. (1987): *Die Gewissheit der Chirurgie: Grundlagen klinisch-therapeutischer Bewertung um 1750*, Schweiz. Rundschau Medizin (Praxis) 76, pp. 958-61.

Tröhler, U. (1988): 'To improve the evidence of medicine: arithmetic observation in clinical medicine in the eighteenth and early nineteenth centuries', *History & Philosophy of the Life Sciences*, 10, Supplement, pp. 31-40.

Tröhler, U. (1999): 'L'essor de la chirurgie', in Grmek MD (ed): *Histoire de la pensée médicale en occident* (Paris: Ed. Du Seuil), vol. 3, pp. 958-61.

Tröhler, U. (2000): *'To improve the Evidence of Medicine': quantification in British medicine and surgery, 1750-1830* (Edinburgh: RCPE).

Turnbull, M. (1991): *The Edinburgh Graveyard Guide* (Edinburgh: Saint Andrew Press).

Turner, A. Logan (1937): *Story of a Great Hospital: the Royal Infirmary of Edinburgh 1729-1929* (Edinburgh: Oliver & Boyd).

Watson, J. G. (1937/8): 'The Gregorys and Andrew Duncan', *University of Edinburgh Journal* IX, pp. 160-63.

Wemyss, H. L. W. (1933): *A record to the Edinburgh Harveian Society* (Edinburgh: A. Constable).

Wilkins, F. (1993): *The Smuggling Story of the Two Firths* (Kidderminster: Wyre Forest Press).

Withering, W. (1785): *An account of the foxglove and some of its medical uses* (Birmingham: Robinson).

Young, J. H. (1963): 'James Hamilton (1767-1839) Obstetrician and Controversialist', *Medical History* 7, pp. 62-73.

Zachs, W. (1998): *The first John Murray and the late eighteenth-century London book trade.* (Oxford: Oxford University Press, for the British Academy).

Miscellaneous publications

Annual Medical Review and Register (1809) in CRC, EUL.

Collection of pamphlets owned and bound by Mr Colin MacLaurin Advocate, c.1822, NLS ABS.2.94.55 (12).

Gregory, James (1804): Review of the Proceedings of the RCPE 1752-1804.

Gregory, James (1805): Censorian letter, 25 January 1805.

Gregory, James (1806): Reasons of Protest.

Gregory, James(1811): Defence before the RCPE.

Harveiana: Volume of miscellaneous papers in RCPE Library.

Laws and List of Members, Medico-Chirurgical Society of Edinburgh, 1821, CRC, EUL, GD3/1/1.

Memoirs of the Caledonian Horticultural Society, volumes I-IV, 1814-29.

Resolution of the RCPE (1805).

RCPE report (1809), Narrative of the Conduct of Dr Gregory.

Royal Commission Report (1831).

Royal Medical Society, Bound Dissertations 4, 1774-75.

Transactions of the Medico-Chirurgical Society of Edinburgh (1824).

Transactions of the Royal Society of Edinburgh. General Index to first thirty four volumes (1783-1888) with History of the Institution of the Society, Royal Charter, List of contents of each volume, etc. (1890) (Edinburgh: Neill and Co., printer; Robert Grant & Son).

Minute books

Aesculapian Society, RCPE.
Caledonian Horticultural Society, RBGE.
City of Edinburgh.
Council of the RCPE.
Harveian Society, RCPE.
Medico-Chirurgical Society of Edinburgh (1821), CRC, EUL, GD3/2/1.
Medico-Chirurgical Society of Edinburgh (1821-41), CRC, EUL, GD3/3/1.
Royal College of Physicians of Edinburgh.
Royal College of Surgeons of Edinburgh.
Speculative Society.
University of Edinburgh.
University of St Andrews.

Archives

The Duncan Archive, British Library.
The Duncan Archive, Edinburgh University Library (EUL).
The Murray Archive (includes the Charles Elliot Archive), National Library of Scotland.
Royal College of Physicians (RCPE) Library.

Selected Index

Image and Text Credits

IMAGES

THE AESCULAPIAN SOCIETY

for art section – *fig.* 14

JOHN CHALMERS

for art section – *figs* 29a, 30, 31, 34 (Courtesy of Napier University), 37, 38

EDINBURGH CITY LIBRARY

(By courtesy Edinburgh City Library)

for art section – *figs* 1, 4, 6

EDINBURGH UNIVERSITY LIBRARY

(With permission Lothian Health Service Archive)

for art section – *figs* 9, 13a, 13b; for text page – 113

(© Special Collections Department)

for art section – *figs* 7a, 7b; for text page – 71

JAMES GRANT (1881-83): *Old and New Edinburgh*

for art section – *figs* 3, 17; for text page – 228; for back cover

THE HARVEIAN SOCIETY

for art section – *figs* 15, 16, 39

STEVEN KERR

for art section – *fig.* 45

WILLIAM JARDINE (1833-43): *Naturalist's Library*

for art section – *fig.* 11

THE JOHN MURRAY COLLECTION

for art section – *fig.* 10

MEDICO-CHIRURGICAL SOCIETY, EDINBURGH

for text page – 155

IAIN MILNE

for art section – *figs* 40a, 40b

E. MITCHELL

(With thanks to the Royal College of Physicians)

for text page 219

NAPIER UNIVERSITY

(see John Chalmers)

NATIONAL GALLERIES OF SCOTLAND

(© The Trustees of the National Galleries of Scotland)

SCOTTISH NATIONAL PORTRAIT GALLERY

for art section – *figs* 25 (Auguste Edouart: silhouette of James Hamilton Jr), 35 (David Martin: portrait of Elizabeth Duncan) [detail]

NATIONAL LIBRARY OF SCOTLAND

(Reproduced with kind permission of the Trustees of the National Library of Scotland)

for text pages – xiv-xv, 32 (and inset)

NATIONAL MUSEUMS SCOTLAND

(© National Museums Scotland)

for art section – *fig.* 18; for text page – 180 (with thanks to Royal Company of Archers)

ALEXANDER NISBET (1892): *Heraldic Plates*

for text page – xvi

ROYAL BOTANIC GARDEN EDINBURGH

(Copyright of the Royal Botanic Garden Edinburgh (2008)/ Photographer: Lynsey Wilson)

for art section – *fig.* 41

ROYAL CALEDONIAN
HORTICULTURAL SOCIETY
(Copyright of the Royal
Caledonian Horticultural
Society)

www.rchs.co.uk

for art section – figs 20, 42

ROYAL COLLEGE OF
PHYSICIANS OF EDINBURGH

(By courtesy Royal College of
Physicians of Edinburgh)

for art section – *figs* 8a, 8b,
12, 32, 33, 44; for text page
53; for front and back cover
images

ROYAL COLLEGE OF
SURGEONS OF EDINBURGH

(By courtesy Royal College of
Surgeons of Edinburgh)

for art section – *figs* 27, 29b

ROYAL COMPANY OF
ARCHERS
(see National Museums
Scotland)

ROYAL SOCIETY OF
EDINBURGH
(© Reproduced by permission
of Royal Society of Edinburgh)

for art section – *figs* 19, 43

THOMAS H. SHEPHERD
(1831): *Modern Athens*

for art section – figs 2, 5

UNIVERSITY OF EDINBURGH
FINE ART COLLECTION

for art section – *fig* 36

TEXT

BIRLINN LTD

With thanks to Birlinn Ltd for
permission to quote from
David Stevenson (2001): *The
Beggar's Benison, Sex Clubs of
Enlightenment Scotland* on
page 175 of this book.